An Obsession with History:
Russian Writers Confront the Past

An Obsession with History

Russian Writers Confront the Past

Andrew Baruch Wachtel

Stanford University Press
Stanford, California

Stanford University Press, Stanford, California
© 1994 by the Board of Trustees of the
Leland Stanford Junior University
Printed in the United States of America

Stanford University Press publications are
distributed exclusively by Stanford
University Press within the United States,
Canada, Mexico, and Central America; they are
distributed exclusively by Cambridge University
Press throughout the rest of the world.

CIP data appear at the end of the book

Original printing 1994
Last figure below indicates year of this printing:
04   03   02   01   00   99   98   97   96   95

For my parents,
Dr. Fred Wachtel and
Mrs. Miriam Wachtel

Acknowledgments

My first thoughts on this project came while I was completing my tenure at the Harvard University Society of Fellows. Special thanks are due to my Junior Fellow colleagues and to Jurij Striedter, who was always and remains an inspiration. I continued to work on the project at Stanford University, where my colleagues Lazar Fleishman, Joseph Frank, Grigory Freidin, Hans Ulrich Gumbrecht, and the late Edward J. Brown and students Sam Eisin, Larry Joseph, Judith Kalb, Sally Kux, and Kevin Platt provided scholarly and moral support.

I was able to finish the book with the help of grants from the Social Sciences Research Council and the National Endowment for the Humanities. Northwestern University's College of Arts and Sciences graciously allowed me to spend my first year at the university on leave in order to complete the manuscript. Many other colleagues around the country read or listened to parts of the work in progress and their judicious criticism helped me when I began to go off track—in particular I would like to acknowledge Boris Gasparov, Irina Gutkin, Hugh McLean, Elliott Mossman, Kathy Nepomnishchy, Irina Paperno, Irina Reyfman, Stephanie Sandler, William Mills Todd III, and Michael Wachtel. I received invaluable assistance at various points from Caryl Emerson. Saul Morson read every word a number of times, argued with me frequently, and tried to keep me from saying crazy things about Bakhtin. The staff at Stanford University Press did their usual stellar job: special thanks to Helen Tartar, Julia Zafferano, Ellen Smith, and Jan Spauschus Johnson. Finally, Elizabeth Calihan tried as hard as she could (and mostly succeeded, I hope) to make me think logically.

A.W.

Contents

Note on Transliteration and Translation

I have used the Library of Congress system of transliteration except in two cases: widely known names (e.g., Gogol, Tolstoy) and all names, first and last, ending in "ii," which are rendered here by "y" (e.g., Vasily for Vasilii, Zhukovsky for Zhukovskii). All translations are my own unless specified otherwise.

An Obsession with History:
Russian Writers Confront the Past

Chapter One

⚘

Introduction

*Russia never had anything in common with the rest of
Europe. Her history demands a different thought and a
different formula.*

Alexander Pushkin [1]

That Russians have frequently seemed transfixed with the idea
of the singularity of their own history and with the relationship
of that history to the history of the outside world—that Russians are, let us say, obsessed with the idea of history itself—is a
thought that has undoubtedly struck many observers of Russian
culture. In particular, three notions stand out, related to each
other to be sure, but by no means unproblematically so. First
is the conviction, expressed by Pushkin in the above epigraph,
of absolute difference; Russians insist, sometimes even in the
face of evidence to the contrary, that their nation's past is unlike
that of any other country. Second is the belief that Russia will
somehow be able to overcome history, to jump out of time, as
it were, and thereby escape the perhaps overly strong allure of
her history. And third is the frequent assertion that though all
may not be well with her in the present, Russia's unusual past
ensures that she will have a unique role to play in the future; she
is the messiah among nations, it is believed, whose time will
come after the apocalyptic crash of the present order.

Needless to say, none of these ideas is by any means recent.
As early as the 1820's, Petr Chaadaev asserted that Russians
"belong to none of the great families of mankind; we are neither
of the West nor of the East, and we possess the traditions of
neither. Somehow outside of time [*vne vremeni*] we have not

been touched by the universal education of mankind."[2] Initially, to be sure, Chaadaev believed that this particularity was a catastrophe: "Our first years, spent in immobile brutishness, have left no traces on our minds; we have nothing that is ours on which to base our thinking; isolated by a strange fate from the universal development of humanity, we have also absorbed none of mankind's ideas of traditional transmission. Yet it is on those ideas that the life of nations is founded; it is from those ideas that their future develops and that their moral growth derives."[3]

A few years later, however, starting from the same initial premises, Chaadaev came to a startlingly different conclusion—that Russia's unique history was not a drawback but an advantage. He now claimed that Peter the Great had been the first person to recognize Russia's peculiar potential:

[Peter] saw that a historical foundation was wholly lacking to us, that consequently we could not rest our future on such an empty ground; he understood that, confronted by the ancient civilization of Europe, the final expression of all previous civilizations, we could not afford to drown ourselves in our own history, we could not afford to drag ourselves, like the people of the West, through the chaos of national prejudice, along the narrow paths of local ideas, across the ruts of national tradition; that we had to seize our promised destiny by a spontaneous leap. . . . And so he freed us from all those precedents that clutter historical societies and put a stop to their forward motion; he opened our minds to all the great and fine ideas that exist among men; he gave us the entire West, as the ages had made it; for our history he gave us its entire history, and for our future he gave us its entire future.[4]

Russia, it is opined, can choose from the past whatever is valuable and, avoiding the mistakes of other countries, can leap outside of history.

Whether interpreted positively or negatively, the myth of Russia's unique history became firmly entrenched in the national self-perception. By the 1840's, the influential literary critic Vissarion Belinsky could state without much fear of being contradicted: "It is precisely one of the greatest intellectual achievements of our age that we have at last begun to realize that Russia had a history of her own that in no way resembled that of a single European state, and that it should be studied and judged on its own merits and not in the light of the history of European nations with which it has nothing in common."[5]

In the twentieth century, the conviction that, because her history is unlike any other, Russia does not have to play by the chronological or historical rules that govern the development of other countries has, if anything, strengthened. Marxist doctrine held that every economy must and would pass through defined and orderly stages of development. But Lenin declared that in Russia the bourgeois-capitalist phase of development could be more or less skipped over, and he proceeded to construct a new type of state on that premise. Stalin had even less respect for chronology; five-year plans could, it seems, always be completed in four. Disregard for chronology led easily to the belief that the past could be manipulated just as well as the future. After 1937, it became common practice for people who had made important contributions to the Russian Revolution to simply disappear—their names were erased from books, and their faces were airbrushed in or out of pictures.

The idea that Russia is somehow historically unique reaches its zenith in the worldview of Stalinist culture, which "looks upon itself as postapocalyptic culture—the final verdict on all human culture has already been passed, and all that was once temporally distinct has become forever simultaneous in the blinding light of the Final Judgment and the ultimate truth revealed in Stalin's *Short Course* of party history. . . . Socialist realism . . . regards historical time as ended and therefore occupies no particular place in it."[6] But for all its seemingly monolithic strength, this view was never able to mask completely the traditional heightened Russian concern for history, even in the minds of those who created Soviet culture. The fact that folders containing information on nonpersons were marked "preserve forever" is perhaps the best expression of this paradox. There was always a suspicion that history would someday return to take its revenge. As a result, as one eminent American historian puts it, "History in the old Soviet Union was like cancer in the human body, an invisible presence whose existence is bravely denied but against which every conceivable weapon is mobilized."[7]

Given a belief in the uniqueness of Russia's historical experience, it was relatively easy to predict that her destiny would also differ from that of other countries. She had not trod the same path of development earlier, and she would not do so in the future. This corollary allowed Dostoevsky to predict that Russia would not fall victim to the collapse he foresaw awaiting Europe. Instead, after Europe's imminent destruction, Russia would emerge to pronounce the word of universal salvation: "Our mission and our role are not at all like those of other nations, for there each separate people lives exclusively for itself and in itself, while we will begin, now that the time has come, precisely by becoming the servants of all for universal peacemaking."[8] Not surprisingly, Russia's suitability for the role of universality lies in her unique historical past: "I dare to state that the fact that Russia will be able to say the word of living life to humankind in the future lies in the foundations of the Russian nation and in her Orthodoxy."[9]

But of course, Dostoevsky was only restating here a conviction that had been part of Russian Orthodox doctrine since the sixteenth century: "The Church of ancient Rome fell because of the Apollinarian heresy, as to the second Rome—the Church of Constantinople—it has been hewn by the axes of the Hagarenes. But this third, new Rome, the Universal Apostolic Church under thy mighty rule radiates forth the Orthodox Christian faith to the ends of the earth. . . . Hear me pious Tsar, all Christian kingdoms have converged in thine alone. Two Romes have fallen, a third stands, a fourth there shall not be."[10]

Now, as Russia struggles to rejoin the world, it does so by tearing down the monuments to its past 75 years in a desperate attempt once more to escape its own history—statues are pulled down, cities and streets receive their pre-Revolutionary names. It is as if Russians think that by erasing the physical traces of the past they will be able to return to 1917 and start all over. At the same time, some Russians continue to assert their nation's uniqueness, insisting that Russia's historical mission in the twentieth century was to show the world how not to live. And even in this dark stage the belief in Russia's unique and messianic historical destiny has not been abandoned. Voices are heard echoing Alexander Solzhenitsyn's assertion—expressed most forcefully in his Harvard commencement speech of 1979—that Russia's great suffering in this century has given her people deep reserves of spiritual energy, lacking in the West, that will allow her to play a messianic role at some time in the future.

Surely, for anyone who wants to understand Russia, the questions of how the peculiar set of historical convictions touched on above came into existence and how they have been maintained—that is, the basis for and the development of the Russian obsession with history—must be of cardinal importance. In this book, I will not attempt a comprehensive analysis of these questions. Instead, I will examine a phenomenon that at first glance might seem somewhat tangential to the broader issue—the obsession with history of major Russian writers of belles lettres in the nineteenth and twentieth centuries. However, on closer consideration, we will see that the practice of authors, a group that has "traditionally enjoyed far greater prestige in Russia than in most Western countries," [11] quite frequently illuminates the peculiarities of the broader Russian attitude toward history. Indeed, with respect to history, it is difficult to tell whether authors are echoing broader cultural patterns, actually creating these patterns, or a combination of both.

Before going any further, it would perhaps be a good idea for me to lay my cards on the table and mention just which authors and works will concern me. I will begin with a consideration of the historical plays and the history written by Catherine the

Great. Although nowadays Catherine is usually studied as an historical figure, in her lifetime she was also known as a prolific writer (and not only because she more or less controlled the Russian publishing industry). She managed to take enough time out from ruling her empire to produce a history of Russia and two plays on historical themes, among many other literary works. Even though the writing of both history and imaginative literature was not uncommon in her day, her approach is interesting enough to merit attention. Following Catherine, and perhaps influenced by her to some extent, Nikolai Karamzin gave up a career as Russia's most acclaimed author of fiction to become imperial historiographer at the court of Alexander I. His *History of the Russian State (Istoriia gosudarstva Rossiiskogo)* is still both a classic and a joy to read.

Pushkin wrote both a historical novel and a narrative history on material from the Pugachev uprising at the same time that Nikolai Gogol was writing his historical novel *Taras Bul'ba* and a history of Ukraine. With *War and Peace*, Tolstoy maddened both his contemporaries and ours by combining a novel with a disquisition on history. Dostoevsky, following and modifying the Slavophiles, integrated the utopian historiography of his multigeneric *Diary of a Writer (Dnevnik pisatelia)* with his last and greatest novel, *The Brothers Karamazov*. The Futurist poet Velimir Khlebnikov embedded his theories of history in essays on the subject and in his "supersaga," *Zangezi*. Using literary history as his base, Iury Tynianov produced both "scientific" studies and novels to explore the workings of the historical process. And in our own day Solzhenitsyn, perhaps the most acclaimed living Russian novelist, thinks nothing of inserting a 200-page essay on history in the middle of a novel.

The unusual character of the individual works I will consider here has, of course, been remarked on frequently, although, perhaps because of their supposedly anomalous nature, they have not been deemed worthy of scholarly inquiry as a group. Pushkin scholars have wondered what role *The History of Pugachev (Istoriia Pugacheva)* plays in Pushkin's oeuvre, but have rarely considered it in a broader context.[12] Ever since the initial publication of *War and Peace*, its seemingly strange mix of history and fiction has been obvious even to casual readers.[13] *The Diary of a Writer* has been examined from the point of view of utopian fiction and political prophecy.[14] It has been noted that Khlebnikov incorporates the same historical material in his essays and plays, and that Solzhenitsyn conflates history and fiction. What I hope to show is that this many anomalies of the same kind add up, not to random weirdness, but to a tradition.

If we view these works and writers as a tradition rather than as unrelated anomalies, we may come up with some preliminary observations on the relationship between the writing of history and of imaginative literature in Russia. For almost 200 years, Russian writers of belles lettres have not only produced fiction, drama, and narrative poetry on historical material, but they have also turned to what they consider to be nonfictional genres, particularly history and the philosophy of history. Rather than assert the primacy of poetic experience, a romantic strategy that, considering the great prestige literature has had in Russia, one might have expected, they have produced complementary texts on the same historical subject, at least one claiming to be nonfictional and one claiming to be "poetic." This has allowed them to exploit the differences in tone, approach, and authority that by convention have separated imaginative literature and history. The result is a tradition of intergeneric dialogue in which a chosen historical period is illuminated through multiple competing narrative perspectives.

My analysis of this tradition has a dual purpose: on the one hand, I think that it provides a window onto the peculiar Russian attitude toward history; on the other, I believe that it will allow us to read some major works of Russian literature in an entirely new light. I am interested here only in those writers who attempted, by various strategies, to escape what they perceived as the overly rigid distinctions between history and imaginative literature. What is more, I have tried to focus on the central representatives of this tradition, hoping that the depth of analysis of the works considered makes up in part for the lack of comprehensiveness. It should be clear that I am not concerned with either the rich traditions of the Russian historical novel or with those of Russian historical writing per se. From the works of Ivan Lazhechnikov and Mikhail Zagoskin through A. K. Tolstoy and Petr Boborykin, from A. N. Tolstoy through Valentin Pikul', the Russian historical novel exists as a recognizable and productive genre, differing little in approach from its counterparts in Europe. The same can be said of the full-scale narrative history as practiced by Sergei Solov'ev or Vasily Kliuchevsky, and of the specialized historical monograph. Studies of the history and development of these genres in Russia already exist, and although much work remains to be done in that area, I will not be doing it.[15] Rather, the historical novel and the history form the background against which the works I treat stand out. Even Pushkin's *The Captain's Daughter* (*Kapitanskaia dochka*) which is most clearly in the tradition of the historical novel, is discussed here not in that context, but in the light of its dialogue with *The History of Pugachev* and Karamzin's *History of the Russian State*.

I will begin with the prehistory of this approach in Russia. This will require an examination of the period at the end of the eighteenth century and the beginning of the nineteenth when the question of which genres should be used to represent historical events was entirely open. In part, we will see that intergeneric treatments of Russian history could ultimately thrive because this question remained open. A discussion of Karamzin's *History of the Russian State* forms the link between the prehistory and the history of this approach. The rest of the book consists of case studies, each of which will, I hope, illuminate another stage in the evolution of the intergeneric Russian approach to history. Thus, we will be concerned both with those aspects of the system that have remained more or less constant over time and with those that have changed. For while the basic intergeneric approach has remained remarkably constant, the historiographical assumptions underlying these works have changed considerably over time, usually in response to new ideas (often imported from Europe) on the role of history in national culture.

The concept of intergeneric dialogue has been invoked a number of times in the preceding discussion. Because an analysis of the multifarious ways that Russian authors have exploited intergeneric dialogue for the purposes of historical narration will be of central concern throughout the book, and because this phenomenon has rarely been studied, it seems advisable to provide a basic theoretical exposition at this juncture.[16] Since the explosion in popularity enjoyed by the work of Mikhail Bakhtin in the 1980's, references to and reliance on his key concepts—unfinalizability, heteroglossia, carnival—have become so commonplace that I am vaguely embarrassed to invoke the word *dialogue* at all. Nevertheless, I do so here because it seems to me a most appropriate term, as long as we keep in mind that the kind of dialogue I am describing is not one with which Bakhtin was primarily concerned. For both ethical and aesthetic reasons, Bakhtin favored texts that were *internally* dialogic. And as Caryl Emerson and Saul Morson point out, Bakhtin's philosophical belief in the moral imperative for dialogue caused certain problems in his literary criticism: "Bakhtin's dismissal of the creative uses of authoritative discourse in novels weakens his readings of certain texts. . . . Clearly the charge to make novels analogous to selves can work to crimp Bakhtin's own critical imagination and to narrow the types of novels he can accommodate." [17]

For Bakhtin, the most significant kind of dialogue occurs when the position of the other is taken into account overtly. In the classic case, the underground man anticipates and attempts to answer the queries of an implied interlocutor, and it is precisely his recognition of and need to confront another, potentially different, point of view that drives the dialogue.[18] There is, however, another potential type of dialogue. A text that is, in and of itself, monologic (i.e., dominated internally by authoritative discourse) can be dialogized by another equally (but differently) monologic text on the same subject. Since the monologic truths of the two are, on the face of it, incompatible, the result is an unusual form of dialogue: intergeneric dialogue. This observation, it is true, did not entirely escape Bakhtin: he classifies genres on the basis of their "naiveté," their greater or lesser questioning of their own mode of expression, and he suggests that "in principle, all genres can force rival genres to become more self-conscious, 'to better perceive their own possibilities and boundaries, that is, to overcome their *naiveté.*' " [19] Nevertheless, Bakhtin chose not to focus on the nature of the dialogue engendered by clashing generic paradigms, and he did not discuss its potential in the works of a single author.

Although Bakhtin was not concerned with its systematic analysis, the phenomenon of intergeneric dialogue has been the starting point for one Bakhtinian study of Russian culture. And it is certainly not accidental that the book I have in mind, Caryl Emerson's *Boris Godunov: Transpositions of a Russian Theme*, deals with various treatments of a historical theme—although this aspect was not Emerson's primary topic. What she describes and theorizes about so brilliantly is a specific instance of what I am claiming to be a more general phenomenon of Russian culture. Emerson calls the reworking of the same story "transposition," and defines it as "one category of 'translation' where coauthorship is not hidden but rather celebrated, where the independence of the second voice is guaranteed by the new genre or medium, and where dialogue among versions is inevitably explicit. A good part of the audience's interest lies precisely in watching a multiple *co*authorship at work." [20]

The situation Emerson describes involves multiple authors and is not really unique to Russian culture; even in nineteenth-century Europe fictional, operatic, and dramatic treatments of stories that were part of the national historical memory continued to be produced. The right of a novelist or poet to use historical material was never in dispute. [21] The result in Europe, however, was not intergeneric dialogue. Literature and history were simply different animals. The writer of fiction promised to make accurate use of historical material, but he did not take for himself the position of one who could divine a historical truth unknowable by a historian. Certainly, no European writer of belles lettres could have allowed himself the indulgence of saying with Tolstoy, "I was afraid that the necessity to describe the significant figures of 1812 would force me to be governed by historical documents rather than the truth." [22]

The specificity of the Russian situation does not lie, therefore, in the transposition of a historical theme into various genres by various authors. What makes Russia unique is that major Russian authors tend to produce their own transpositions of historical themes. That is, Russian writers traditionally write multiple monologic narratives on the same historical material. In most cases, one of the texts is fictional (in the pre-postmodernist understanding of the term) and the other is nonfictional. The dialogue is not only intertextual and intergeneric but its existence defies the conventional split between the expected professional segregation of the historian and the writer of fiction. In some cases, fictional and nonfictional narratives are kept apart through the production of entirely separate texts. This, for example, was what Pushkin did with his *History of Pugachev* and his novel *The Captain's Daughter*. But in other cases an equivalent degree of separation is achieved through the interaction of competing generic approaches within the same text: Tolstoy's *War and Peace* provides an example.

In either case, the important thing to recognize is that the separate generic narrative voices do not take other potential ways of narration into account. The competing textual voices seem unaware of each other's existence. They remain aggressively monologic. Thus, the narrator Grinev in *The Captain's Daughter* does not realize that the story of the Pugachev uprising could be told in an entirely different manner. And in *War and Peace* we do not feel that the narrator of the second epilogue knows or cares about the relationship of his understanding of history to that of the fictional narrator. To use Bakhtin's terminology, each of the genres or voices remains "naive," unaware of the possibility of narrating the world differently.

Of course, this is not to say that the authors in question do not recognize the essential clash of the narrative paradigms inherent in the genres they employ. Quite the reverse is true. They consciously exploit the narrative possibilities afforded by different genres, and they deliberately choose not to embody a recognition of the other within their separate texts (or parts of texts). In doing so, they place the onus to recognize dialogue on the reader, who cannot and should not remain naive when confronted by these competing narratives.[23] In this tradition, then, there is an implicit recognition that historical truth cannot be achieved through any one perspective, no matter how convincingly presented. Instead, whatever truth can be achieved emerges from the uneasy coexistence of multiple ways of seeing and narrating the past. It is constituted not through the authority of a single genre but instead through the principle of intergeneric dialogue.

As a rule, Russian writers rarely made direct theoretical statements indicating that they thought intergeneric dialogue the best way to present historical material. This understanding seems usually to have been implicit. Nevertheless, there are instances of such statements, particularly from earlier periods. In a pseudonymous article he wrote for his journal *The Russian Herald* (*Russkii vestnik*), Karamzin claimed: "If a historical personage is depicted vividly on canvas or in marble, then he becomes more fascinating for us in the chronicles themselves."[24] And it seems that it was the assumption that historical material could be presented most effectively in more than one genre that drove and continues to drive the system of intergeneric dialogue.

The Russian intergeneric tradition of history writing rests on a number of paradoxes. First, as a rule, Russian writers derive their initial social authority as an outgrowth of their success and popularity as fiction writers, yet at some point in their careers they decide that fiction alone is inadequate to express all they wish to say, and so they choose to supplement their fictional work with what they offer as nonfictional writing. Second, the intergeneric tradition requires that authors recognize the strength and importance of a European genre system that makes a sharp distinction between history and literature—for when they are working within a single genre they remain true to its conventions—but at the same time they must ignore the fact that, according to those same conventions, one person is not supposed to write both history and fiction. Third, instead of considering famous fiction writers misguided for turning to a profession for which, from a Western European point of view, they are entirely unqualified, Russian readers accept and seemingly expect this of their authors.

A quote taken from Dostoevsky's notebooks for his *Diary of a Writer* is, perhaps, emblematic of the Russian writer's attitude toward history: "One can express incomparably more about our history through fidelity to poetic truth than through fidelity merely to history." [25] On the one hand, the nation's history (perceived, as we have come to expect, as unique—"our history," as opposed to that of any other country) is, for whatever reasons, too difficult or complex to be left to historians. Mere history, however constituted, can never do justice to this crucial topic. And yet, on the other hand, Dostoevsky's own practice indicates that he did not by any means advocate a *purely* poetic version of history. As we will see in Chapter 6, Dostoevsky did not feel that his novels alone were capable of expressing his views on Russian history. Instead, he developed his historical philosophy primarily in the nonfictional sections of *The Diary of a Writer*, a generically heterogeneous work that incorporates essays, feuilletons, journalistic polemic, and some fiction. This quote, had it actually been used in the *Diary*, would certainly have appeared in a nonfictional essay. Thus, the "poetic truth" about history could not be stated exclusively through poetry either (no matter how loosely we construe the term "poetic truth"). At the same time, we see a marked suspicion of historians and the pretensions of nonfictional writing to express the truth about the nation's past, coupled with the (at least implicit) realization that poetry alone is also insufficient to do the topic justice.

This entire Russian tradition, with all the vicissitudes of its development, stands in stark contrast to the practice in European and American culture in the nineteenth and twentieth centuries. In the West, in the course of the first half of the nineteenth century, "the historian became king, all of culture heeded his decrees; history decided how the *Iliad* should be read; history decided what a nation was defining as its historical frontiers, its hereditary enemy, its traditional mission. . . . At a stroke, the historian supplanted the philosopher as guide and counselor."[26] The historian's newfound power grew out of a radical realignment in European culture in the period after the French Revolution, characterized by the gradual disappearance of the eighteenth-century man of letters and the appearance of "literature" and "history" in the generally accepted contemporary definitions of these terms. The chronology of this process of differentiation is summarized neatly by Lionel Gossman: "In the course of the 19th century historians withdrew more and more to the university, to be followed by historians of literature and literary critics; and thus history, like literary scholarship, passed from the hands of the poet and man of letters into those of the professor. . . . The old common ground of history and literature—the idea of mimesis, and the central importance of rhetoric—has thus been gradually vacated by both."[27] In the eighteenth century it had been possible, indeed normal, for a person to produce both fictional and nonfictional narratives. Both Voltaire and Schiller did so, for example. But by the middle of the nineteenth century this was no longer accepted practice.

Although I agree with Gossman's basic characterization of this process, a few caveats should be introduced. It is important to recognize that the rhythm of this separation was different in different countries. In Germany, for example, Leopold von Ranke had already effected the separation of the historian from the man of letters by the 1830's.[28] In France, Jules Michelet was the last historian to straddle the rising generic boundaries that separated historians and writers.[29] To quote Gossman again: "The fragile synthesis that Michelet struggled to sustain fell apart among his successors into a popular novelistic practice of historiography on the one hand, and a more or less academic positivism on the other. History after him was either lively narrative or scholarly disquisition."[30] Thus, the break occurs somewhere in the 1840's or 1850's. In England, where Thomas Macaulay and Thomas Carlyle were active into the late 1850's and mid-1860's, respectively, the process of separation stretched on a bit longer.

Even more important is to recognize that those figures who remained true to the dying tradition of the historian/man of letters (Michelet, Carlyle, Macaulay) were primarily historians who also happened to be excellent prose stylists. Writers of what was coming to be called "literature" in European countries had much earlier abandoned attempts to wear the historian's hat. There were at least two reasons for this. On the one hand, the rise in esteem of the newly recognized historical profession left the writer of imaginative literature little historical space in which to work. Once professional study had become a prerequisite for writing history, the novelist was excluded. On the other hand, the incredible popularity and influence of the Scottian historical novel made that genre (which, after its basic principles had been codified by Sir Walter Scott, had little or nothing to say about history as such) too tempting for most novelists to resist after the 1820's.[31] The net result was that by the 1830's and 1840's, European writers of belles lettres simply did not enter the historical lists at all (or if they did venture forth it was with works that had no pretensions to be taken seriously as history, like Charles Dickens's *A Child's History of England*).[32]

In Russia, the situation was reversed. The major writers of belles lettres never stopped writing history. Indeed, it turns out that at some point in their careers practically all of Russia's most famous writers took it upon themselves to write the nation's history. The literature/history boundary was and continues to be straddled primarily by writers of belles lettres trying their

hand at history, rather than by historians/men of letters of
the Michelet or Carlyle variety.[33] And the historical profession,
although it did produce a few academic historians of great stature, remained relatively weak, especially when compared to the
astonishing prestige afforded novelists and poets.[34] As a result,
Russia looks something like those countries outside the West
that are characterized by Edward Shils as "societies without historiography," in which "belief in the primacy of rational and
empirical cognitive validity has not been accepted . . . to the
extent that they have been disposed to entrust the image of
their past to professional scholars."[35] But as is so often the case,
on closer examination Russia turns out to be a strange hybrid:
it is not exactly that Russians do not believe in the importance
of historical narrative, it is simply that they have not trusted
historians to provide it. When history is provided by novelists
it is frequently accepted willingly. Ultimately then, the Russian
case looks extremely strange when compared to either Western
European or non-Western traditions.

Anyone who has followed developments in European and
American post-structuralist theorizing and postmodernist literary production will certainly appreciate that one of the central
moments in such thinking has been to expose theoretically the
artificiality of the barriers that have separated fiction from nonfiction, literature from history, and to explode them artistically.
Michel Foucault, Hayden White, Umberto Eco, and a host of
others all seem bent on exposing the artificiality of the genre
system that has dominated European art and culture for at least
the last couple of hundred years. This radical reappraisal is one
of the most characteristic and important contributions of the
post-structuralist movement. With respect to the separation of
history and literature, the battle to undermine or at least expose
the artificiality of the old system has been particularly fierce.
Gossman reminds us that this distinction is actually quite recent, a development of Enlightenment thought. Hayden White
tells us that for all intents and purposes novelists and historians

do exactly the same things. Finally, new literary works or even whole genres have sprung up to close the gap between these areas, a fine example of which is the recent novel/history *Dead Certainties*, by Simon Schama.[36] Whether or not one finds postmodernist works that break down the boundary between history and literature convincing is, from my point of view, unimportant. What is crucial is to recognize that the virulence of the attack on this border points up the extent to which its existence has been a fact of European culture.

In Russia, this kind of postmodernist attack would be unthinkable. As opposed to their western European and American counterparts, Russian writers never allowed themselves to be marginalized from the scene of history writing. Employing the tradition of intergeneric dialogue, they continued throughout the nineteenth and twentieth centuries to produce works devoted to Russian history in both fictional and historical genres. The refusal on the part of Russian authors and readers to recognize any one discourse type as most appropriate for the writing of history led to a situation in which various genres, each possessing its own authoritative viewpoint, could, through their interaction, dialogize the presentation of historical material. And now the basis for one of our paradoxes becomes clear. For this approach to succeed, writers and readers must believe that different genres do indeed represent different ways of understanding the world. Difference must be recognized, otherwise dialogue will not be achieved. At the same time, there must be a belief that historical truth is not the exclusive property of any one authoritative discourse. Thus, we can say that in the area of historical narrative, eighteenth-century European culture did not yet recognize difference; hence there was no significant tension between literary and historical genres and no possibility for real dialogue. In the nineteenth century, on the contrary, difference was perceived, but historians succeeded in convincing their audience that theirs was the authoritative discourse. The result, again, was a lack of real dialogue between history and literature.

In Russia, an appreciation of difference had grown up by the beginning of the nineteenth century, but for a number of reasons the discourse of historians failed to become authoritative.

What caused this anomalous situation? Did it result, as many Russians might have claimed, from the uniqueness of the Russian historical situation? the relative weakness of the historical profession in Russia? the peculiarly powerful role of imaginative literature there? the influence of censorship? the unpredictable interaction of native Russian traditions and borrowed European genres? I am afraid that even after having completed this book I cannot provide a neat answer. In the Conclusion, I will speculate on the causes of this unusual Russian tradition, providing overlapping and perhaps contradictory explanations. For now, however, it seems appropriate to begin my investigation by examining what Russian writers have actually done with history. For until we appreciate the full richness of the Russian intergeneric tradition, we cannot even begin to speculate as to why Russian writers have wanted to become historians for the past 200 years.

❦

A Historical Character in Search of a Genre: Vadim of Novgorod and the Prehistory of Intergeneric Dialogue in Russia

In the Nikonian Chronicle, the following entry can be found under the year 864: "In that same year Riurik executed the courageous Vadim and killed many of his [Vadim's] advisors."[1] This terse line marks the only appearance of Vadim in the Russian annals. He is not mentioned in any other historical source, and by all rights he should have been consigned to oblivion along with hundreds of other figures of dubious historical authenticity whose names are scattered throughout the annalistic accounts of Russia's early history.[2] Yet this rebel, who, if he existed at all, accomplished next to nothing in his own time, was destined to play a crucial role in the literary and historical debates that raged in Russia from the last decades of the eighteenth through the first third of the nineteenth century.

In the period from the end of the eighteenth century into the 1830's, the story of Vadim appeared in plays, poetry, prose fiction, history, and even an opera libretto by writers as diverse as Catherine the Great, Iakov Kniazhnin, Petr Plavil'shchikov, Vasily Zhukovsky, Karamzin, Kondraty Ryleev, Aleksei Khomiakov, Stepan Shevyrev, and Pushkin. Because the Vadim story was presented in so many genres and by authors of such differing schools, styles, and temperaments, it provides an unparalleled test case for examining the processes by which a historical theme acquired meaning for Russian culture, underwent a series of adaptations, and finally faded away as it lost cultural relevance. It also gives us a window onto a literary scene in flux, for each new treatment of the Vadim story was, in effect, an attempt to assert the right of a different genre to treat historical material. Ultimately, no consensus was reached, and no genre was able to gain the upper hand as the single appropriate vehicle for the expression of historical truth. Rather, the project came to be seen in terms of complementarity, in which a historical subject took on new meaning and significance through the dialogic interaction of the different genres in which it appeared.

In order to appreciate fully the role that various treatments of the Vadim story came to play in Russian culture, it is important to keep in mind the breakdown in the genre system of Russian literature that occurred in the last decades of the eighteenth century. One of the central concerns of the "legislators" of modern Russian literature—Mikhail Lomonosov, Vasily Trediakovsky, and Alexander Sumarokov—had been to provide the nascent national literature with a solid generic system. Sumarokov's "Instructions for Those Wishing to Be Writers" ("Nastavlenie khotiashchim byti pisateliami"), a text filled with specific prescriptions on what was and was not acceptable in each literary genre, is a typical expression of this desire. Such an approach made sense both in terms of literary history, since the Russians took as their primary model the French normative neoclassical poetics of the seventeenth century, and in pragmatic terms, for it is difficult to see how a Europeanized version of Russian literature could have gotten off the ground without recourse to some kind of imitative poetics. By the 1770's, however, cracks had already begun to appear in the generic edifice erected by the initial literary legislators: for example, much to the disgust of the aging Sumarokov, sentimentalist features were appearing in tragedy. And by the 1780's, even such well-codified genres as the solemn ode were being subverted.

In the generic system of neoclassical Russian literature there were a number of options for writers who wished to deal with historical figures. One was the epic poem. In Russia, the most celebrated epic of the eighteenth century was Mikhail Kheraskov's *Rossiada*, which commemorated the capture of Kazan' by Ivan the Terrible in 1553. It is noteworthy for my investigation that Kheraskov makes no claims regarding the truth value of his epic. Indeed, in the introduction he specifically disavows any such claim: "It is necessary not to forget that one should not search for historical truth in an epic or in the historical descriptions in a poem."[3] Although he uses historical material, Kheraskov acknowledges that his epic is not about history—historical figures appear strictly to fill the epic roles allotted them by the genre. The epic is a source of emotional and spiritual uplift, not a true representation of historical events.

The other neoclassical genre appropriate for the depiction of historical characters was, of course, the tragedy. Many Russian tragedies dealt nominally with historical figures from Russia's past. As a rule, however, this genre also made no claims to historical accuracy, as can be seen from a statement made by Sergei Glinka in the introduction to his tragedy *Mikhail, Prince of Chernigov* (*Mikhail, kniaz' Chernigovskii*): "A tragedian is not a historian. Therefore, one cannot demand from him historical exactness."[4] The sentiment here is, of course, quite similar to that expressed by Kheraskov in the preface to his epic.

Taken together, these two quotes suggest that although neoclassical Russian writers did not believe it was to be gotten at through literary works, they did have some notion, however vague, of historical truth. In turn, this would naturally imply the existence of works of history. And indeed, although history writing was not part of the official neoclassical literary canon, a number of histories were published in Russia in the eighteenth century. Among these, Vasily Tatishchev's *Russian History from the Earliest Times* (*Istoriia rossiiskaia s samykh drevneishikh vremen*), which was presented to the Russian Academy of Sciences in 1739, deserves to be mentioned. This work, a compilation drawn from an impressive variety of sources, was a new departure for Russia: "With Tatishchev, it can be said, historical science in Russia begins to move forward from the simple

annalistic accounts to a more modern form of historical narrative."[5] However, for a variety of reasons, Tatishchev's work was
not published in his lifetime, and so it was not accessible even
to the small Russian reading public that might have wished to
sample its contents.[6] The first volume was eventually published
in 1768 and, among much else, we note that under the year
869 Tatishchev repeated the story of Vadim from the Nikonian
Chronicle, adding a bit of motivation for it: "In these times
the Slavs fled from Novgorod to Kiev, away from Riurik, who
killed the courageous Vadim, a Slavic prince, for not wanting to
be a slave to the Varangians."[7]

Almost simultaneously with the appearance of the first volume of Tatishchev's history, Russian readers were treated to
the first volume of what would eventually be an eight-volume
set entitled *Russian Historical Library Containing Early Chronicles
and Various Notations, as an Aid to the Understanding of the History
and Geography of Early and Medieval Russia* (*Drevnaia rossiiskaia
vivliofika*, 1767–92). The appearance of this set was significant
because for the first time Russians were able to read for themselves the chronicles that formed and have continued to form
the single largest source of material on the history of Rus'. This
material had hitherto been extant only in manuscript form. In
particular, Russian readers might well have noticed the generic
heterogeneity of the chronicles, a quality that sharply separated
them from European history writing of the eighteenth century.
In addition to annalistic descriptions (which themselves present
a variety of perspectives), the chronicles contain interpolated
treaties, a will and testament, folk elements, and so forth. As
Dmitry Likhachev puts it: "There is no single authorial point
of view in the chronicles, they rather express the views of many
authors, which were more or less cursorily edited by the final
chronicler, the person who unified the chronicle texts of his
predecessors. Polyphony is characteristic of the pre-sixteenth-
century chronicle."[8] Indeed, one factor that may well have
played a significant role in preventing the split between the
writing of belles lettres and the writing of history texts in Russia

was precisely the ambiguous generic nature of these chronicles. In any case, this feature was certainly appreciated by Karamzin. Even so, since the language of the chronicles differed sharply from modern Russian, and since the Russian book-buying public was tiny, only a few of the best-educated Russians of the day could have appreciated the chronicle texts.

This, then, was the general situation by about 1780: on the one hand, there were literary works that were vaguely based on historical material but that made no claims to tell the truth about history; on the other, there were learned histories and published historical documents that for linguistic and economic reasons remained mostly inaccessible to Russian readers. This literary/historical equilibrium was upset by what at first glance seems a most unlikely perpetrator: the Empress of Russia, Catherine the Great.

Although she is known in the West and in Russia primarily for her political achievements, Catherine, true to the model of the ideal Enlightened Despot, produced a varied corpus of literary work. Early in her reign, in the late 1760's, she introduced the Addisonian satirical journal to Russia with her *All Kinds of Things* (*Vsiakaia vsiachina*). In the 1770's, she began writing comedies for the stage, and while they are perhaps not literary chefs d'oeuvre, they are certainly no worse than the average Russian comedy of the period.[9] In the 1780's, Catherine turned her attention to history. In her secretary's notes of December 4, 1783, we find the following order: "Her Imperial Highness has deigned to order that, under the direction and supervision of Count Andrei Petrovich Shuvalov, a few people be appointed to work together to compile useful notes about ancient history, most particularly concerning Russia."[10]

Catherine first published the results of these researches starting in 1783 under the title *Notes Concerning Russian History* (*Zapiski kasatel'no Rossiiskoi Istorii*) in the journal *Collocutor of Lovers of the Russian Word* (*Sobesednik liubitelei rossiiskogo slova*). The notes were prefaced by the following observation: "These notes concerning Russian history are composed for our youth at a time

when books calling themselves histories of Russia have been
appearing in foreign languages. But these books should really
be called biased creations, since every page bears witness to the
hatred with which they were written." [11] The clearly implied
goals for the work were that it be national in character (as opposed to the works of "foreign authors"), sympathetic to Russia (in distinction to their alleged "hatred") and, presumably,
accurate. What would happen if these three imperatives were
incompatible was not stated, nor was the irony in the situation
of a German-born Empress taking on the role of nationalist historian for her adopted country acknowledged. However, as we
will see when we examine Catherine's work more closely, tensions between nationalism, nationality, and historical accuracy
would prove to be of paramount importance.

Although it is generally conceded that Catherine did not take
her literary efforts that seriously, she was evidently quite pleased
with the history. In a letter to F. M. Grimm on the subject, she
managed to be regally aloof and ironic, but a certain authorial
pride cannot be overlooked: "This history is being published
in a Russian journal . . . which comes out once a month; so
many reigns a month. This gives the history to everyone, and
I cannot deny that it is successful; it is considered the most
palatable of the ones that have appeared, and people find that
it inculcates a zeal for the fatherland that touches the emo-
tions." [12] Two thoughts are central here: the history is for a mass
audience (for the day, anyway), and it is nationalistic. This combination of qualities had been notably lacking in the serious
historical works of her predecessors, both Russians (who were
not writing for a general audience) and foreigners (who were not
nationalistic).

At first glance then, it would seem that Catherine imagined
herself as nothing more than a popularizer of Russian history
for a more or less mass audience. And indeed, considering the
fact that she could not and did not do any of her own research,
it is hard to imagine how she could have hoped to accomplish
anything more. Nevertheless, as we will see on closer exami-

nation, Catherine's *Notes* were not merely randomly assembled facts pasted into readable narrative form. At least in some areas, she developed a very specific interpretation of Russian history, informed by the historical debates of her time and marked by a clear ideological attitude. In this regard, her use of the story of Vadim of Novgorod, which had been practically insignificant for her predecessors, took on major importance.

In her *Notes* we read the following concerning Vadim:

> While Oskold kept in shape with campaigns against the Pechenegs and Kriviches, and Grand Prince Riurik dealt with the security of his borders, disorders occurred in Novgorod as a result of the Novgorodians' envy toward the Varangians. The leader of these disorders was a brave man named Vadim, a Slavic prince.
>
> It is opined that the complaint was that the Slavic people were allegedly humiliated, and that Slavs were rarely in important positions because Varangians were sent everywhere and employed for everything.
>
> But Grand Prince Riurik quickly quieted the disorders and punished the ringleaders.[13]

One's initial response to this passage is to note that Catherine limits herself to a bare-bones historical account: basically nothing more than a rewriting of Tatishchev. Still, the emphasis has shifted significantly; in Catherine's version right and the author's sympathy are clearly and unequivocally on the side of Riurik. The rebels are filled with "envy"; they stir up trouble while Riurik is out defending the frontiers; the word "allegedly" is obviously meant to indicate the spuriousness of the Novgorodians' claims. Of course, that Catherine supports the ruler against a rebel is hardly surprising.

What is more important to keep in mind, however, is that Riurik was not simply a ruler, but a non-Slavic ruler who had been invited into Rus' from a foreign country. That is, the conflict can be seen in ethnic rather than in political terms. Considering the fact that Catherine herself was a German princess who had acceded to the Russian throne only after a palace coup that resulted in the deposition and murder of her partly

Russian husband, and considering that the Pugachev uprising of 1773–74 had been led by a rebel who claimed to be that very husband, it is not too much to assume that Catherine identified with Riurik to a greater extent than with most other figures from Russia's past. As we will see, the play that she wrote on the Riurik theme serves to support such a contention.

But Catherine's position vis-à-vis the Riurik/Vadim conflict had deeper historiographical implications as well. In supporting Riurik while emphasizing his non-Russian background, Catherine was aligning herself with the so-called Norman theory, which "came to regard the Varangians (Normans) as true founders of the Russian state. The founding of this Norman school dates back to the first half of the eighteenth century, traced largely to a group of German scholars" that included "Bayer, Müller, Schlözer, and others." [14] Historians of Russian descent, including Tatishchev and Lomonosov in the eighteenth century, rejected this theory, primarily because of "its tendency to consider the Slavs not only a backward people, but as incapable of governing themselves." [15] Catherine, then, in addition to coming out on the side of Riurik against Vadim in a particular case, turns out to be by implication a supporter of the Norman theory in general.

Further evidence that this was the case can be seen from an ironic letter written to herself and published with the third installment of the historical *Notes*, in which she speaks as if from the point of view of a reader disappointed by the dryness of her *Notes* in general and by her less-than-glorious view of the early history of the Slavs in particular. "For example, what a dry and insignificant account you give of the ancestry of the Russians! Could you really not have given such a glorious people a more miraculous cradle than this?" [16] Here we see Catherine tempering the Norman theory a bit, for she goes on to say specifically that Russian patriotism and national pride are not incompatible with borrowing from the outside. Considering that Catherine became an ardent Russian patriot while remaining both a foreign ruler and a partisan of Western European ideas of enlightened despotism, it is not surprising that she would attempt some kind of synthesis of Normanist and anti-Normanist views.

Evidently, however, Catherine was not entirely satisfied with the nonfictional prose history as a genre for expressing her interpretation of Russia's past. What she needed was a genre that could allow her more freedom in portraying historical actions but that would, at the same time, retain some of the truth value (seen, of course, in contemporary terms) of the history. In 1787, two plays now generally attributed to Catherine appeared anonymously in the journal *The Russian Theater* (*Rossiiskii featr*, vol. 14). The first was entitled *Imitation of Shakespeare, a Historical Representation Without the Retention of Standard Theatrical Rules, from the Life of Riurik* (*Podrazhanie Shekspiru, Istoricheskoe predstavlenie bez sokhraneniia featral'nykh obyknovennykh pravil, Iz zhizni Riurika*), and the second *The Beginning of Oleg's Reign* (*Nachal'noe upravlenie Olega*).[17] Here, Catherine fleshes out the story of Russia's earliest history, gives her characters psychological motivations for their action, and adds or changes certain details of the story. That she consciously appreciated the different possibilities afforded by the two genres can be seen in one of her notes: "I did not dare to put my conjectures regarding Riurik in my history, for they were based solely on a few words hidden by Nestor in his chronicle and one passage in Dalin's history of Sweden. But while reading Shakespeare in German I dreamed up the idea of putting my conjectures in a drama, which was printed in 1786."[18]

Quite clearly, Catherine had a well-developed sense of the different levels of historical accuracy required by the history and the drama. At the same time, she found it perfectly reasonable to produce both. Evidently, however, the fact that certain aspects of the plays are based on conjecture did not, in her view, invalidate the drama entirely as a source of historical knowledge. In the long introduction to the play about Oleg, the author remarks: "In this historical representation there is more historical truth than invention."[19] Of course, whether or not these plays really deal in historical facts is unimportant; what is crucial is the claim. Whereas Kheraskov and Glinka emphatically disavowed any attribution of historical truth to their literary works, Catherine demands that the reader recognize her plays as historically valid. Not completely so, of course, for she does not deny or try to hide the fact that she has made some things up. Her choice of genre, an imitation of Shakespeare, is a further indication of the uniqueness of her claim for the historical authoritativeness of her literary work. Before this, serious drama in Russia had been restricted to neoclassical tragedy, which was not assumed to have any necessary connection to historical fact. By choosing a new genre (new for Russian literature, anyway) for her history play, Catherine freed herself of the fictiveness expected of the tragedy and at least allowed for the possibility of a literary genre that could tell historical truth and provide valid historical interpretation.[20]

More important, from my point of view, than the claim to historical truth in the introduction to the play about Oleg is the strategy Catherine adopted to force readers to notice the connections between her plays and her historical *Notes*. Her strategy was to weave the exact words she used in the *Notes* into the speeches of the characters in both historical plays. This, for example, is how Vadim's revolt is characterized by one of the characters in the play:

Prince Vadim is starting to spread rumors among the people that *supposedly the Slavic people are humiliated and that Slavs are rarely in important positions*; that a large number of Varangians will come to Rus' with the Grand Prince; that *they will be sent everywhere and employed for everything* and that they will oppress the Slavs and the Rus; that the Varangians are more skilled on the sea than on dry land and that they don't know or understand Slavic military affairs; that Vadim grew up and was brought up in Novgorod by Gostomysl; that in the old days they didn't look at order of birth so much as at who the people would derive the most good from; and that Vadim was born to be just what the people need.[21] (emphasis mine)

In this excerpt one can see clearly Catherine's basic technique. She repeats the essential nugget of information gleaned from her historical sources, and then she adds a more or less psychologically motivated embellishment. Evidently, Catherine took Aristotle's famous distinction between the poet and the historian to heart. In her play she is happy to show us what might have happened, while in the history she limits herself, more or less, to her sources, qualifying her interpolations carefully. Furthermore, changes are dictated by the exigencies of the genre. The Shakespearian history play is primarily psychological. For it to work, we must be given clues as to the motivations of the characters. This is not true for the kind of mixed chronicle/history that Catherine was writing. Such a work was supposed to provide facts, and these were not seen as requiring psychological explanation.

What, we must ask, is the effect of this unusual device on the reader (assuming, of course, that the device is recognized)? First and foremost, repetition of textual elements inevitably strengthens the dialogue that would probably be the natural result of the existence of two works on the same theme by the same author. It emphasizes both identity (thereby strengthening the connections between works) and lack of identity (because the presence of some repeated elements invites the reader also to notice what is not repeated or what is changed). As a result, reader response, both to the play and to the history, must change. Because most readers take works entitled "histories" to be basically true, the presence of elements lifted from the history helps buttress Catherine's claim that the plays contain "more historical truth than invention." They lend an air of verisimilitude to the plays and force readers to contemplate the possibility that a fictional work can be a carrier of historical truth.

At the same time, the Riurik play reveals the limitations of history (at least history as Catherine wrote it) when it comes to explanation. In her *Notes* Catherine was willing to provide a conjecture as to the cause of Vadim's revolt (about which the Nikonian Chronicle is silent), but when it came to the outcome there was not much she could do. In the play, however, she could be much freer, allowing herself to make additions that would turn the suppression of a revolt into an ideological statement. In the play, after the revolt is put down Riurik shows himself to be a generous and noble victor. Instead of executing Vadim, as Catherine's historical sources had it, Riurik pardons him, and, surprisingly enough, Vadim agrees to be a loyal subject henceforth.

What are we to make of this harmonious, reconciliatory closure? It is clear that we are meant to see Riurik as an ideal despot of the type Catherine fancied herself. He is slow to anger, decisive when necessary, and merciful in victory. Indeed, he is a dramatic endorsement of the monarchical principle. As one of the characters puts it: "In a large country with a big population, can you expect everyone to think alike in all cases? . . . But a reasonable ruler who judges someone not by biased accounts but rather by his qualities and merits will easily be able to tame our envy and disaccord." [22] There is, however, one additional important polemical point being made here. Catherine's play illustrates, allegorically if you like, what her history could only hint at: that a foreigner is perfectly fit to rule Russia, assuming that this foreigner is an enlightened ruler. The historical play encourages the audience to draw a direct parallel between hero and author, to appreciate their psychology, and to see both as perfect rulers called from abroad to lead the Russians to greater glory. The play then is, in great measure, about the legitimacy of autocracy, and particularly of a foreign-born autocrat. History, when viewed properly, can provide a lesson for the present day, and the historical drama, while lacking some of the truth value of a history, is perhaps a more useful vehicle for its presentation. It partakes of the truth of history insofar as it incorporates historical material into its fabric, but it is not limited by that material.

Ultimately then, what Catherine has done is to create an intergeneric dialogue between her works. The device of direct self-quotation invites the reader of the play to recall the history and to compare the possibilities that the various genres allow for the presentation of historical material. To recall the terminology borrowed from Bakhtin in the Introduction, each of these methods of presentation calls into question the "naiveté" of the other genre. At the same time, no single genre is valorized as the most appropriate for the presentation of historical material. Indeed, the implication is that both are necessary, for if one would do, why bother to write the other? If the reader happens also to be a writer, the dual treatment of the Vadim story encourages the production of other versions of the story either in the same or in different genres. It was this literary potential that became the most important legacy of Catherine's writing. Long after the debates that interested her had become insignificant, the principle of intergeneric dialogue as a means for treating historical material in Russia remained. Indeed, it remains until this day, although Catherine's role in originating the process has been completely forgotten.

Catherine the Great's influence on Russian literary developments of the nineteenth and twentieth centuries must be recognized as equal to that of any of Russia's more celebrated eighteenth-century writers. Her historical *Notes* and historical dramas must also be seen as an early contribution to the Russian literary search for a viable national past. Her efforts are representative of a Russian cultural nationalism that manifested itself only weakly in the eighteenth century. The pattern we see here is, of course, not unique to Russia: it was and is standard practice for nations to defend themselves culturally through the creation of a glorious national past.[23] Specific to Russia, of course, is that fact that the ruler took a direct part in the process. And if we recall that Catherine and her court were the only viable consumers of cultural products in this period, it is hard to overemphasize the impact that her personal involvement would have had.[24]

It did not take long for a reply to Catherine's implicit invitation to generic dialogue to appear. In 1789, Iakov Kniazhnin wrote a five-act verse tragedy entitled *Vadim of Novgorod* (*Vadim Novgorodskii*). The play went into rehearsal in 1790 but, perhaps feeling that in the wake of the French Revolution it would be misinterpreted, the author withdrew the work. Kniazhnin died the next year. In 1793, his heirs asked Princess Dashkova, the head of the Russian Academy of Sciences, for permission to publish *Vadim*. After checking with a censor she agreed, and the play appeared both in *The Russian Theater* (the same annual publication of new plays in which Catherine's dramas had appeared a few years earlier) and as a separate edition.

The story of what happened next has been recounted many times. Someone informed Catherine's last lover, Platon Zubov, that the play was subversive. He brought the matter to Catherine's attention, and she was outraged to the point of insanity. As Simon Karlinsky puts it: "Her reaction to Zubov's accusations was spectacular indeed. She ordered a copy of *Vadim of Novgorod* burned by an executioner in a public ceremony. All copies of *The Russian Theater* that contained the play were ordered destroyed. All purchasers of the play were directed to turn their copies in to the authorities. Private homes were searched to ensure that no copy of the play survived." [25]

What could it have been in Kniazhnin's play that drew Catherine's hysterical wrath? The usual explanation is, of course, political. The Soviet literary historian G. R. Gukovsky, for example, attempting as always to rescue another writer for the proto-Communist pantheon, attempts to prove that Kniazhnin did indeed write with revolutionary intent and that Catherine's reaction was simply based on a logical desire to preserve her personal and class interests. [26] Karlinsky, more convincingly, tries to show that the whole scandal was merely a misunderstanding, but that Catherine indeed interpreted the play as a political attack. [27] Is this position tenable?

In Kniazhnin's play the center of gravity is shifted from Riurik and his reign to Vadim, a change in focus indicated by the title. In Catherine's play the action takes place immediately after Riurik has arrived, and is motivated primarily by Vadim's desire to have the throne for himself. Kniazhnin's tragedy is set three years after Riurik's reign has begun and the crisis is precipitated by Vadim's belief that Riurik is a tyrant who is trampling on the ancient democratic rights of the Novgorodians. It is true that Kniazhnin's play contains a number of ringing speeches against tyranny, both by Vadim himself and by some of the secondary characters. These speeches are usually cited by Soviet commentators as evidence that the play was meant as a political attack on Catherine. In our view, of course, such an interpretation would be strengthened by the fact that Catherine is strongly identified with Riurik.

Nevertheless, there are certain problems with a straightforward political explanation of Catherine's reaction. First, a glance at the pages of *The Russian Theater* in the years immediately following the French Revolution shows it to contain other plays in which tyrants are denounced, including a five-act drama by Kniazhnin himself called *Vladistan*. Set in mythical Slaviansk, this play is entirely about efforts to overthrow a tyrant.[28] It drew no response from Catherine as far as can be ascertained. Second, in the course of *Vadim* it becomes clear to the reader that Vadim's perception of Riurik is not shared by his fellow citizens. Rather, Riurik considers himself an exemplary ruler, and the Novgorodians concur with this estimation. Riurik's goodwill and benevolent reign would seem ultimately to be proved at the close of the play when, having put down the revolt, Riurik not only offers Vadim his personal liberty, but even offers to return his crown to the Novgorodian people. They then reaffirm the social contract, it would appear, by requesting him to continue to rule. As opposed to the harmonious resolution in Catherine's play, however, Vadim spurns Riurik's offer and takes his own life.

Given the tragedy's conclusion, it would seem that a relatively dispassionate reading could not possibly provoke the interpretation that it was antiautocratic or anti-Catherine. This, clearly, was the judgment of Princess Dashkova, of the play's original censor, and of its only contemporary reviewer. Dashkova, who should certainly have known which way the winds were blowing at court, seems to have been quite surprised by the scandal. In her memoirs, admittedly written after the fact, she says that she gave the play to an advisor: "According to Kozodavlev, the tragedy presented exactly historical events that had occurred in Novgorod and ended with the triumph of the Russian tsar and the submission of Novgorod and the rebels. So then I ordered the play printed."[29]

It seems likely then, that Kniazhnin's crime may have been something other than incorrect political thinking, actual or perceived. I would suggest that what drew Catherine's fury was as much literary jealousy as political fear. Having initiated the potential for intergeneric dialogue, Catherine seems to have been enraged when this potential was activated. Kniazhnin had presumed to reinterpret and rework a story that Catherine had taken to heart. He gave that story new form (changing it from Shakespearian history to French tragedy), focused attention on a different hero, and turned the audience's attention away from the problem of whether autocracy in Russia had been legitimated by a social contract to whether autocracy could be legitimate *even* if it had been ratified by a social contract. Finally, he revised the ending from one stressing integration to one showing a radical inability to integrate.

It is my view that Catherine was more angered by the literary and historical polemic proposed by Kniazhnin than she was by the work's ambiguous political content. This reaction was one that Dashkova and the play's censor (who were, quite reasonably, only worried about "revolutionary" content) failed to anticipate. It should be noted in this context that this was not the only time in her career that Catherine expressed and acted on a certain literary jealousy. She did the same in 1769–70 when competing satirical journals (whose appearance she had initially encouraged) presumed to reinterpret some of her themes and methods. Psychologically, this response is understandable. In theory an author invites dialogue with other authors on a footing of equality. However, for an autocrat, explicit dialogue, even if only in literature, represents a denial of hierarchical relations and is therefore unacceptable. Implicit dialogue was fine, but when writers engaged in explicit polemics Catherine felt challenged, not as a fellow writer but as an autocrat, and she acted accordingly.

That Catherine's fury was the result of literary rather than strictly political objections is borne out by an examination of the first and only contemporary review of Kniazhnin's *Vadim*, published in Ivan Krylov's journal *The St. Petersburg Mercury* (no. 3, 1793). The reviewer, the minor playwright A. Klushin, does not make any reference to the play's potential ideological unsuitability. He does suggest that the play would be better if it had a different ending. "Wouldn't it have been preferable for Mr. Author to have depicted a break in Vadim's character in the denouement? . . . Wouldn't it have been preferable for Vadim to have recognized Riurik as the Novgorodians' benefactor[?] . . . It would seem that this action would have been more vivid, more unexpected, more reasonable, and more edifying." In effect, what the reviewer is doing is proposing Catherine's ending for Kniazhnin's play. Catherine, of course, had more effective methods than literary criticism for dealing with Kniazhnin's play. On the pretext of political unsuitability, she banned a rival literary treatment of "her" theme.[30] However, as is usual in such cases, the effect of the ban was just the opposite of what was intended. Because it was forbidden, *Vadim of Novgorod* lived on as an underground text long after all of Kniazhnin's other tragedies had been forgotten, while Catherine's own plays fell into oblivion.

The scandal surrounding Kniazhnin's play had important consequences for later literary and historical developments. The conflicting treatments of Vadim highlighted the advantages and disadvantages of various genres for the treatment of historical material. Having already appeared successfully in a history, a "Shakespearian" history play, and a classical tragedy, Vadim was liberated from the constraints of any single genre. The Vadim story became a natural choice for genre experiments, and the story would be used and abused for the next quarter of a century in all manner of literary and historical guises.

Equally important, the scandal lent the Vadim story immense contemporary significance in the Russian cultural mind. It was transformed from a hazy legend of the ninth century into a burning cultural issue. In effect, the scandal surrounding Kniazhnin's play allowed events of 1793 to be projected onto the events of the original story: Kniazhnin was linked to his Vadim and to his *Vadim*, and Catherine was equated with Kniazhnin's Vadim's vision of Riurik, thus doubling the story's symbolic potential. For many writers of the first quarter of the nineteenth century, the Vadim story could easily be connected not to the question of the legitimacy of autocracy (its original literary raison d'être), but rather to the question of the right of the individual to express himself in an oppressive state. This was a natural development because it underscored a belief about the value of history that was standard for the time: that history serves as a model for the present. As Karamzin put it at the beginning of the influential preface to his *History of the Russian State*: "Leaders and legislators act according to the suggestions of history and look on her pages as navigators study charts of the sea. Human wisdom has need of experience, while life is short." [31]

The next stage in the development of the Vadim story sees the character move from drama to prose fiction. Such a trajectory is consistent with general trends in Russian literary culture. [32] With only one major exception, the plays of Vladislav Ozerov, neoclassical tragedy dried up as a productive genre, and Catherine's "Shakespearian" example was not followed. Russian writers turned increasingly to lyric poetry, a genre not conducive to historical material, and to the prose tale. Vadim appears in at least three prose works of the first decade of the century, and in each of them one can see the problems that the still-developing genre had in incorporating historical material. At the same time, one can sense what attracted authors to prose fiction. Particularly important was the freedom to re-create more fully the general tone and atmosphere of the past. Of course, the atmosphere actually re-created had in fact very little to do with historical reality. Nevertheless, writers were struggling to escape the constraints of the dialogue and stage directions in drama and the necessity to keep within the bounds of the known in history. The prose tale injected new potential into the intergeneric dialogue. Unfortunately, however, at this stage in the development of Russian prose, authors were as yet unable to integrate atmosphere with action, and in most cases their stories have a static quality.

The least successful of these works is the dreadful fragment of juvenilia "Vadim Novgorodskii" that Zhukovsky published in 1803 in Karamzin's journal *Herald of Europe* (*Vestnik Evropy*). It begins with several pages of effusive elegiac laments from the "author," who claims to be isolated from the world and all who love him, including the inevitable dead friend. This treacly paean to friendship leads the author into historical free association, and the era in which he descends is the ninth century. Zhukovsky does create an appropriately portentous, mist-covered, and starkly suggestive landscape. He peoples the scene with an old man who, like the "author," is wasting away alone in the wilderness. This similarity between "author" and historical character, created by the story's frame narrative, points to a potential equation between events of ancient history and those of Zhukovsky's day, a potential that is not exploited here, however.

The old man's solitude is broken by the appearance of a handsome youth who asks for shelter. It turns out that this young man is Vadim and the old man is Gostomysl, the same Slavic prince whose death in earlier versions of the story led to the disturbances that precipitated the calling of the Varangians. In this version, Vadim's father and Gostomysl were exiled from Novgorod, a fact that would presumably call into question the voluntary nature of the Slavs' submission to Riurik. Unfortunately we never learn just what happened, because the rest of the story is taken up by the two characters' recalling Vadim's father and shedding sentimental tears. Zhukovsky is so busy trying to create atmosphere that he fails to provide any forward narrative motion. The story breaks off at this point with the promise of a continuation. It is not clear whether this is simply a device for closure or whether the author actually intended to continue (it is probably just as well that he did not). Still, despite its deficiencies, Zhukovsky's fragment initiates the development of a new version of Vadim as the innocent youth. This version would become standard for poetic treatments of the subject in the 1820's.

Most of the same criticisms apply to Mikhail N. Murav'ev's story "Oskol'd." It lacks Zhukovsky's sentimentalist clichés, but this story too is all atmosphere and preparation as warriors gather to begin Oskold's legendary campaign against Constantinople. Once again, the fragment breaks off just when the author would have had to depict some action, confirming the suspicion that prose writers of this period had not quite figured out how to do this. Still, Murav'ev's story was appreciated in its time by at least one qualified reader, precisely for its re-creation of historical atmosphere, something that neither drama nor history could match.[33] Vadim plays only a bit part in "Oskol'd." This Vadim, presumably more or less the one whose life was spared by Riurik at the end of Catherine's play, shows up as the sullen leader of the Novgorodian troops: "A martial fortress, gloomy, silent, and consumed by injured pride, Vadim cannot forget his exile from the Novgorodian throne. He leads those whom he once considered his subjects."[34] We are given no further details about this Vadim, but it is clear that neither he nor historical material in general fits very comfortably in the confines of the preromantic prose fragment.

A far more successful prose treatment both of history and of Vadim is Karamzin's story "Martha the Posadnik, or the Subjugation of Novgorod" ("Marfa-posadnitsa, ili pokorenie Novagoroda"). This version actively encourages dialogue both with previous treatments of the story and with Karamzin's own presentation of it in his *History of the Russian State* (see Chapter 3). At first glance, "Martha the Posadnik," which describes events that occurred some 500 years after Vadim's death, seems an unlikely place for his appearance. He is physically present, however, in the form of a marble statue, which stands in the main square of Novgorod. And it is to his memory that Martha appeals when she stirs the Novgorodians to resistance. This is not the Vadim of Catherine and of Murav'ev; this is Kniazhnin's rebel and by extension any rebel against the tsar's autocratic power, including, perhaps, Kniazhnin himself. Here is an excerpt from Martha's initial call to arms:

Vadim! Vadim! This is where your sacred blood flowed. Here I call you and the heavens as witnesses that my heart loves the glory of the fatherland and the good of my fellow citizens. A woman dares to speak at the Veche, for my ancestors were friends of Vadim's. . . . Riurik wanted to rule autocratically . . . but the courageous Vadim called him before the people's judgment. "Let the Gods and the sword be our judges," answered Riurik,—and Vadim fell at his hand, saying: "Novgorodians! Come to this place that is crimsoned with my blood to cry over your lack of understanding—and to glorify freedom when it again appears triumphantly within your walls." [35]

Vadim's statue becomes a symbol for rebellion against authority. This leitmotif is carried through consistently to the story's end, when the crushing of the revolt is coupled with the toppling of the statue.

Thus, a new figure of Vadim arises. As opposed to the earlier, more ambiguous versions, this Vadim was justified in opposing Riurik, who, it turns out, really was a tyrant. Kniazhnin himself, as a victim of authority, has been grafted onto a portrait of Vadim. It must be pointed out that Karamzin lets the reader know that he is not in sympathy with the revolt led by Martha, but this fact fails to undercut the association of Vadim with revolution that the story creates. The actual winner, ultimately, is the principle of intergeneric dialogue, for now a whole new method of treating historical material—the full-blown prose tale—has entered the equation.

How did the next generation of Russian writers deal with Vadim's story? Ironically, as more attention was focused on Vadim, it became clear that the story was probably only a legend. More "scientific" historians began to question their sources and to realize that the Nikonian Chronicle was extremely untrustworthy. Russian historians in general, including Karamzin, began to cast doubt on the authenticity of the Vadim legend just as it began to take on crucial significance for contemporary Russian culture. In his *History of the Russian State*, for example, following his description of the "calling of the Varangians," Karamzin asks a series of rhetorical questions before introducing Vadim:

Did the people approve of the changes in their civic code? Did they enjoy the happy quiet that is so rarely known by human societies? Or did they miss their ancient freedom? Although the newest Chroniclers say that the Slavs soon became unhappy with their slavery, and that a certain Vadim, called "the Brave" fell, together with many of his adherents, in Novogorod at the hand of the powerful Riurik—a likely event: people who were used to freedom might have wished for Rulers to save them from the horrors of anarchy, but they could have easily repented *if* the Varangians, the countrymen, and friends of the house of Riurik persecuted them—however, this story, as it is not based on the ancient writings of Nestor, is probably just a guess and an invention.[36]

Karamzin gives a far more psychologically convincing explanation for Vadim's actions than did his predecessors, but a question arises, nevertheless: if Karamzin did not believe that Vadim existed, why does the story appear here at all? The answer, of course, is that while Vadim's story may no longer have been considered historical fact, it was unquestionably still literary fact, and Karamzin's *History* belongs to a literary as well as to a historical genre. Vadim was an expected part of the Riurik story, canonized by literary practice, and he could not just be left out of the narrative. By including the story and simultaneously denying its historical truth, Karamzin drains it of historical content while allowing it to function as literary text. As a result, Vadim is liberated not just from any specific historical genre, but from history itself, eventually becoming a purely literary character.

One might imagine that after the historical wind had been

taken out of Vadim's sails the theme would have lost its value for Russian culture. This was not the case, however, and the further transformation of the theme in the 1820's illustrates the potential that narratives have to move from one context to another, adapted by a culture for new purposes and taking on new levels of meaning even as they lose their original ones. In Russian literature of this period the Vadim theme becomes more popular than ever. Ryleev starts a lyric poem on it, Pushkin begins his version a number of times, the very young Khomiakov writes part of a narrative poem on the subject, and Mikhail Lermontov writes a prose *Vadim* (although he echoes the theme only in his title and subject matter, without using the "historical" story).

What is clear from these treatments is that the story of Vadim's revolt has by this time been freed entirely of historical constraints (probably as a result of Karamzin's debunking of the story's historical veracity), and that the figure of Vadim has become invested with a positive revolutionary aura (almost certainly born of the identification of Vadim with the "martyred" Kniazhnin). Questions concerning the legitimacy of autocracy and the foreign ruler (Catherine) and tyranny and its definition (Kniazhnin) are no longer as important as they had been.

In Ryleev's fragments, Vadim becomes a model Byronic hero.[37] The requisite surroundings of gloom, waves, cliffs, thunder, and lightning are present. However, Ryleev's Vadim is a Byronic hero with a political purpose. He is attempting to free his people:

> Несмотря на хлад убийственный
> Сограждан к правам своим
> Их от бед спасти насильственно
> Хочет пламенный Вадим.[38]

> Despite the murderous coldness
> Of his countrymen toward their rights
> The fiery Vadim wants
> To save them from their misfortunes.

Or, as Vadim says to himself in a different variant:

Ах! если б возвратиться я мог
Порабощенному народу
Блаженства общего залог
Былую праотцев свободу.[39]

Ach! if I could only return
To my enslaved people
That pledge of common happiness
The erstwhile freedom of their forefathers.

What is interesting here is the fact that Vadim simply assumes Riurik is a tyrant, "князь самовластительный" (autocratic prince), and so, one presumes, does the author. There is no longer a question of tyranny or legitimacy. Riurik is considered illegitimate simply by virtue of his presence on the throne.

The same assumptions underlie Khomiakov's long poem *Vadim*. The work is unfinished, and large pieces of it are unconnected or only loosely connected to each other. Nevertheless, some important transformations of the Vadim story seem to be on the verge of taking place here. Other than the existence of Vadim, Riurik, and a revolt, little trace of the story as it had been told in eighteenth-century accounts remains. Instead, Vadim is made the son of a man who had been exiled unfairly from Novgorod some twenty years before the action of the poem begins.[40] The young Vadim has grown up to become a cross between a noble savage and Childe Harold. Despite having never been in Novgorod, upon hearing that the city is being ruled by a Varangian Vadim leaps to his feet, ready to defend the freedom of his almost-native city. He sees a vision:

Всечасно пред его очами
В тяжелых Новоград цепях
И торжествующий варяг
Над хладными славян гробами.
В Вадиме пылкий дух кипит,
Но кто за родину отмстит?[41]

At all times before his eyes
Are Novgorod in heavy chains

And the Varangians exulting
Over the cold graves of Slavs.
A fiery soul boils in Vadim,
But who will take revenge for the fatherland?

Vadim goes off to fight for Novgorod, and after a battle (which is described in Homeric terms and shows clear influences of the *Iliad*), the democratic forces in Novgorod triumph (!), and Riurik is apparently driven out of the city ("И струи Волхова священны / И град славян освобожденный" [And the holy Volkhov flows / The Slavs' city is liberated]).[42] It is clear at this point that Khomiakov has left any concerns for history far behind, for, no matter how legendary the story of Vadim, it is difficult to see from any of the extant sources how Vadim could have won this battle and driven out the Varangians.

It is at this point, perhaps a bit confused over how to proceed, that Khomiakov interrupts the Vadim story and introduces a fascinating digression. What he does in canto 3 is to create an equation between ancient Novgorod and Petersburg, between Vadim and Peter the Great, and between Riurik and Charles XII. It now becomes clear why the question of Riurik's foreign origin was so important for Khomiakov's Vadim, and why it was such a negative trait (recall that in Catherine's play foreignness was an asset). Riurik is a bad ruler in the universe of Khomiakov's poem not because he is a tyrant, but simply because he is a foreigner. If we recall that Khomiakov would later become one of the leading spokesmen for the Slavophile view of history, the undesirability of a foreign-born ruler and the need for the native Slavic element to triumph over him becomes clear. For Khomiakov, Vadim is a hero as much for his racial qualities as for his democratic leanings.

By the time Lermontov takes up the theme, the original story has disappeared entirely. Indeed, although Lermontov's Vadim is a rebel, he belongs not to pre-Christian Russia, but instead to the time of the Pugachev uprising. Evidently the last of his literary line, Lermontov's unfinished Vadim has lost all of his original historical context and remains merely a name signifying rebellion.

A similar fadeout awaited Vadim in history. Karamzin found it necessary to repeat the story in his *History*, although he clearly disbelieved it, but Nikolai Polevoi does not even mention Vadim in the first volume of his *History of the Russian People* (*Istoriia Russkogo naroda*, 1829). Of course, it must be recalled that Polevoi was writing under circumstances completely different from Karamzin's. The Decembrist revolt took place between the appearance of Karamzin's *History* and Polevoi's. Vadim had been one of the chief heroes in the Decembrist poetic pantheon, and after the suppression of the revolt Polevoi might well have decided that mentioning Vadim was too dangerous to be worth it. Indeed, one imagines that had critical readings of historical sources not already shown that Vadim never existed, Polevoi would have been forced to disinvent him.

The struggle to find a genre appropriate for conveying the story of Vadim of Novgorod points to an interesting aspect of Russian literary history of this period. In their desire to Europeanize, Russian writers naturally tended to import genres by imitating model works rather than by re-creating a genre's evolutionary history. In Russia, genres like neoclassical tragedy, the preromantic prose fragment, and the romantic narrative poem, which in Europe belonged to distinct periods and did not overlap, were all productive and attempting to incorporate the same historical material simultaneously. The outcome of this literary aberration was somewhat unexpected. Russians seem, as a result, to have accepted the notion that history should not be the exclusive province of any one genre. They appreciated the intergeneric dialogue that resulted from the ahistorical telescoping of the borrowed genres, and although Vadim disappeared and all of the genres in which he had appeared eventually became unproductive, the principle of intergeneric dialogue remained.

In the first decades of the nineteenth century the ways in which history could be used in Russian belles lettres were still fluid. Various authors and schools favored different genres, and there was no single work with the prestige to serve as an authoritative model. This situation was to change radically in the course of the 1820's, however, as literate Russian society digested the full import of Karamzin's monumental *History of the Russian State*, a work that foregrounded the intergeneric strategies that had been used more or less unconsciously before its appearance.

≈⁓⦿⁓≈

Karamzin's *History of the Russian State* and the Codification of the Principles of Intergeneric Dialogue

At one point in his *Letters of a Russian Traveler* (*Pis'ma russkogo puteshestvennika*), the still young Karamzin mentions meeting the French writer Pierre Levesque, author of an *Histoire de la Russie* which, according to Karamzin, "despite having many shortcomings is better than all the rest." Karamzin then continues, "It is painful, but in all fairness necessary, to say that at this time we still do not possess a good Russian History, that is, one written with noble eloquence, critically, by a philosophical mind. Tacitus, Hume, Robertson, Gibbon—they are models!" [1]

And as every educated Russian reader knows, Karamzin eventually did more than bemoan the lack of a good Russian history. In the wake of the publication of *Letters of a Russian Traveler*, Karamzin became Russia's best-known author. In the decade or so that followed, he wrote poetry, short stories in sentimentalist style, and founded *The Herald of Europe*, the first of the Russian "fat" journals. But then, in 1803, Karamzin requested and received a post that had never before existed in Russia, that of imperial historiographer. He remained in this post until his death in 1826, producing along the way twelve volumes of his magnum opus, *The History of the Russian State*. The first eight volumes of the *History* (which cover Russian history from its beginnings to 1560) appeared in 1818 and created a gigantic stir in the educated circles of Moscow and St. Petersburg. In Pushkin's words, the *History* "made a splash and produced a powerful impression. Three thousand copies disappeared in a month. . . . Society people rushed to read the history of their fatherland. It was a new discovery for them. It seemed that Karamzin had discovered ancient Russia as had Columbus America."[2]

Although the *History* was widely read, it was by no means received uncritically.[3] Many Russian liberals were upset by Karamzin's ringing endorsement of the autocratic principle. The historian's central thesis, that Russia had flourished in periods of strong central rule and had declined in its absence, rankled many members of the younger generation who, in the years after 1815, hoped that Alexander I might introduce a form of constitutional monarchy.[4] In addition, some historians, particularly Polevoi, whose competing *History of the Russian People* began to appear in 1829, objected to Karamzin's almost exclusive concern with the role of Russia's rulers. Nevertheless, despite critical carping, the *History* quickly became a classic.

Of course, the very fact that Russia's leading fiction writer would choose to take up history was significant. Karamzin himself was inclined to think that this shift signaled a broader change in Russian sensibilities. As he said in an essay just before he started work on the *History*: "In several years history will occupy us considerably more than novels; for the mature mind, truth has a special charm which does not exist in fictions."[5] Yet although Karamzin was correct in predicting the rise to prominence of history, he was wrong to think that Russians would be satisfied exclusively with the brand of historical truth provided by nonfictional narrative. The influence of his own work is a case in point. True, *The History of the Russian State* proved a source of inspiration for Russia's professional historians.[6] At the same time, it turned out to be just as influential in belles lettres, because instead of overshadowing fictional narrative on historical themes, Karamzin's *History* was read as one more artistic work. Generations of Russian writers, including Dostoevsky and Tolstoy, gained their first exposure to and love of history from Karamzin.[7] In Karamzin's day and beyond, Russian writers of belles lettres mined the *History* as a model of prose style and as a source of plot material. Ultimately, Zhukovsky's prediction that "a new epoch has opened up for Russians with the appearance of this history! What a treasure house for language, for poetry, not to mention all the activity it will generate for the intellect" came true.[8] As a result, as late as the 1820's, precisely when in western Europe the split between history and literature was being codified, Karamzin provided Russia with a work that could be read as both. From the point of view of this book, it is difficult to overestimate the significance of this fact. In this chapter, I will examine two types of intergeneric dialogue whose presence was essential for this dual reception: one between Karamzin's own fictions and his historical prose, and the other internal to the *History*.

Karamzin's central task in the *History of the Russian State* was to create a viable Russian version of narrative historical discourse and to differentiate it clearly from competing methods of presenting historical material. As discussed in the previous chapter, modern Russian literature had no tradition of sustained narrative on historical themes, either in fiction or in nonfiction. The fragmentary prose études of Zhukovsky and Murav'ev, for example, which successfully created a historical atmosphere, foundered when it came to dealing with plot. Perhaps the only real exceptions were the historical stories of Karamzin himself—"Natalia the Boyar's Daughter" ("Natal'ia, boiarskaia doch'," 1792) and "Martha the Posadnik" (1803). Because of this relative weakness in the area of prose narrative, when Karamzin turned to writing a history he was, inevitably, creating a dialogue not with a developed tradition, but with his own earlier fiction. There were, of course, both advantages and disadvantages to this position. On the one hand, Karamzin must have known that readers' memories of him as the author of sentimental historical tales would make it difficult for them to appreciate his new method. Like a comic actor who suddenly switches to tragic roles, Karamzin had to dissolve audience expectations of his writing persona as playful and lightweight. At the same time, Karamzin could count on his authorial prestige to provide him with an instant audience, and he could be sure that his readers' knowledge of the historical tales would allow them to perceive the contrast in narrative modes between fictional story and history if that contrast were drawn sharply enough.

The key here is that the existence of the earlier stories allowed for the possibility of dialogue between the narrative modes and expectations of history and fiction. There is no need, it seems to me, to see the *History* as Karamzin's attempt to overcome his earlier stories, to escape his previous method, if only because escape was impossible. As the Russian tradition suggested and as Karamzin was aware, each narrative strategy has its own strengths and weaknesses, and although one can be more or less appropriate at a given time, there is no absolute reason to prefer one over the other. Thus, in an initial attempt to explore Karamzin's achievement and to explain his dual legacy as historian and writer of belles lettres, I would like to turn to the dialogue between the competing modes of historical presentation represented by the last of Karamzin's historical tales and the *History*.

The story "Martha the Posadnik" is surprisingly well-paced and exciting for its time. It is set in the 1470's, when the city of Novgorod attempted for the last time to assert its traditional independence against the rapidly expanding imperial Muscovite state. The story begins with a note from Karamzin, posing as the "editor" of a found manuscript. "Here is one of the most important events in Russian history. For the glory and might of the fatherland, the wise Ivan [Ivan III, the Great] had to join the territory of Novgorod to his state: Praised be he! Nevertheless, the resistance of the Novgorodians was not at all the revolt of some kind of Jacobins: they fought for their ancient laws and rights."[9] The "editor" then goes on to hint that the "author" may have shared this view. Describing the tale's provenance, he opines, "I think that this was written by one of the most distinguished Novgorodians who were exiled to various cities by Ivan Vasilievich. . . . it appears that this ancient author did not fault Ivan even in the depths of his soul" (60). The device of the found manuscript allows Karamzin to present the story as if told by a participant and to evoke some of the tension of lived events.

As Karamzin realized, for a tale of this kind to succeed, it helps to focus on an important historical event that illustrates a clash between two sides that advance equally compelling but, from a historical vantage point, mutually incompatible points of view.[10] Although one or the other of them must inevitably triumph, the author should avoid seeming to take sides; rather, tension should be created by avoiding foreshadowing within the story and allowing the outcome to result from the inevitable logic of events themselves. Thus, more than a decade before *Waverley*, Karamzin had discovered what was to become a central Scottian plot device.[11] In this case, the democratic (almost anarchic) city-state of Novgorod must inevitably fall to Ivan's more rational and powerful program of imperial expansion. The device of pretending that the story was written by a distinguished Novgorodian, probably from personal memories, highlights the narrative tension by imparting a "you were there" feeling. This effect is further heightened by the extensive use of dialogue; the first section of the tale, for example, consists almost entirely of two speeches, one by Ivan's plenipotentiary Prince Kholmsky urging accession to the will of Moscow, the other by Martha urging the Novgorodians to resist. The author can do nothing to change the ultimate outcome, but this method of emplotment allows the reader to feel himself, at least to some extent, inside the historical events being described. And indeed, when reading "Martha," one has a tendency to forget what ultimately happened and is induced to relive the tension of the historical moment.

The "history" presented here is of a type that in the methodological preface to his *History of the Russian State* Karamzin would call "contemporary": either based "on the model of Thucydides, in which an eyewitness speaks about events"; or, possibly, "like Tacitus . . . based on fresh verbal tales close to the time of the actions being discussed." [12] Both of these approaches to Muscovite history were, of course, impossible for the Russian historian of Karamzin's day. But what was forbidden the historian was perfectly acceptable for the writer of fictions, and indeed, Karamzin was well aware of the value of fictions of this and other kinds. As he said in an article entitled "On Events and Characters in Russian History That Could be Subjects for the Arts," "If a historical character is depicted strikingly on canvas or in marble, then he becomes more interesting for us in the chronicles themselves." [13]

In contrast, the modern historian has an entirely different perspective and a different goal as far as Karamzin is concerned. His job is to ensure that the various stories he recounts reflect the overall telos of Russian history. Karamzin expresses this telos frequently in the course of his *History of the Russian State*, but the following passage, inserted in his description of the reign of Ivan Kalita, is perhaps the clearest:

At that time she [Russia] reached the greatest state of calamity, seeing her best lands seized by the Lithuanians and the rest laid waste by the Mongols—that same time was the beginning of the state's renaissance. In a little town, hitherto unimportant, the idea of beneficent autocracy was ripening, the manly courage to sunder the Khan's chains was being discovered, and the means to independence and national greatness were being prepared. Novgorod was famous as the crucible of the monarchy, Kiev as the fount of Christianity, but the fatherland and faith were saved in Moscow. [14]

The task of a history, in Karamzin's view, is not to show exciting moments of conflict from the inside, but rather to depict the monumental and inexorable forward motion of the Russian state. And if passages like the one above encouraged an identification of Russia with Christ, torn and bleeding, only to rise later in a blaze of glory, so be it.

Thus, when Karamzin turned to writing a history, the tactics that had served for fictional tales were clearly not appropriate. When we look at the account of the subjugation of Novgorod in the *History*, therefore, we expect an entirely different mode of presentation, both on the level of the historical information presented and on that of authorial perspective. In particular, we expect more emphasis on the Muscovite point of view. Examining the historical account we discover first of all that in "Martha the Posadnik" Karamzin completely suppressed the fact that the Novgorodians, led by Martha, had formed an alliance with King Kazimir of Poland in order to avoid being swallowed up by Moscow. A revelation of this political situation in the fictional tale would have been inconvenient for at least two reasons. Most obviously, it would have threatened to transform what looked like a balanced internecine conflict between the autocratic centralizing ideal of Ivan the Great and the independent democratic vision of Novgorod into an international conflict in which the Novgorodians might have seemed mere pawns in the larger struggle between Russia and Poland, Orthodoxy and Catholicism. Such a perspective may be fine for a history, in which this episode plays only a minor role, but it would not have served very well as the narrative center of the tale. In addition, this alliance might have been expected to show Martha and her advisors in a bad light; if they were really willing to become vassals of Poland, all of their stirring speeches about independence and old traditions would have sounded hollow. But these facts could be left out of the tale with impunity thanks to Karamzin's simple device of pretending that it was written by a noble Novgorodian. In the hindsight of the dialogue engendered by reading the *History*, we guess that the "author" of the tale chose to suppress the suggested alliance with Poland precisely in order to make Novgorod's position seem more sympathetic and, perhaps, to assuage his own guilty conscience.

From the point of view of the *History*, Martha the Posadnik is not at all a heroic figure. Indeed, her actions opened up the potential for disaster. As opposed to the basically sympathetic portrayal she received in the "eyewitness" account of the anonymous "author" of the tale, in the *History* she is clearly a villain. The passage in which she first appears is worth quoting at length:

> Contrary to the ancient practices and mores of the Slavs, which had kept the female sex at a distance from any participation in civic affairs, a proud and ambitious woman by the name of Martha, the widow of the famous Posadnik Isaak Boretsky and mother of two grown sons, took it upon herself to decide the fate of her fatherland. Cunning, magniloquence, fame, wealth, and luxury gave her the means to influence the government. . . . This proud woman wished to free Novgorod from Ivan's power and, according to the chroniclers, to marry some kind of Lithuanian lord in order to rule her fatherland with him in Kazimir's name.[15]

In addition to demonstrating the importance of the narrator's attitude toward his material, this passage illustrates the difference that the implied reader makes. In his sentimentalist stage, Karamzin was known for his orientation toward the taste of cultivated women. It is not surprising that the main characters of his fictions are frequently women. The titles alone are telling: "Poor Liza" ("Bednaia Liza"), "Natalia the Boyar's Daughter," and "Martha the Posadnik." While women actors were hardly a surprising feature in run-of-the-mill sentimentalist prose, their centrality in Karamzin's historical tales indicates an obvious and marked choice. Presumably he thought that his primarily female audience would appreciate stories in which female characters played central roles, and he sought out such stories. The *History*, on the other hand, was written with a primarily male audience, the tsar himself first and foremost, in mind. The unabashed misogyny of this passage, the historian's heavy-handed attempts to link Martha's sexual charm to her political ambitions, do not merely reveal the political errors of Martha and her Novgorodian allies, but serve as a warning. Autocracy is rational, powerful, and male; democracy anarchic, dangerous, and female.

A comparison of Martha's end in the two works points up

their distinct attitudes to history. In the tale, Martha is recognized as the symbol of Novgorodian resistance, and when Ivan triumphs she is sentenced to death. She confronts her fate bravely: "[She] hurried up onto the high scaffold—and tore the covering from her head herself . . . approached the instrument of death and loudly proclaimed to the people, 'Citizens of Novgorod! I die a citizen of Novgorod' " (98). After the execution, Ivan's herald announces: "Thus die those guilty of revolt and bloodshed! People and Boyars! Do not fear.—Ivan will not break his word; his forgiving right hand is above you. [Martha] Boretskaia's blood will reconcile fratricidal enmity—one victim is needed for your tranquility and she will assure an unbreakable union forever" (99). In this conclusion Martha's martyrdom ensures a tight and satisfying closure. She may ultimately be the loser, but she remains a heroine.

In the *History*, Martha's end is, as one might expect, rather more ignominious. We are told that following the final annexation of the city,

On February 1 . . . [Ivan] ordered the arrest of the Merchant Elder and on February 2 that of the famous Martha Boretskaia and her grandson Vasily Fedorov . . . and among the nobles [of] Grigory Kiprianov, Ivan Kuzmin, Akinf and his son Roman, and Iury Repekhov. He ordered them taken to Moscow and their estates confiscated. These people were the only victims of the awe-inspiring Moscow ruler, either because they were his open and irreconcilable enemies, or because they were well-known friends of Lithuania.[16]

Martha is just one of a number of others, and her death, far from being a symbolic moment of heroism, does not even appear in the main text but is instead relegated to the notes. There we discover that "some have believed" that a tombstone found in the Upper Volotsky district is hers, but Karamzin refutes that theory while providing no concrete information at all about her demise.

Thus, through dialogue with his own earlier fictional works, Karamzin strove to create a new kind of narrative for the presentation of history in Russia. In this he succeeded, and after Karamzin narrative history became firmly entrenched in the Russian generic pantheon. However, Karamzin's "scientific" historical narrative did not displace other potential narrative forms for history, as similarly scholarly works did in Europe. Part of the reason for this had to do with Karamzin's ideas concerning what the historian should be trying to do. Karamzin's task is to "put everything in its place." Thus, in a general discussion of the political history of Novgorod's annexation entitled "A Survey of the History of Novgorod," he comments:

> Although it is characteristic of the human heart to wish republics well, based as they are on deep-rooted principles of liberty which it finds dear; although their very danger and ferment engender magnanimity and captivate the mind, especially one young and inexperienced; although the Novgorodians had a popular government, a general trading spirit, and ties with the best-educated of the Germans, and were doubtless possessed of noble qualities that distinguished them from the other Russians who had been tyrannized by the Mongols; nevertheless, History must in this case glorify the mind of Ivan, because statecraft told him to strengthen Russia by the firm union of its parts into a whole.[17]

Nothing must be allowed to stand in the way of the overall progression of the *History*. The historian's job is not to re-create exciting moments of the past in his prose (although he may sometimes do this), but rather to emphasize from his position in the present the logic of past events. The resulting history, while unquestionably fuller and perhaps more satisfying in its overall sweep, cannot provide the immediacy of a fictional work, nor can it provide the same degree of closure. "Martha the Posadnik" ends heroically, with Martha's martyrdom as the guarantee of future amity. The brief account of her in the *History* merely trails off, for this episode turns out to be simply one in an unending stream of events. After summing up Novgorod's history, Karamzin ends the section by stating: "Here ends Novgorod's *separate* history. We will add now the remaining information concerning her fate during the realm of Ivan."[18] Instead of the satisfying heroic closure achieved in the tale, all we get here is a deflationary list of trivial details.

But perhaps the central reason that Karamzin's *History* did not displace other forms for the presentation of historical material in narrative is that in addition to its dialogue with Karamzin's own historical fictions, it contained an internal version of intergeneric dialogue. I believe that the presence of this dialogue was perceived by Karamzin's contemporaries, although they did not fully understand its nature, and that Karamzin's adoption of this peculiarly Russian technique helped ensure its survival throughout the nineteenth and well into the twentieth century. Furthermore, I believe that the presence of this internal dialogue was what allowed Karamzin to be read both as a model of narrative prose and as a historian.

The dialogue to which I am referring is between the main text of the *History*, which occupies approximately half of each volume, and the notes. The notes are, of course, keyed to specific passages in the main text, and the reader is presumably expected to turn to them each time a number appears in the central narrative. But in practice such a method of reading is almost impossible, and it is doubtful that it has ever been seriously undertaken by any reader. Not only is it annoying to have to flip constantly from one section of the book to another, not only are the notes printed in such tiny type that reading them is torture on the eyes, but to read in this manner makes it extremely difficult to concentrate on the thread of the central narrative. This is so not simply because the narrative and notes are separated by textual space but because they represent essentially incompatible ways of telling stories—different ways of making text out of the historical material Karamzin employed.

Over the years, many readers have noted a split inherent in Karamzin's text. "Each of us who worked on the history of our country did so, perhaps, in part because we had first become acquainted with it in Karamzin's highly artistic narrative. In later years, we turned to these familiar pages many times and found teaching of a different kind here: we learned how to use sources, how to find them." [19] This comment by the nineteenth-century historian Galakhov, for example, indicates that Karamzin's text was perceived as being open to multiple readings, although Galakhov does not explicitly locate the source of that multiplicity in the dichotomy between the main text and the notes. More recently, scholars have focused particularly on the occasional contradictions between the story as it is presented in the main text and as it appears in the notes. [20] And in her *Boris Godunov: Transpositions of a Russian Theme*, Caryl Emerson suggests the possibility of understanding the relationship between main text and notes as one of dialogue, although she does not analyze this phenomenon. "Composing text and notes simultaneously, Karamzin may have envisaged a dialogue between the two that was rather fresh, without privileging either side as more 'true.' This dialogue is worth considering, for it should not be forgotten that Karamzin, as an eighteenth-century man of letters, was quite sophisticated in matters of narrative voice and in the creation of divergent narrative perspectives." [21]

To introduce my own interpretation of the dialogue between main text and notes, I would like to go back to a comment made by Alexander Pushkin in his review of the first volume of Polevoi's *History of the Russian People*. There he makes the enigmatic comment, "Karamzin is our first historian and our last chronicler." [22] At the time, this statement must have seemed intriguingly oxymoronic. It clearly goes against Karamzin's own claims about his work, for in the "Introduction" to the *History* he specifically stated: "The reader will notice that I describe events not haphazardly, by years or days, but I combine them for the most harmonious possible impression on the mind. A Historian is not a Chronicler: the latter considers only time, while the former looks at the character and linkage of events." [23] Nevertheless, in spite of Karamzin's disclaimer, if we interpret Pushkin's remark in the light of our recognition of the dialogical nature of the *History*, we might find that the tension between the categories "chronicle" and "history" does indeed help us understand something of fundamental importance.

In one sense, Karamzin was entirely justified in juxtaposing his method in the main text to that of the Russian chroniclers whose work he knew so well. The central structuring principle of the chronicles is annalistic—events are grouped by the year in which they occurred. Thus, rather than telling the story of a person's life or a king's reign from beginning to end, the chronicler presents in each separate entry only those portions relevant to the year in question. The result is that what would appear to us to be "whole" stories are constantly being broken off, interrupted by seemingly irrelevant descriptions of other events from the same year. By ordering the narrative of his main text around the reigns of individual rulers, Karamzin showed the ability to construct causal narrative chains and to use them in historical interpretation, a hallmark of the modern historian. Karamzin was the first Russian historian to describe Russia's past not as just "one damn thing after another," but as a coherent story with a telos and an internal logic.

The main text, characterized by Karamzin's smooth, flowing prose, tells a simple story: from one among many disorganized primitive tribes, the Russians, thanks to the "happy introduction of monarchical rule," grew in strength and importance.[24] They flourished in times of strong, wise autocratic rule, and declined when autocracy was weakened or the autocrat failed in his duties. Karamzin was well aware that his overall construction was open to criticism, for he adds: "[The historian] may err in his placement of events, but he must try to indicate everything's proper place."[25] What Karamzin is defending here is his decision to subordinate everything in the main text to his overall narrative structure. He admits that errors can occur within the structure, but in doing so he makes the need for such a structure seem beyond criticism; that is, he naturalizes his narrative method.

The problem, however, is that the notes have no place in

this narrative scheme and Karamzin knows it. Far from being an aid to "putting everything in its proper place," the notes are a complete hodgepodge. Each note is a self-contained unit, unconnected to those before and after it, and unpredictable in its contents, which can range from lengthy excerpts taken verbatim from Karamzin's sources, to intricate refutations of the viewpoints of other historians, to outright contradictions of the story as told in the main text. They introduce a strong element of verticality into what would otherwise be a horizontal text. Indeed, when turning to the notes, the reader feels he is descending into a seething cauldron of disagreement that bubbles just under the placid and magisterial surface of the main text. Practically every note is an invitation to break the forward motion of the *History*, to head off on a tangent that will, one way or another, undermine the presentation of events in the main text.

Karamzin was evidently well aware of this potential problem. In the "Introduction" to the *History*, he attempts to downplay the effect that his notes will have on the casual reader: "I myself am terrified of the quantity of notes and excerpts I have provided. The ancients were lucky: they did not know this petty labor that takes up half your time, bores the mind, and deadens the imagination; a heavy sacrifice made to authenticity, but a necessary one." He then adds, "It is left to the reader's desire to look into this colorful miscellany, which serves sometimes as evidence, sometimes as explanation or supplement."[26] Despite this disclaimer, however, it is obvious that Karamzin would not have spent the immense energy needed to collect the notes had he not thought them valuable.

At the same time, the dialogue between chronicler and historian is further complicated by the fact that the methods of the chronicler are not always used in the notes, nor is the main text always that of a modern historian. As Lotman points out, one of the distinguishing features of Karamzin's main narrative, especially in the first eight volumes, is his adoption of the naive moral and political point of view of the chroniclers.[27] He mim-

ics the judgmental tone of the chronicler vis-à-vis the historical
actors, and he seems to come to the same moral conclusions.
However, the notes accompanying these "naive" descriptions in
the main text are anything but. Karamzin casts a discerning
and critical eye on his sources, comparing them one to another,
questioning their veracity or motive, and, with surprising fre-
quency, directly contradicting the point of view of the main
text. Here, then, the equation has been reversed. The chronicler is found in the main text, while the historian inhabits
the notes.

What we see then, essentially, is the cohabitation of two
distinctly opposing ways of telling stories about the past. The
narrator of the main text takes a purposely naive attitude
toward the substance of his sources but changes their story-
telling method entirely, substituting a diachronically ordered
overview for their almost purely synchronic approach. The narrative voice of the notes, on the other hand, tells extremely limited stories that focus on single events at specific moments and
lack any causal connection with their neighbors, while simultaneously employing a sophisticatedly skeptical attitude toward
the sources. There is no way that a reader can legitimately
prefer one of these methods over the other on the grounds of
its truth value (aesthetic grounds are, of course, another matter). The result is a sophisticated narrative dialogue in which
two competing perspectives continually question each other's
authority.

As an example, more or less randomly chosen, let us cite
a historically trivial moment from the reign of Vladimir: the
war between Vladimir and the Norwegian Prince Erik that
is described in Icelandic sources. Karamzin relates that Erik
gathered an army and attacked Vladimir's northwest territories,
laying siege to and overpowering the Russian city Al'deigaburg,
"which is, undoubtedly, today's Staraia Ladoga, where Scandinavian mariners were wont to halt."[28] From the narrative style
of the main text, one would think that Karamzin is simply and
ingenuously repeating information that was in his source text.

But as the appended note indicates, this is not the case. It turns out that the question of the location of Al'deigaburg was not as cut and dried as the "undoubtedly" in the main text might have led one to believe. Karamzin includes in the note a lengthy refutation of an argument by the historian Gerhard Müller, who evidently did not believe that Al'deigaburg really was Staraia Ladoga. To prove his own point, Karamzin cites Scandinavian, Russian, and German sources, etymological analysis, the untrustworthiness of the chronology of the Icelandic source in question, geographical facts, and Müller's faulty logic. This is, of course, the kind of exhaustive research that later historians found so appealing, but Karamzin was obviously aware that such debates were not appropriate in the main text.

Karamzin also used the notes not in order to explicate a point made in the main text, but to include material of doubtful historical accuracy that was nevertheless worth mentioning. As an example, we can turn to Karamzin's descriptions of the sack of Kievan Rus' by the Tatar khan Batu. The historian says: "Having discovered that the Princes of Southern Russia were in Hungary, Batu set off for the provinces of Galitsk and Vladimir; he besieged the city of Ladyzhin." [29] The appended note to this passage tells the legend of St. Mercury. Mercury, it seems, was the servant of the Prince of Smolensk. He killed many Tatars during the siege of Ladyzhin, but was eventually captured and beheaded. After the Tatars left, he picked up his severed head and walked back to Smolensk, where the citizens gave him a decent burial. After telling the story, Karamzin admits that it only appears in two sources, and that one of them cites the date of Mercury's death as 1247, well after the Tatars had left. Clearly, Karamzin did not believe this legend, so he could not include it in the main part of his text. At the same time, he must have found the legend charming enough to include in the notes (along with a careful indication of his disbelief).

Even more interesting, however, are those places in which the information provided in the main text and that provided in the notes conflict. In general, this happens because of a certain hierarchical principle that seems to operate in Karamzin's work. Those stories whose accuracy he does not doubt at all are placed in the main text. The footnotes connected to them, if any, tend merely to reiterate the story and give sources. Those stories that Karamzin considers of doubtful veracity appear straightforward in the main text, but are subverted by being qualified, even contradicted, in the footnotes.

A fine example is Karamzin's treatment of Riurik's accession to the throne. This was, of course, a crucial moment, and one that had played a significant role for Karamzin's predecessors, as we have seen. Did the people, of their own free will, really request Riurik to rule over them? If so, autocracy could be seen in the context not of God's choice of a ruler (the so-called divine right of kings), but in terms of the modish eighteenth-century idea of the social contract. If not, the legitimacy of autocracy itself could be questioned. This same historical story/legend became the basis for further development in Russian historical and political thought when Konstantin Aksakov used it to ground his theories of what separated the Russians from the western Europeans.[30]

As we have already noted, Karamzin considered the monarchical principle crucial, and being a good Enlightenment thinker, he found the social contract aspect attractive. Nevertheless, as a historian, he realized that the story of the calling of Riurik was problematic. He dealt with this conflict between historical truth and his desire for well-made narrative in a creative way. In the main text he says:

Nestor writes that the Slavs of Novgorod, the Kriviches, the Ves', and the Chud' sent an embassy abroad to the Varangian-Rus saying: "Our land is vast and abundant, but we have no order. Come be princes and rule us." Simple, terse, and powerful words! Brothers named Riurik, Sineus, and Truvor, famous for either their lineage or their deed, agreed to take power over people who were able to fight for freedom but not to enjoy its use.[31]

All very well so far. The story makes political and psychological sense and it fits well with Karamzin's basic ideology. However, in the footnote that he places after the quote from the chronicle, things begin to look a bit different. He adds:

Müller . . . thought that the Slavs and the Finns called the Varangians not as rulers, but simply to defend their borders and that Riurik *usurped* power. But the clear words of the Chronicler . . . refute this opinion. Not external enemies, whom the Slavs had happily eliminated, but internal disorders forced them to look for Princes in foreign lands; therefore, they wanted rulers, because only civic power could extirpate the evils of disorder and anarchy.

Once again, so far this looks like the standard tactic of a good historian. Karamzin takes into account opposing interpretations and tries to show why his version is more convincing. Then, however, he concludes the footnote in an entirely unexpected and extremely subversive (to his own narrative) way. He continues: "We don't know if it really happened this way; but that is what the Chronicler says. Only contemporaries really knew the truth." This final caveat throws the entire story into doubt, not just as it appears in the polemical footnote, but as it appears in the main narrative portion of the *History*.

I do not mean to create the impression that the primary purpose of the notes was to contradict the story being presented in the main text. In fact, the dialogue can take many forms, and can perhaps best be characterized as the locus of interaction between smooth and rough texts. I do not mean for these terms to be taken as value judgments, of course. The rough texts are clearly just as important for Karamzin as the smooth ones, but the two simply do not coexist very well. Although examples abound, perhaps the best one is the end of Karamzin's description of the period of Dmitry Donskoi. He ends the section with what Lotman would call an imitation of the chronicler's naive point of view—the recollection of natural disturbances that were thought to be evil omens—although he does ironize a bit at the expense of the credulous. When we turn to the final footnote of the chapter, however, a surprise is in store for us. In the note Karamzin provides "those events of Dmitry's time that we have not spoken about."[32] This heading is followed by a six-page list of events, ordered entirely by chronology and related to each other only by their marginality to the central narrative. Compared to the high drama of the main section on Dmitry, this note can only be seen as comic in its mishmash of seemingly unimportant (but for Karamzin evidently necessary) information.

Ultimately then, *The History of the Russian State* confronts us with two seemingly incompatible ways of narrating history, what Hayden White would call romance and satire. Romance, as White categorizes it, is "fundamentally a drama of self-identification symbolized by the hero's transcendence of the world of experience, his victory over it, and his final liberation from it."[33] In Karamzin's main text there are two transcendent heroes.[34] One is Russia, and the relevant story is how she came to achieve greatness. The other is the historian himself, who struggles with recalcitrant material in order to shape his history.[35] The notes, by undercutting the pretension of the main narrative to completeness and certainty, call into question the very viability of a historical narrative that focuses on a single telos, just as by their constant need to swat away the menacing opinions of other historians they mock the historian's attempt to tell a seamless story. Their position is fundamentally ironic. To put it another way, these narratives give us a poetic and a prosaic text simultaneously. The main text presents a world that is basically neat, orderly, and well formed, while the notes show us messiness, disorder, and sometimes even chaos.[36]

But which of these views of history does Karamzin endorse? The answer can only be, both of them. Just as Russian literature could not choose a single artistic genre for the incorporation of historical material in the period before the appearance of Karamzin's *History*, so even here the author presents us with competing, seemingly mutually exclusive modes of understanding history.[37] The reader, unable to reconcile them, must learn to live with the ambiguity of the dialogue. And it is precisely this dialogue, lying at the center of Karamzin's monumental *History*, that made it such a fecund source for generations of

Russian writers. By refusing to limit himself to a single emplotment of history, Karamzin opened his text not only to those
who chose to write using one or the other of his emplotments (a
route many would follow), but also to those who chose to continue down the path of intergeneric dialogue. What Karamzin
did was to take the principle of intergeneric dialogue for historical narrative that had been latently present in Russian literary
culture and codify it in a single monumental work. From then
on there were not only multiple acceptable genres available for
writers who wished to exploit history, but there existed a model
for their combination in the work of a single author.[38]

Ultimately then, Karamzin was quite right when he predicted that the Russian reader had matured sufficiently to appreciate history. He was wrong, however, to think that the
newly mature reader would be satisfied solely by "scientific"
history. Instead, Russian readers wanted both the scope and
depth of nonfictional narrative history and the immediacy and
excitement of fiction. In this regard, of course, they were no
different from their counterparts in Europe who read both history and historical novels. But what Karamzin gave Russia,
both through the dialogue between his history and his fictions
and through the history's internal dialogue, was an authoritative example of a single individual producing both. Karamzin's
immense prestige, both as writer of belles lettres and historian,
ensured that *The History of the Russian State* would remain standard reading for Russians throughout the nineteenth century
and that his model of intergeneric dialogue would be developed
further. The model of Karamzin certainly must have been on
the mind of Russia's next imperial historiographer, Alexander
Pushkin.[39]

❧❦❧

Chapter Four

Incarnations of Intergeneric Dialogue in the Age of Pushkin

It seems to me that it will be beyond the powers not only of an average historian but even of the most wonderful historian to describe this criminal.

Platon Liubarsky [1]

In order to approach the complicated question of how the historical method that Karamzin codified was continued, modified, and transformed in the 1830's, I will focus on Alexander Pushkin's use of history in two works concerning the events of the so-called Pugachev uprising: the nonfictional *History of Pugachev* (1834), and the novel *The Captain's Daughter* (1836).[2] Specifically, I am concerned with why Pushkin chose to encode the story of the Pugachev rebellion in two radically different genres. I will claim that for Pushkin, who was following in the intergeneric tradition of Karamzin, both versions were equally important, and that ultimately neither of them can be read adequately without a knowledge of its twin; that is, Pushkin forces his readers to consider these two different encodings of the same events in tandem. Neither one of them can be considered Pushkin's final word on the subject of the Pugachev rebellion in particular or on the best way of writing on historical themes in general. I will, therefore, be arguing against a possible reading of *The History of Pugachev* as a work of fiction written in the guise of a history, and, equally, against the corollary, a reading of *The Captain's Daughter* as a history cloaked in novelistic form. At the same time, I will attempt to show that there is a level on which the two works, despite their generic differences, express a view of history that is characteristically Russian.

Pushkin was nineteen when the first volumes of Karamzin's *History of the Russian State* appeared, but this publication did not mark the beginning of their acquaintance. In fact, Karamzin was a friend of the Pushkin family, one of the figures who populated Pushkin's childhood world.[3] Later, when the budding poet was still at the Lycée, Karamzin followed his progress, and by 1816 Pushkin was visiting the Karamzin family on his own.[4] Until his exile to the south in 1820, Pushkin spent much of his time with members of the literary society "Arzamas," a group whose idol and ex officio leader was Karamzin.

Pushkin read the *History of the Russian State* avidly. His reactions to it varied depending on the times, his mood, and the volume he was reading. As a young man he seems to have sided with Karamzin's liberal detractors. Thus, in a famous epigram of 1818, he commented acidly:

> В его «Истории» изящность, простота
> Доказывают нам, без всякого пристрастья,
> Необходимость самовластья
> И прелести кнута.[5]

> His *History*, so simple and so graceful
> Proves to us without a doubt
> The need for autocratic rule
> And the wonders of the knout.

There is evidence, however, that the more mature Pushkin found this epigram embarrassing.[6] In any case, we know that he made extensive use of the *History* when he was writing *Boris Godunov* in 1825. And based on comments in his letters, as in the following to Nikolai Raevsky, it seems that he intended his play to be read in dialogic counterpoint to Karamzin: "Here is my tragedy, since you absolutely must have it, but before you read it I insist that you skim through the last volume of Karamzin. My play is full of good jokes and allusions to the history of the time . . . it is a *sine qua non* that they be understood."[7]

At more or less this same time, in a biographical sketch devoted to Karamzin, Pushkin defended his great predecessor from critics in words that, a few years later, he could well have applied to himself: "They forget that Karamzin published his *History* in Russia; that the Tsar freed Karamzin from censorship, but by this sign of trust placed on him the obligation to be as modest and measured as possible" (11, 57). By the time Pushkin wrote his own history, of course, Nicholas I had appointed himself personal censor of Pushkin's works, thereby freeing him from the normal censorship while, presumably, demanding of him the same level of modesty as had been required of Karamzin. In this regard, it is interesting that through a fairly elaborate ruse on Pushkin's part, *The Captain's Daughter* passed through the regular censorship.[8] The significance of this move will be discussed in more detail later. For now, however, it is sufficient to note that when Pushkin turned to history later in his career, he must have been well aware of the extent to which he was following in Karamzin's footsteps. This in itself does not prove that Pushkin was consciously aware of the intergeneric dialogic inherent in Karamzin's own work, or that he tried to emulate it, of course. The evidence for this will have to come from our analysis of the works on historical material that Pushkin produced.

The History of Pugachev is a work very much in the tradition of Karamzin's *History*. It begins with an extensive geographical, ethnographical, and historical survey of the area in which the revolt took place and then continues with a discussion of tensions in the Cossack regions before the outbreak of the rebellion. Finally, Pushkin turns his attention to the uprising itself, tracing its course in gory detail. He concentrates on military history, so the reader is presented with detailed descriptions of fort stormings, troop movements, and strategy discussions. At the same time, in the style of Karamzin, Pushkin keeps the narrative flowing with pithy anecdotes and allows himself liberties that modern readers might find unbecoming to a historian. For example, he goes well beyond historical evidence in permitting his characters to speak for themselves. This is how Pushkin builds narrative tension in his description of the state of the Cossack region just after the initial disturbances had been put down and just before the appearance of Pugachev: "The government's stern and necessary measures restored external order, but the tranquility was illusory. 'Just you wait!' said the pardoned rioters, 'We'll shake Moscow yet'" (9, I, 12). In general, however, Pushkin stays fairly close to his source texts, sometimes even introducing them verbatim into his narrative.[9]

For our purposes the actual course of events of the rebellion is not as important as the question, what conception of history does Pushkin's work convey? First and foremost, historical events are presented within a tight narrative structure. The uprising is presented as a completed and well-formed story consisting of a prologue (the historical overview, chapter 1), a beginning (the appearance of Pugachev and the start of the uprising, chapter 2), a middle (the actual course of the rebellion, chapters 3–7), and an end (the collapse of the rebellion and the execution of Pugachev, chapter 8). Moreover, the beginning and end of the work mirror each other. *The History of Pugachev* starts with the title of course, and the first sentence of the prologue is "The Iaik, which by order of Catherine II was renamed the Ural, issues from the mountains" (9, I, 7). The last lines of the work are: "Catherine, wishing to efface all memory of this horrible epoch, eliminated the ancient name of the river whose banks were the first witnesses of the disturbances. The Iaik Cossacks were renamed Ural Cossacks, and their town was renamed correspondingly. But the name of the frightening rebel still sounds in the areas he ravaged. The people still remember that time they expressively call the 'Pugachevshchina'" (9, I, 81). Pushkin the historian discovers Pugachev for Russian society, just as Karamzin had discovered ancient Russian history. His narrative serves to bridge the gap between the people's memory and educated society's forgetfulness.

Though Pushkin is definitely concerned with telling a good story, he resists the verbal hyperbole characteristic of Karamzin's almost sentimentalist narrator. The sympathies of Pushkin's narrator evidently lie with the government forces who put down the rebellion. Those generals and common soldiers who did their duty in resisting Pugachev are commended, but are rarely placed on heroic pedestals. At the same time, although Pugachev's army is called "scum" and "a band of robbers" on a number of occasions, Pushkin avoids turning Pugachev and his rebels into a pack of demons. Particularly interesting is the treatment of the figure of Pugachev himself. Pushkin attempts to show that Pugachev was far more the instrument of the historical process than its instigator. This, for example, is how Pugachev's position in his own army is characterized: "Pugachev was not all-powerful. The Cossacks who had initiated the rebellion directed the actions of this scoundrel, who had no capacity other than some military knowledge and unusual bravado" (9, I, 27). Pushkin was particularly proud of his unromanticized treatment of Pugachev, as a letter to the poet Ivan Dmitriev shows: "As for those thinkers who are annoyed at me because I depict Pugachev as Emel'ka Pugachev and not as Byron's Lara, I happily send them to Mr. Polevoi who, for a reasonable price, would certainly be willing to idealize this personage according to the latest fashion" (16, 21).[10] In general, the historical voice that emerges from the text of Pushkin's *History* is that of a man convinced that history makes sense, that it is a process not directed by larger-than-life figures, that it flows in a series of identifiable narrative patterns.

This conclusion, which emerges from an analysis of the wealth of detail in the main text of the history, is underscored by footnotes, mostly containing lengthy excerpts from Pushkin's sources, that are as copious as those in Karamzin's *History*. Unlike Karamzin, however, Pushkin does not allow the material in the notes to contradict his own interpretation of events directly. When he wants to make a point that his evidence might not sustain, he simply does not footnote the passage at all.[11] He does not, therefore, take advantage of the potentially divergent perspectives of main text and notes to create dialogue. *The History of Pugachev* and the accompanying notes comprised the first volume of Pushkin's work. In the second volume, Pushkin went even further than had Karamzin in providing readers with a view of the raw materials from which his history was written. He published, in unabridged form, hundreds of pages of eyewitness accounts and documents relating to the uprising. The curious reader could, if so inclined, examine practically in toto Pushkin's sources. Unfortunately, curious readers, or any readers at all, for that matter, were few and far between. The *History of Pugachev* might have fallen into almost complete oblivion had Pushkin not decided to exploit the Russian tradition of producing multiple versions of the same historical material. In this case, Pushkin chose to create intergeneric dialogue by writing a "competing" fictional work set in the time of Pugachev. Thus, Pushkin's version of intergeneric dialogue, like Catherine's, occurs across the boundaries of separate texts rather than within the confines of a single work.

Today's readers of Russian literature know that *The Captain's Daughter*, a first-person "memoir" by one Petr Grinev, is actually a novel by Alexander Pushkin. But for Pushkin's contemporaries this was, perhaps, not so clear. The work was originally published anonymously in the December 1836 issue of Pushkin's journal *The Contemporary* (*Sovremennik*). The author himself took credit only for the editing. The importance Pushkin placed on convincing readers that "Grinev's" manuscript was indeed written by an eyewitness can be seen in the efforts he made to distance himself from the manuscript (see note 8 to this chapter). It is, of course, likely that few readers were fooled by this rather transparent ruse into thinking the story was actually written by some unknown Grinev. Nevertheless, Pushkin's use of the "found manuscript" device hints at a possible dialogic relationship between this account and *The History of Pugachev*.

That the reader of *The Captain's Daughter* was meant to recall *The History of Pugachev* is made crystal clear in the frame epilogue provided by the "editor" at the very end of the "memoir." After the happy ending described by Grinev, Pushkin announces: "The notes of Petr Andreevich Grinev break off here." Then he continues, "Petr Andreevich Grinev's manuscript was presented to us by one of his grandsons, who discovered that we were occupied with a work about the period described by his grandfather" (8, 374).[12] That is, Pushkin pretends that Grinev's account of the uprising is merely another of the lengthy interviews, eyewitness accounts, and memoirs that had comprised the second volume of *The History of Pugachev*, and that he simply received it too late to include it with the others. In reality, however, this frame is provided by Pushkin the historian to motivate a text produced by Pushkin the novelist.

When we turn our attention to *The Captain's Daughter*, we find an entirely different view of history from the one provided in *The History of Pugachev*. Indeed, the novel seems almost like an illustration of a theoretical point that Pushkin had made in a review of Polevoi's *History of the Russian People*: "Do not say: 'It could not have been otherwise.' If that were true then the historian would be an astronomer and the events of human life, like solar eclipses, could be predicted by calendars" (11, 127).

The Captain's Daughter is narrated in the first person by Petr Grinev, the ultimate "little man" caught up in the maelstrom of great historical events. Grinev's account of the Pugachev rebellion becomes an intimate look at events that Pushkin the historian, working in a different genre, was neither able nor desirous of incorporating into the text of his history. Through a complicated series of coincidences, Grinev unwittingly helps Pugachev before the beginning of the uprising and is then caught up in the revolt itself. In Pushkin's *History*, the uprising occupied center stage; here, it forms the background against which Grinev tells his own story. It is not merely that the novel recasts the events of the uprising; rather, Pushkin seems to be saying that, depending on one's point of view and narrative purpose, the entire story can change. Given their contrasting foci it is not surprising that Pushkin's novel and *History* contain almost no common material. Grinev the "autobiographer" is simply not concerned with the same things Pushkin the historian is, and therefore their narratives do not coincide. What seemed of crucial importance in the narrative of the *History*—why did the revolt take place? what were the plans of Pugachev and his band? how did the government defend itself?—does not interest Grinev. Instead, the mundane details of everyday life become central, and the position of an individual buffeted by history comes to the fore. We see that although Grinev lived amidst momentous historical events (from the point of view of a historian, that is), he never really noticed them. For Grinev, and, by extension, for any individual in history, private life (in this case the outcome of his love affair with Masha Mironova) is far more significant than are "historical" events. As we will see in the following chapter, a similarly prosaic view of history formed the basis for one level of Tolstoy's narrative in *War and Peace*.

The novel plays up the role of accident and coincidence in history, factors completely absent in the controlled and orderly narrative of *The History of Pugachev*. At the very beginning of the novel, Grinev is rescued from a blizzard by the prerebellion Pugachev and gives the unknown Cossack his coat as a reward. After the revolt has begun, when his men take the fort in which Grinev is garrisoned, Pugachev happens to arrive just in time to recognize and save his former benefactor. Later in the novel, Pugachev again happens to arrive in the nick of time and prevents Shvabrin from marrying Grinev's beloved. All of these devices for creating suspense are, of course, unremarkable, the stock-in-trade of any novelist. But when they are contrasted to the approach of the narrative historian, as they inevitably are here, they point up the divergence in the assumptions of these two genres. Pushkin's approach to dealing with the ultimate incompatibility of the perspectives of an eyewitness and a future historian is to present both of them.

The ultimate irony of history, the fact that things "could have been otherwise," which Pushkin emphasizes throughout the novel, is another factor separating the historical conception of *The Captain's Daughter* from that of *The History of Pugachev*. Pushkin's primary method of encoding irony is by superimposing obvious literary patterns onto the historical events described by Grinev. What seems unique and historically important to

Grinev is revealed as conventional and commonplace by the putative editor. For example, the historicity of Grinev's descriptions is tempered by the editor's addition of literary epigraphs, which form an ironic commentary on the events described by the narrator. Thus, Grinev's overly melodramatic and somewhat comic account of the siege of Orenburg is presaged by an epigraph taken from Kheraskov's bombastic patriotic epic, *Rossiada*. The epigraph, which describes Ivan the Terrible's successful siege of Kazan', implies (incorrectly, as it turns out) that Pugachev's corresponding siege of Orenburg will ultimately succeed, and that there is some meaningful connection between the figures of Pugachev and Ivan. When this proves not to be the case, the reader is left with frustrated expectations and the gnawing feeling that the "editor" is making fun of the simple narrator.[13] Whereas one might conclude that historical events had a strict logic of their own after reading the *History*, the novel's reader is impressed with the artificiality of the historical narrative, with the extent to which historical events can be modeled by literary works.

Given the major and seemingly irreconcilable differences between the historical conceptions of these two works, the question arises, why did Pushkin feel the need to write both a history of the Pugachev rebellion and a novel on the subject? An obvious psychological explanation springs to mind, namely that Pushkin was stung by the failure of his history and that he turned back to the more familiar ground of literature to produce a popular masterpiece. When the creative biographies of these two works are examined, however, this hypothesis becomes untenable. Pushkin's letters make it clear that the idea of writing a historical novel set during the rebellion did not arise in the wake of the failure of his *History*, but was present from the outset.[14] Indeed, in his first letter alluding to the project, Pushkin informed Tsar Nicholas I that he intended to begin a work of fiction: "Perhaps the Sovereign will wish to know precisely what kind of book I want to finish writing in the village; it is a novel, the greater part of the action of which takes place in Orenburg and Kazan."[15]

However, as Pushkin began to work with the documents relating to the uprising, the idea of writing a history became increasingly attractive. In September 1833, he set off for the areas in which the revolt had occurred. He relished interviewing the last remaining eyewitnesses of those frightening times. Indeed, he asked about Pugachev so zealously that some suspicious Cossacks denounced him to the local police as the Antichrist.[16] By the time Pushkin returned home in the late fall of 1833, he was ready to inform the tsar about a change in plans. As he wrote in a letter to Alexander Benkendorf, his conduit to the tsar: "I once thought of writing a historical novel relating to the times of Pugachev, but after finding a multitude of materials, I abandoned that notion and wrote *The History of the Pugachev Affair*." [17] In the end, Pushkin did not finish the novel he had originally intended until 1836. Thus, *The Captain's Daughter* was not written in response to the failure of *The History of Pugachev*. Rather, it seems that Pushkin was unable or unwilling to write the novel before he had completed the history.[18]

One way to understand why this was so is to compare Pushkin's situation in 1833 with that in 1825, when he was working on *Boris Godunov*. At that time, Karamzin's wildly popular historical account of the rise and fall of Boris had just appeared, and Pushkin was able to transpose Karamzin's version of the story at will, secure in the knowledge that his audience would recognize and appreciate the differences between Karamzin's version and his own dramatic one.[19] Because Karamzin included most of the available material relating to the events of Boris's reign in a coherent narrative account, Pushkin could afford to be elliptical, confident that his target audience could easily fill in the gaps that were the inevitable result of his decision to concentrate on specific scenes. The result was a generic dialogism in which the inclusivity and distanced perspective of Karamzin's history illuminated the specificity and intimacy of Pushkin's play and vice versa.

But as opposed to the story of the rise and fall of Boris, that of the Pugachev rebellion was almost unknown in Pushkin's day.[20] After the investigation of the uprising was completed and the guilty had been punished, Catherine the Great ordered the archives on the subject sealed, and as a result no history of the rebellion had ever been written. Pushkin was evidently the first person to be given access to the documents relating to the revolt.[21] Thus when Pushkin began working on the Pugachev uprising there was, in effect, no preexisting plot for it in the Russian cultural memory. Pushkin's novel was narrated in the first person; this inevitably meant that it would be perceived as presenting an individual point of view. But how could this point of view work effectively if readers were unable to recognize the points at which the fictional narrative called the history of the events of the uprising into question?

Of course, the problem was not merely one of familiarity with the facts, although audience knowledge of the historical story line is almost as important for the success of a historical novel as for that of a drama; I say "almost" because the novel's frame has the potential to (and in the case of *The Captain's Daughter*, actually does) allow for the inclusion of more background material than can be presented dramatically. But the real problem is that the lack of a history meant the absence of a generally accepted reality, and Pushkin's creative imagination was always most stimulated when he was working against the canons of the generally accepted, be it a literary genre, a historical theme, or a social situation. The lack of history meant there was nothing for him to call into question ironically through a fictional perspective; that is, it made impossible the potential for mutual illumination that Pushkin had exploited so skillfully when writing *Boris Godunov* in the light of Karamzin's *History*. In the end, Pushkin seems to have realized that if he wanted the benefits of intergeneric dialogue for his Pugachev tale, he was going to have to provide both genres himself.

There is a danger, however, in assuming that Pushkin's need for a traditional historical account, a need which probably provided the initial stimulus for writing *The History of Puga-chev*, remained the only raison d'être for the work. This would imply that the history was merely a necessary evil, a preliminary operation that prepared the ground for Pushkin's literary masterpiece. In a more complicated form this seems to be the opinion of N. N. Petrunina, who has written the most recent comprehensive treatment of Pushkin's prose. She suggests that Pushkin initially wished to borrow from Walter Scott, who had begun the novel *Rob Roy* with a long historical introduction. In her opinion, this "introduction" eventually outgrew itself and became an independent work.[22] But her ingenious hypothesis, even if true, reveals nothing more than the evolutionary connection between two works, one that Pushkin might well have chosen to downplay. It does not help us understand the nature of their dialogic relationship, a relationship that Pushkin chose to force his readers to note in the epilogue of *The Captain's Daughter*. In Petrunina's account, *The History of Pugachev* is merely one more source text for *The Captain's Daughter*, no more essential for understanding the novel than Zagoskin's *Iury Miloslavsky* or the novels of Walter Scott. The relationship is seen as entirely one-way—from the history to the novel.

This, I think, is to downplay the importance of *The History of Pugachev* both for Pushkin himself and for an understanding of *The Captain's Daughter*. If we turn again to Pushkin's letters it becomes obvious that whatever his initial reasons for writing the history might have been, he became quite fond of it in its own right. In his letters of 1833–36, Pushkin writes about *The History of Pugachev* more frequently than about any of his other works, and he mentions it with obvious affection. This is true in the first place because he was handsomely paid for the history. He joked about this in a letter to his friend Pavel Nashchokin: "What do you think of these times? Pugachev has become a reliable payer of quitrent: Emel'ka Pugachev, my serf, paid in full" (16, 6). In another letter, to his hostess in Kazan', he jested, "I don't understand how it is that my vagabond, Emel'ian Pugachev, didn't make it to Kazan', a place he remembers well; he must have wandered off along the way and gone on a spree, as is his wont" (16, 87).

At the same time, there were certain ways in which the strict narrative form of history as Pushkin practiced it could not have been entirely satisfying. For one thing, the grudging affection that Pushkin evidently developed for Pugachev in the course of his research went unreflected in the text of his *History*. This is not surprising, considering that *The History of Pugachev* was more or less paid for by the imperial treasury, and one can imagine that Nicholas I would have been less than happy with a sympathetic portrayal of a peasant rebel. Perhaps we are seeing the "modesty and moderation" that Pushkin felt were required of the historian as thanks for having been freed from regular censorship. In the more subjective novel, Pushkin was under no such obligation and here, hiding behind the voice of his narrator, he was able to show some sympathy toward the rebel hero. Pugachev treats Grinev well, and Grinev is able to appreciate this streak of humanity in the otherwise bloodthirsty Pugachev.

Building off the story laid out in Pushkin's *History*, the novel can delve into areas of character and psychology that must remain outside the objective historian's realm, particularly if the historian is in the employ of the state. The desirability of a reading that would consider the history and the novel in tandem was noted by P. V. Annenkov as early as 1855: "Together with his historical work, Pushkin, led by the immutable demands of his artistic nature, began a novel. *The Captain's Daughter* presented the other side of the subject—the side concerning the mores and habits of the age. The terse, externally-dry-seeming manner of presentation that he chose for the history found its complement, as it were, in his exemplary novel, which has the warmth and charm of historical jottings."[23] Thus, each version of the rebellion had advantages and disadvantages. The history allowed for a seemingly distanced, objective, inclusive version of the story, while the novel lent a personalizing, subjective view of events. The "true" historical narrative is, of course, not to be found in either work. Rather, historical truth is seen as dialogic, and is to be found in the interaction of these (and, potentially, other) perspectives.[24]

It should also be pointed out that in the mid-1830's the

problem of integrating objectivity and subjectivity was hardly limited to Pushkin or to the sphere of history. As Boris Eikhenbaum pointed out, one of the most important tasks for Russian literature of the 1830's was sorting out "the relationship between private life ('the story of the heart') with historical life, the life of the people." [25] Eikhenbaum sees Lermontov's novel *Hero of Our Time* (*Geroi nashego vremeni*) as the work that really begins to resolve this relationship, and, as far as the history of the Russian novel goes, he is probably right. But when it came to the presentation of historical material, a smooth Lermontovian synthesis of the private and public spheres was not the method of choice in Russia. Instead, following in the tradition of Karamzin, Russian writers chose intergeneric dialogue. The relationship between *The History of Pugachev* and *The Captain's Daughter* can be seen precisely in the terms Eikhenbaum suggests, with the novel concentrating on the former side of Eikhenbaum's equation and the history on the latter. The integration of the points of view represented in Pushkin's separate but equal texts was left up to the reader.

But why, we might ask, did Pushkin turn specifically to these two genres to emplot the events of the Pugachev rebellion? After all, earlier in his career he had successfully used completely different ones for a similar purpose. In fact, he considered his historical narrative poem, *Poltava*, and his historical drama, *Boris Godunov*, to be among his crowning achievements. To answer this question we must recall Pushkin's constant tendency to appropriate those genres that were most in the public eye at a given time and to transform them to fit his personal literary needs. In the 1820's the long poem and the drama had been central, but by the 1830's the two obvious available genres for encoding historical events had become the history and the historical novel. [26] Of course, the first volumes of Karamzin's *History of the Russian State* had appeared and been appreciated as early as 1818, but the question of how the national history should be treated by historians was debated with new intensity after the publication in 1829 of a work whose author advertised his radical departure from Karamzin: Polevoi's *History of the Russian People.*[27] The historical novels discussed in this period were, of course, generally those of Walter Scott or his numerous Russian imitators.[28]

The advantages and disadvantages of these various methods of treating historical material were endlessly debated in the Russian journals in the 1830's. Indeed, discussions of this sort had become a cliché of Russian cultural life in this period, as can be seen in the following excerpt from the preface to a long-forgotten historical novel by a (deservedly) obscure author named Konstantin Masal'sky:

> The historian discovers the truth in the past, the eternal laws governing the world, and contemplates events like a philosopher, concerning himself not so much with the pleasure of his readers as with their enlightenment. The historical novelist tries to present the past in an intriguing and attractive fashion, concerning himself principally with the readers' pleasure, without too strongly exhibiting the philosophical or educational purpose which must be present in any novel.[29]

One imagines that Pushkin, always a keen follower of literary politics, might have felt challenged to prove the conventional wisdom wrong—to show that the truths of fiction and of history were not mutually exclusive, but, rather, complementary. In any case, he took an active if somewhat ambiguous part in polemics on the subject of how to treat history. He voiced his approval for the works of the man he called "the Scottish sorcerer" in both personal letters and articles. In the draft of an article on Walter Scott's novels, he said: "The most wonderful thing about the novels of Walter Scott is that in them we come to know the past not with the *enflure* of French tragedy,— not with the priggishness of sentimental novels,—not with the dignity of history, but as if it were contemporary, quotidian" (12, 195). In Pushkin's mind, it would seem, the specificity of the novel has nothing to do with pleasure, as Masal'sky would have it. The novel's strength lies in its ability to make history come alive from the inside, as it were, and from a particular perspective. This is more or less the same attitude we found in

Karamzin's historical tales, but, of course, in the intervening thirty years Russian prose had made great forward strides in sophistication.

However, Pushkin never felt that Scott's approach was the only possible one. The desirability of other approaches became particularly clear after 1831, when Pushkin began working with original sources and archival materials in preparing *The History of Pugachev* and the unfinished *History of Peter the Great*. He gained increased respect for Karamzin's monumental history. In an article criticizing Polevoi, Pushkin specifically defended Karamzin. Pushkin attacks Polevoi for writing badly in general, but more specifically, he charges that "having been enthralled by the novelistic vividness of the truth which is placed before us in the naked simplicity of the chronicles, he [Polevoi] fanatically denied the existence of any other history" (11, 121). Evidently Pushkin realized the advantages inherent in each genre but felt it most important for the writer to be aware of the multiplicity of ways in which historical material could be encoded.

At the same time, Pushkin's reluctance to choose a single genre to express his views on history can be seen as part of a general pattern in his creative biography. He always had a tendency to encode the same material in two forms, one elevated and serious, the other ironic and comic, more or less simultaneously. One recalls, for example, the conjunction of the lyric "I Remember a Wonderful Moment" ("Ia pomniu chudnoe mgnovenie") and the salacious letter about Anna Kern that Pushkin wrote to Sobolevsky. Another example is Pushkin's encoding apocalyptic scenes comically in *Count Nulin* and heroically in *Poltava*.[30] Thus, Pushkin's dialogic approach to history in *The History of Pugachev* and *The Captain's Daughter* can be seen as part of a larger pattern of intergeneric dialogue characteristic of his work in general.

It might seem that I do not believe there to be any way to reconcile the historical philosophies of Pushkin the historian and Pushkin the novelist. This is true if we limit ourselves to questions about what must be included in the narrative and how historical material should be presented. On this level, I believe that Pushkin's choices were dictated primarily by considerations of genre; what was crucial for one genre was unnecessary for another and Pushkin wished, if anything, to emphasize the incompatibility of the historical perspectives that his various genres required in order to encourage intergeneric dialogue between them. However, if we turn to the larger question of what it means to write a history, I think we can find a thread connecting all of Pushkin's historically oriented work. The crux of Pushkin's attitude can be found in the speech of one of the historical personages he created: the monk and historical chronicler, Pimen, in *Boris Godunov*.

In his famous monologue, Pimen predicts the future fate of his chronicle:

> Someday an indefatigable monk
> Will come upon my sedulous, anonymous work;
> Like me, he will illuminate his lamp
> And shaking from the scrolls the hoary dust,
> He will rewrite [*perepisat'*] these tales in all their truth,
> That the descendants of the Orthodox
> May know their native land's past fate. (7, 17)

The word *perepisat'*, translated here as "rewrite," is somewhat ambiguous in Russian. It can mean either "to rewrite" or simply "to copy." However, as Pushkin and Pimen both knew, later generations of monks never merely copied the chronicles, they added new material and removed or adapted old material as necessary, which is why I have opted for "rewrite."[31] And while Pimen's words certainly cannot be taken as an accurate depiction of how and why the Russian chroniclers worked, there is a sense in which they can be seen as Pushkin's own historical credo.

Let us examine what Pimen thinks about his work. Obviously, he realizes that he is writing narratives that will tell a story to future generations. He does not consider his own contribution a work of genius—it is merely "sedulous" and "anonymous." Perhaps even more importantly, Pimen knows and expects that it will all be rewritten by some future chronicler: that is, there will inevitably come to exist multiple encodings of the same event. Indeed, as Jurij Striedter has shown, within *Boris Godunov*, Grisha Otrep'ev's actions can be seen as a reencoding of Pimen's story from the mode of passive chronicle to that of active rebellion.[32]

Turning to the introduction that Pushkin wrote for *The History of Pugachev*, we see a number of important similarities between Pushkin the historian and Pimen the historian. Pushkin acknowledges the fact that he was not able to look at all of the sources but does not find this a problem. He says that "a future historian will find it easy to correct and add to my work which is, of course, incomplete although sincere" (9, I, 1). Once again, we have the idea that this encoding of events is neither the only possible one nor the final one. Inevitably, some future historian will shake the dust off *The History of Pugachev* and will reemplot the events of the uprising in light of new data or a different perspective. As it turned out, the introduction to the history foreshadowed the novel, for it was Pushkin himself who decided to reencode the events of the Pugachev rebellion in a different genre.

To sum up our discussion of Pushkin, we might say that while *The History of Pugachev* and *The Captain's Daughter* represent entirely different methods of encoding history, there is no evidence that either was meant to be seen as privileged. The view of the Pugachev rebellion and the attitude toward history displayed in the novel are in no way meant to supersede the very different point of view of the history. Rather, Pushkin implies that the two works are meant to be read in tandem. The clash of their separate monologic narratives leads to an intergeneric dialogue that emphasizes the multiplicity of possible historical interpretations. Each belongs firmly to its own genre, but the two are linked to each other, and to all of Pushkin's work on historical themes by his conception of history as a series of possible stories. Each individual work of history should be imbued with what Pushkin called a "unified spirit,"[33] but ultimate historical truth, if it exists for Pushkin, arises not from the synthesis of genres, but from their juxtaposition. In this respect, Pushkin was consciously or unconsciously following the lead of Karamzin, reinterpreting his initial *maître*'s approach in light of the new possibilities available in the 1830's.

It might be argued, of course, that such a continuity is not surprising considering Pushkin's close ties with Karamzin. However, if we look at the larger cultural context, it turns out that the use of intergeneric dialogue for the presentation of historical material was also characteristic for writers who were never part of Karamzin's orbit. For example, intergeneric dialogue is foregrounded in the poetics of Ryleev's *Dumy* (1825), a cycle of patriotic historical lyrics. Here the dialogue is not constructed around the clash between smooth-flowing and fragmentary narratives or between internal and external perspectives on historical events, but rather between synchrony and diachrony. Each lyric presents a slice of history in the form of a brief verse scene. As a rule, the poems are named not for the specific scenes described, but for the central actors. "Dmitry Donskoi," for example, does not tell the reader anything about most of the events of Dmitry's life; instead, it concentrates exclusively on the 1380 Battle of Kulikovo. Of course, one might argue that such a narrow focus is justified given Ryleev's choice of genre. This is certainly the case; in a 50-line poem it would be absurd to present more than one incident. But what is interesting given the Russian penchant for intergeneric dialogue is that Ryleev is unwilling to settle for the limitations of the lyric.

His method of overcoming these limitations is twofold. First, he gathers what had initially been scattered and, from the point of view of most readers, unrelated poems into a single collection.[34] This serves to enhance the connections between the lyrics, to create an overarching thematic structure and to allow for the emergence of a specific view of history. That this was indeed Ryleev's motive can be seen from the preface to the collection, in which he claims to have published the work with the same goal as that expressed by the Polish poet Niemcewicz: "To remind our youth of the feats of their ancestors, to acquaint them with the brightest epochs in the people's history, and to link love for the fatherland with the earliest recollections of memory."[35]

Second, and more important from our point of view, is that when Ryleev published the lyrics as a collection, he chose to preface each one with a short prose fragment giving an overview of the hero's life; that is, he places the specific event described in each poem in a diachronic context. He does this even though he could reasonably expect that, given the popularity of Karamzin's *History*, every reader would already know the information presented in the capsule biographies.[36] Presumably, then, what was important to Ryleev was not simply making the information available; rather, he was trying to balance the synchrony of his lyric genre with the diachronic principle of the prose biography.[37]

It is also worth noting that for Ryleev and his fellow Decembrists, there was a second intergeneric dialogue at work here, this one between genres of literature and genres of life.[38] The actions of the freedom-loving heroes of Ryleev's poems were not described merely to provide aesthetic pleasure. They were meant to be emulated in the real world, and, at some level, the Decembrist uprising was the fruit of that emulation. Naturally, the failure of the Decembrists made the actual relationship of literature to life problematic. The course of events caused the poems to be read in a tragic rather than a triumphant light, but the inevitable references to the Decembrist rising that accompany any discussion of the *Dumy* show that intergeneric dialogue did in fact result.

Finally, at almost the same time that Pushkin was laboring as imperial historiographer, Nikolai Gogol was having himself appointed adjunct professor of history at St. Petersburg University.[39] Gogol the professor was an abject failure, as numerous eyewitness accounts describing his lectures attest.[40] Nevertheless, the mere fact that he would aspire to such a position says a great deal about the prestige of history in Russia in the 1830's, and the fact that he could win the post despite his lack of formal training indicates the extent to which Russian writers were accepted as historians.

Nor was Gogol's interest in history confined to the classroom. While Pushkin was writing *The History of Pugachev* and *The Captain's Daughter*, Gogol was treating the history of Ukraine in the same two genres.[41] Unlike Pushkin, Gogol never finished his history, but he did publish what was billed as an excerpt from the *History of Little Russia* (*Istoriia Malorossii*) in 1834. More or less simultaneously, he was working on the historical novel, *Taras Bul'ba*, which appeared in 1835. Also unlike Pushkin, who left no obvious programmatic statements on the relationship between historical and literary genres, Gogol, in his article "On the Teaching of Universal History" ("O prepodavanii vseobshchei istorii"), discussed the problem directly. According to Gogol, the purpose of universal history is "to gather as one all the peoples of the world, scattered as they are by time and happenstance, mountains and seas, and to unite them in a single elegant whole; to make of them a single, full, magnificent poem."[42] This poem could not be achieved, however, merely by writing an actual work of poetry (even in the broadest sense of the term). As Gogol points out later in his essay, one needs history for poetry: "A quick survey of the history of each part of the world . . . is necessary, because it leads one to ideas, forces the listener to think. The mind develops faster when it can put great and poetic questions to itself."[43]

As far as one can ascertain from the excerpt Gogol published, his history of Ukraine was designed to be just the kind of "brief survey" that would allow the mind to pose poetic questions. Of course, Gogol's survey is nothing at all like the great professional histories of Karamzin or Pushkin.[44] But neither is it a work of fiction. Although its language is quite elevated in some places, it is clearly meant to complement the highly rhetorical *Taras Bul'ba*, a historical novel that is singularly lacking in history. The novel, for which, incidentally, Gogol cribbed quite a lot of descriptive material from his history, represents the poetic version of the history of Gogol's motherland. What is crucial, however, is that one evidently could not have existed without the other. Even though he never published the history, the act of imagining the history of Ukraine in a nonfictional genre is what allowed Gogol to write the novel.[45]

Thus, to return to some of the questions that interested us at the beginning of this chapter, we can see that Pushkin's intergeneric dialogue was by no means unusual. It was deeply rooted in Russian cultural and literary tradition. As the hierarchy of genres that had characterized Russian literature through the early part of the nineteenth century finally disintegrated completely, writers and readers were unable to decide which genre, if any, was the proper one for dealing with perhaps the most burning cultural issue of the day: the national history. Karamzin and his *History of the Russian State* provided a model of intergeneric dialogue for the next generation of Russian writers, and in their own ways, Pushkin, Ryleev, and Gogol all extended that model. Of course, many writers continued to practice only one genre, either because they did not worry about questions of genre, or because they counted on their readers' knowledge of Karamzin's history to fill in the nonfictional gap.[46] But Pushkin, Ryleev, and Gogol were important enough figures that their experiments did not go unnoticed. In particular, it seems that Lev Tolstoy had their generic dialogism in mind when he began *War and Peace*, a work that achieved a truly successful intermingling of historical and literary genres in one magisterial whole.

⚜

Chapter Five

War and Peace:
Intergeneric Dialogue in One Text

I was afraid that the necessity to describe the significant figures of 1812 would force me to be governed by historical documents rather than the truth.

Lev Tolstoy [1]

War and Peace has always been a difficult book to classify. Generations of readers and critics have been mystified by the peculiarities of this "loose baggy monster." [2] Tolstoy himself announced that it was "not a novel, still less a poem, still less a historical chronicle," [3] but he failed to provide any positive generic indication for it. In the context of the Russian tradition that has been sketched out in the first chapters of this book, however, such interpretive difficulties seem a bit bizarre. From our perspective, it is obvious that *War and Peace* is constructed around an intergeneric dialogue between fictional and historical voices, a standard technique of Russian writers of belles lettres for the treatment of history. But whereas previous authors had segregated their historical and literary narratives into discrete units, Tolstoy writes fiction and history more or less simultaneously; he elevates intergeneric dialogue to the principle of literary and historical organization *within a single work.*

A closer examination shows that this transformation was not an easy one to effect. Tolstoy's bold but inherently dangerous combination of fictional and historical narrative within the confines of a single text necessitated major modifications in the Russian tradition we have been examining. Intergeneric dialogue is far more complex and harder to sustain when genres are not segregated, for if a book is to function simultaneously as fiction and history, a way has to be found both to keep the separate genres recognizable and to promote their interaction. How could the interaction of multiple and, from a normal generic point of view, mutually exclusive presentations of history be fused into a single text? Of Tolstoy's predecessors only Karamzin (in a sustained way) and Ryleev had attempted anything like this, and both had solved the problem by a graphic separation of their various narratives. But this meant that readers were free to ignore the potential for dialogue: it is easy, for example, to read all of Karamzin's main text without ever looking at the notes. The segregation of genres thus tends to mask precisely the kind of interaction that intergeneric dialogue has the potential to foster. I would suggest that Tolstoy, here as always a maximalist, wanted to thematize overtly the different kinds of historical knowledge made available by each of his separate genres and thereby to force his reader to recognize the full potential of intergeneric dialogue as a literary/historical method.

There is ample evidence from Tolstoy's writings to indicate that he, like his predecessors Karamzin, Pushkin, and Gogol, believed fictional and historical narration to be fundamentally different, and that he felt called to be both novelist and historian. Strong evidence for the former can be seen in a published defense that appeared while *War and Peace* was still unfinished. Here Tolstoy acknowledges the criticism that his presentation of the Napoleonic period is not in accord with the descriptions of historians. But he ripostes with an appeal to the artist's right to his own kind of truth: "When describing a historical epoch the artist and the historian have two entirely different objectives. Just as the historian would be wrong if he attempted to present a historical figure in all his entirety, in all his complicated connections to all aspects of life, so an artist would not be doing his duty if he presented that figure in all of his historical significance" (13, 57). Taken by itself, this passage would seem to indicate that Tolstoy recognized the differences and wished to avoid the burden of being a historian in addition to being a writer of fictions: that he renounced the temptation, always present for major Russian writers of belles lettres, to cross the boundary separating literature from history.

Yet by the time he was reaching the conclusion of *War and Peace*, approximately a year later, Tolstoy had evidently undergone a change of heart. In his notes for the epilogue he wrote: "I understand the entire difference between my stated view of history and that of all historians. The difference is such that it is clear: either I had the misfortune to go out of my mind and to couple an insane discussion of history to a work that was having great success, or else all that is called historical science, that is written, taught, and published so seriously is empty and idle chatter. . . . Either I am crazy or I have discovered a new truth. I believe I have discovered a new truth" (15, 242). Considering the tone of the epilogue, it seems likely that the truth Tolstoy has in mind here transcends the truth accessible to the "mere" fiction writer. Tolstoy now sees himself as a historian.[4] What is more, he sees himself as superior to all other historians.

But Tolstoy's statements, whatever they might tell us about his personal view of his accomplishment in *War and Peace*, are by no means incontrovertible evidence that the book actually creates a successful intergeneric dialogue of fictional and historical voices, nor do they tell us how he accomplished this feat if indeed he did. For this we must turn to an attentive reading of *War and Peace* itself. The solution Tolstoy hit upon, I would argue, was to observe the basic subject of his narrative, the Napoleonic period, not from two but rather from three distinct monologic narrative positions. I will call them the fictional, historical, and metahistorical voices. The fictional and historical voices correspond, more or less, to the positions of Pushkin's fictional and historical narrators in *The Captain's Daughter* and *The History of Pugachev*. The function of the metahistorical voice is to mediate their interaction within a single text.

Fortunately for Tolstoy, the technical problems of how to arrange multivoiced texts were familiar. He had run into them when writing his first published book, the pseudo-autobiographical *Childhood* (*Detstvo*), more than a decade earlier. The pseudo-autobiography, as Tolstoy developed it, is a first-person narrative in which the narrator shares much of the author's life but does not share his name. This creates a narrative situation that allows the story to be presented from three distinct points of view: that of the child hero, that of the adult narrator, and that of the implied author. The resulting structure is analogous to musical counterpoint.

The following passage gives an idea of how the system works when all three voices are present at the same time:

At the time I was amazed at the change from touching emotion, with which she spoke to me, to grumbling and trivial calculation. [*The child's voice is speaking here: it does not analyze or seek to explain, but merely to present what happened. Of course the words "at the time" show a sense of lost time.*] Thinking about it later, I understood that despite what was happening in her soul she still had enough spirit left to take care of her work. . . . Grief had affected her so strongly that she did not find it necessary to hide the fact that she could take care of other things: she wouldn't have even understood how such a thought could arise. [*Here we are in the presence of the adult narrator's voice, which looks back on the raw material of the child's perception, interprets it, and sometimes even tries to "correct" the child's impression.*]

Vanity is the feeling most incompatible with true grief but, at the same time, the feeling is so deeply embedded in human nature that it is very rare that even the strongest grief can drive it out. Vanity in grief is manifested in the desire to seem either afflicted or unhappy or firm. [*This is the implied author's voice, which extrapolates from the story of Natal'ia Savishna and the child's reaction to it in order to show a general truth about mankind.*] (1, 91)

In *War and Peace* Tolstoy would again use three interpenetrating voice positions, this time distributed among novelist, historical narrator, and metahistorian. But before discussing how Tolstoy achieved intergeneric dialogue employing his separate voices, it is important that the reader be able to identify them.

The Fictional Voice

The standard model for using historical material in fiction had been provided by the "Waverley novels" of Sir Walter Scott almost 50 years before Tolstoy began to write *War and Peace*. Like every other nineteenth-century reader, Tolstoy knew the Scottian conventions well and was quite capable of reproducing them effortlessly. For an example, one can turn to almost any passage in part I of *War and Peace*.

In part I, chapter 23, Prince Andrei arrives with his pregnant wife Liza at his father's estate, Bald Hills. Also present, in addition to his father, are his sister Maria and assorted retainers. The interactions of the characters are developed with all the verisimilitude of psychological and physical detail that the realist novelist can muster.

The grey-haired valet was sitting in the waiting room dozing and listening to the prince's snoring in his immense study. From a far-off part of the house, through closed doors, came the sound of difficult passages of a Dusseck sonata being repeated twenty times over.

At that moment a carriage and a little cart drove up to the steps, and Prince Andrei got out of the carriage, helped his little wife out, and let her pass into the house before him. Grey Tikhon in his wig, popping out at the door of the waiting room, informed him in a whisper that the prince was taking a nap and quickly closed the door. Tikhon knew that neither the arrival of a son nor any other extraordinary event should break up the order of the day. Prince Andrei evidently knew this just as well as Tikhon. He looked at his watch as though to be certain that his father's habits had not changed during the time he had not seen him, and satisfying himself that they had not changed, he turned to his wife. (9, 118)

Details like the Dusseck sonata help re-create the specificity of the historical period. Those pertaining to the daily routine of the household and its inhabitants, and particularly to its longue durée (here the fact that the old prince's habits have not changed over the years), evoke the prosaic ordinary world that the fictional characters seem to have created by themselves (and which is, of course, an artifact carefully crafted by the fictional narrator). The mimetic illusion is strengthened both by the blurring of narrator's and character's perception (here we view the house through Andrei's perception, more or less) and by the sense of presentness this kind of narration engenders.[5]

Within this framework, Andrei and his father discuss specific historical events, namely the upcoming war with Napoleon and the probable European response to events. The old man asks his son for fresh news from the capital.

> Prince Andrei, seeing the urgency of his father's questions, began explaining the plan of operations of the proposed campaign, speaking at first reluctantly, but becoming livelier as he went on, and unconsciously, from habit, switching from Russian into French in the middle of his narrative. He told him that an army of ninety thousand was to threaten Prussia in order to drive her out of neutrality and draw her into the war, that some of these troops were to join up with Swedish troops at Strahlsund, that two hundred and twenty thousand Austrians were to combine with a hundred thousand Russians for action in Italy and on the Rhine, and that fifty thousand Russians and fifty thousand English troops were to disembark at Naples, and that thus, in the end, a five-hundred-thousand-man army was to attack the French from different sides. The old prince did not exhibit the slightest interest during the narrative. He went on dressing while walking about, apparently not listening, and unexpectedly interrupted him three times. Once he stopped him and shouted, "The white one! the white one!"
>
> This meant that Tikhon had not given him the waistcoat he wanted. Another time he stood still and asked, "And will she give birth soon?" and shook his head reproachfully: "That's not good! Go on, go on." (9, 122–23)

Through this passage the fictional narrator is able to introduce historical material into his narrative. Of course, we know that the "facts" are being provided by the fictional character Andrei, and are at best suspect as a source of historical knowledge. Nevertheless, there is an unwritten compact between historical novelist and reader that either the facts in passages like this one be accurate or inaccuracies be motivated by the bias of the character. What the fictional narrator cannot do is to change facts completely (as opposed to interpreting them): we can be fairly certain that Andrei could not tell his father that the American army was going to take part in this campaign, for example. This pact is not a problem for Tolstoy in this case, since he evidently has no desire to dispute these particular facts here (either because their accuracy is unimportant, or because if they are wrong the mistake can be attributed to Andrei's lack of knowledge). However, the inability on the level of the fictional text to dispute the facts of history in any meaningful way is one of the weaknesses of the standard historical novel and, as we will see, it is one that Tolstoy gets around by presenting his disagreements with the standard presentation of the facts of the Napoleonic campaign not through his fictional but rather through his historical narrator. At this point there is no discrepancy between received fact and Tolstoy's opinion, though, and the characters in their fictional world go on discussing the "real world." In this respect Napoleon is no different a marker of the period than is Dusseck.

This passage and hundreds like it in *War and Peace* illustrate how history, in the sense of information about famous events and people, is integrated into the daily life of almost everyone. The old prince's approximately equal concern with troop movements, the pregnancy of Andrei's wife, and the proper waistcoat is emblematic of the fictional narrator's main point: that history is just a part of daily life, and, ultimately, far less important than people imagine.

Tropologically speaking, the fictional narrator is a believer in metonym. It is implied by the fictional narrator that the actions and observations of a tiny group of closely related characters (after all, the vast majority of the book's fictional characters are either Rostovs or Rostov in-laws) in some way capture the experience of all Russians during the years 1805–13. Tolstoy was of course aware that this aspect of his work was open to criticism—in one of the drafts he acknowledged that some would attack him for describing "only princes, counts, ministers, senators and their children"—but on the fictional level he made little effort to do anything about this potential weakness.[6] Nor was there very much he could have done. The only way to achieve a level of detailed description of the mundane details of daily life sufficient to re-create present-tense experience in a fiction that covered such large quantities of space and time was by sharply limiting the number of fictional characters.

The Historical Voice

The historical narrator narrates historical events. This means that the historical voice is employed to relate those events over which the writer does not have ultimate control. When Tolstoy is writing about Prince Andrei or Pierre Bezukhov, he is relatively unconstrained. He does not have to know how their plots will turn out, and from the evidence of Tolstoy's drafts and his statements, it seems likely that he did not. This, however, is not the case with the Battle of Borodino. No matter how much freedom Tolstoy allows himself within the battle description, the end result of the battle is fixed. He cannot write it to conclude with the immediate retreat of the French to Paris, or with the death of Napoleon.

This may seem a trivial detail considering, on the one hand, the wealth of freedom Tolstoy has within his depictions of historical events, and, on the other, the boundedness that results from every fictional decision (after Andrei has been killed off, for example, his plot can no longer be modified). For both Tolstoy and his reader, however, this difference leads to some crucial and palpable narrative contrasts. As opposed to the fictional narrator, who tells his stories from the inside out, the historical narrator takes a stance outside his text, perched far enough above it to take in its broader perspectives. The illusion this voice presents to readers is that of the existence of a finished product: a history that has already happened, without the uncertainties that an individual perspective would perceive. Indeed the analogy one comes away with is that of viewing a film clip. It is as if the historical narrator has access to a movie taken at the time in question and is simply providing a commentary: "Look, over there, at the right of the screen you glimpse the French," and so on.

Most important, we must keep in mind that this narrator has a completely different view of the historical process than does the fictional narrator, and as a result, their functions in the text are entirely different. The historical narrator comes to the fore when Tolstoy wants to set the historical record straight, in scenes like those at the Shevardino redoubt, which we will consider later. In the early stages of the book, however, the role of this narrator is limited, and his presence is muted.

It is not at all difficult to distinguish the voice of the historical narrator from that of the fictional. Let us briefly examine the opening section of part II of *War and Peace*. It stands a mere ten pages from the passages we have just considered, but in tone, concern, and attitude it is light years away: "In October of 1805 the Russian troops were occupying the towns and villages of the Austrian archduchy, and fresh regiments kept arriving from Russia and encamping about the fortress of Braunau, burdening the inhabitants on whom they were billeted. Braunau was the main headquarters of the commander in chief, Kutuzov" (9, 137). Most obvious here and in the pages that follow is the absence of fictional characters, although as we will see, their absence is not as important as one might think. More interesting is the perspective of the narrator. In passages presented by the fictional narrator there is always the possibility (actualized quite frequently) of a melding of the perspective of the narrator with that of one of the characters. Thus, in the description of Andrei and his father quoted earlier, the reader feels for much of the passage as if he is observing the old prince through the filter of Andrei's perception. This is a function of Tolstoy's use of a kind of perspectival *style indirect libre*, which allows the narrator to seem at times to be inside his text looking outward. When a fictional character thinks (narratively speaking) this way, readers tend to place themselves inside the character's consciousness and to see the world unfolding from that perspective, with the same degree of unpredictability that the character does. Ultimately all this means is that fictional texts, even when narrated in the past, seem to readers to be occurring in a narrative present. All realist writers use this to their advantage, although Tolstoy was perhaps the most successful with it.

Passages presented by the historical narrator, in contrast, seem entirely in the past; we are completely outside of them. They do not unfold with any unpredictability, but rather march purposefully toward a goal: the fullest possible presentation of the event in question. Of course, this feeling of closed wholeness is no less an illusion than the seeming open-endedness of the fictional passages, but it is a very different kind of illusion.

Two rhetorical features are characteristic of the historical narrator—the frequent use of first-person plural pronouns, and the equally frequent use of rhetorical questions. These features of Tolstoy's style have been noted by many, but it is worth pointing out that they do not appear at every level of the text. When the historical narrator uses the pronoun "we," he aligns himself with his narrative in a way that neither of the other narrative voices can. On the one hand, the "we" allows for an exclusivity denied the absolute voice (which claims to speak in universals), while on the other, it allows for some escape from the subjectivity of a fictional narrator speaking through the perceptions of individuals. The "we" places Tolstoy's historical narrator firmly in that tradition of national history whose great exponent in Russia had been Karamzin.[7] There can be no doubt that the historical narrator in *War and Peace* roots for the Russians, glories in their triumphs, and disparages the French. This is not to say, of course, that he agrees with the way Russian historians have presented the campaign. Nevertheless, he unquestionably shares with them a spirit of patriotic nationalism, now deflected from individual heroes (except Kutuzov) onto the people (*narod*).

The rhetorical question is used primarily as a tool for destroying the arguments of other historians. The discussion of the Russian army's so-called flanking march is typical:

Historians attribute the glory for this brilliant feat to various people and they dispute over to whom, in fact, the glory belongs. Even foreign, even French historians, admit the genius of the Russian generals when they speak about this flanking march. But it is extremely hard to understand why it is that military writers and, following their lead, all others think that this flanking march was some individual's very sagacious invention, one which saved Russia and destroyed Napoleon. First, it is difficult to understand what constituted the sagacity and genius of this movement, since to guess that the best position for an army (when it is not being attacked) is wherever there is the most provender does not take much mental effort. . . . Even a stupid thirteen-year-old boy could have guessed without any difficulty that the most advantageous position for the army in 1812 after the retreat from Moscow was the Kaluga road. . . . Second, it is even more difficult to understand why the historians credit the deliverance of Russia and the destruction of the French to this maneuver. (12, 67)

If we can permit ourselves a military metaphor in discussing *War and Peace*, such passages can be called frontal assaults. The arguments of a historian or historians are taken (they are usually paraphrased rather than quoted directly, a practice that gives Tolstoy more control over them) and demolished. As a rule, the demolition is accomplished not by introducing new information to invalidate the paraphrased argument, but rather by asking the defenseless paraphrase questions it cannot or did not ever intend to answer.

Tolstoy lays out his objections to preexisting theories in a series of questions. He emphasizes the supposedly dispassionate nature of his "simple" queries by numbering them. His methodology, however, is not quite Socratic; the truth as he sees it is first stated by the historical narrator, and the arguments that follow serve merely to confirm it, while Socrates' no less coercive method lets the facts themselves reveal their implications.

The Metahistorical Voice

The last voice to be considered here is also the last one to appear in *War and Peace*: the philosophical voice, or what I will call the metahistorical voice. This narrative position, corresponding to what Saul Morson has identified as Tolstoy's "absolute voice," takes on an unusual spatio-temporal position vis-à-vis the narrative.[8] It speaks in an eternal, unchanging present tense, not the present tense of a fictional narrator, which implies a future, but what might be called a timeless or unmarked present. Passages in the voice of the metahistorian pronounce "not one man's truth but the Truth."[9] Spatially, the metahistorian claims to have discovered a kind of Archimedean point from which he is able to observe everything that occurs in the world. Rhetorically, the statements of the metahistorian are characterized by metaphor. Historical situations are generalized by being likened to mathematical, physical, or agronomic problems.

The metahistorian expresses what Isaiah Berlin called the "hedgehog" side of Tolstoy's personality, the side that wished to reduce the chaos of experience to simple, coherent laws.[10] This side of Tolstoy's personality became more and more dominant in the course of his life, and by the 1880's and 1890's it had more or less triumphed, allowing him to claim that there are simple answers to questions like *What Is Art?* (*Chto takoe iskusstvo?*). In *War and Peace*, however, this voice is curiously paradoxical. While its tone is omniscient, its statements are curiously empty of content. For all its assertiveness there are many things the metahistorian does not know. In fact, surprising as it may seem, within its purview, the metahistorical voice actually knows less than do the fictional and historical narrators—for although their fields of vision are far narrower, they know everything that falls within them. Indeed, it is almost as if Tolstoy hopes his rhetorical bluster will be so convincing that readers will fail to notice that the metahistorical statements are almost empty of content. And this strategy, if it is a strategy, worked reasonably well. Perhaps because of its peremptory tone and because it gains in strength as the end of the work approaches, the statements of the metahistorical voice have often been equated with Tolstoy's own views of history.

As an example of how the metahistorical voice operates, let us turn to the question of historical laws, one to which this narrator returns frequently. I am convinced that Tolstoy's metahistorian actually believes in the desirability of discovering the laws that govern history, though he suspects that in practice this may be impossible. A typical passage can be found at the beginning of volume 3, part III. Here the absolute voice discusses the insight made possible by the invention of calculus and alludes to the increase in understanding that would come about through the discovery of analogous historical laws. He closes by asserting: "The motion of humanity, arising from an innumerable multitude of individual wills, is continuous. The discovery of the laws of this motion is the goal of history" (11, 267). At the same time, he does not claim to have found such laws, and later in the chapter he questions whether they can be found at all: "No one can say how far it has been given to humankind to achieve an understanding of the laws of history in this way" (11, 269). But the lack of positive laws in the present does not make the desire to discover them any less strong. If anything, the reverse is true.

The same desperate desire for rule-bound explanation is expressed even more vehemently when the metahistorical narrator tries to develop an algebraic formula for determining the relative strength of armies:

Ten men, battalions, or divisions, fighting against fifteen men, battalions, or divisions, overcame the fifteen. That is, they killed them all or took them prisoner, and they lost only four men; therefore, on one side four were lost and on the other fifteen. Consequently, four were equal to fifteen, and consequently, $4x = 15y$. Consequently, $x:y = 15:4$. This equation does not give the value of the variables, but it gives the ratio between the two variables. And by treating various historical units (battles, campaigns, periods of war) in such equations, we get a series of numbers in which laws must exist and can be discovered. (12, 122–23)

Again, the metahistorian does not actually claim to have discovered any laws, but in his use of nineteenth-century scientistic discourse (a type that Tolstoy often reviled when it was used by others) he makes their discovery seem desirable and inevitable. We seem to have reached a frustrating paradox: on the one hand, a call for laws and a tone that implies their existence; on the other, a complete lack of any kind of coherent statement of these laws.

If the metahistorical voice does not, in fact, provide any kind of coherent position, what, we might ask, are its functions in *War and Peace?* Primarily, I believe, these passages are meant to sensitize the reader to problems that receive more subtle and complicated treatment on other narrative levels and in the intergeneric dialogue between levels. Thus, such problems as free will and necessity, the place of the individual in history, and the role of the "great man" are all afforded complex dialogic treatment in the historical and fictional narration. Were they not mentioned so obviously on the metahistorical level, however, the reader might fail to notice this aspect of the text. In their blatancy, the metahistorical tirades ensure that we will not be able to read *War and Peace* simply to discover the fates of Natasha, Pierre, and Andrei, nor even to find out what really happened during the Napoleonic invasion. We are forced to acknowledge that Tolstoy has other fish to fry here. But, it may be objected, this would be obvious in any case. Who needs this commentary, particularly since it provides no solutions to the questions it poses?

To answer this question it is necessary to digress for a moment to the history of the composition, publication, and reception of Tolstoy's work. In *Tolstoy in the Sixties*, Eikhenbaum, working from the observation that the comments of the metahistorian appear only in the third and fourth volumes of *War and*

Peace, concluded that their appearance coincided with a change in Tolstoy's plan. Tolstoy, claimed Eikhenbaum, had initially started to write a "picture of morals" of the Napoleonic age, but by the time he reached volumes three and four he had changed course and was writing an epic.[11] However, since the first parts had already appeared in serial publication, he couldn't very well go back and revise them completely when he published *War and Peace* in book form. The result is a book that changes genre in midstream.

The only problem with this explanation is that it is contradicted by an examination of the drafts, which reveal that passages in the metahistorical voice were actually present in the sketches for volumes one and two.[12] Thus, it is not that the metahistorical voice appeared later; rather, for some reason, Tolstoy stopped suppressing that voice when he wrote final drafts for volumes three and four. Why? The answer, I think, lies in the way Tolstoy responded to the criticism of the early volumes. Although serial composition does have its drawbacks, it has the advantage of allowing the author to get what we now call "feedback" as a work is being produced.

In this case the feedback Tolstoy got was that readers were unable to figure out what his fictional and historical narratives had to do with each other.[13] Originally, I suppose, Tolstoy had used the metahistorical voice to allow himself to understand better the interactions of the fictional and historical narratives. Reviews that indicated readers' puzzlement over these connections convinced him to stop suppressing the mediating metahistorical voice. Evidence for this can be seen in Tolstoy's notes for the epilogue. He divides his readers into three groups. His favorites are the "artistic readers," those who find the metahistorical meditations boring and unnecessary: "Without meditating, they will read between the lines and perceive everything that I wrote in the meditations, and that I would not have written had all readers been like them. In the presence of such readers I blame myself for having disfigured my book by inserting the meditations" (15, 241). Of course, throughout his career Tolstoy feared being misunderstood, so it is not surprising that he ultimately concluded that there were not enough "artistic readers" and jumped at the chance to help all the others understand his book. Still, the fact that the second edition of *War and Peace* was published in 1873 with most of the metahistorical commentary removed to the oblivion of an appendix makes one suspect that Tolstoy was never entirely certain that this voice was necessary. In the end, though, the metahistorical voice could not be excised, because ultimately it is through interaction with it that the dialogue between fictional and historical narrative voices becomes intelligible.

Calls for historical laws that would explain power, free will and determinism, and the role of the individual leave a strong rhetorical residue in the minds of Tolstoy's readers. True, the pronouncements of the metahistorical narrator tend to be extremely frustrating; the most obvious thing that can be said about them is that, taken by themselves, they are incoherent. But this is not surprising, because rather than expounding a finished methodology, the metahistorical comments are meant to encourage readers to seek connections between the historical and the fictional narratives. They focus the dialogue by providing philosophical underpinnings for the two central voices. Indeed, one might say that the fictional and narrative lines of *War and Peace* are attempts to find a workable means to deal with the insoluble philosophical contradictions raised by the metahistorical voice.[14] How precisely they do this we will see when we turn a bit later to questions of the interrelationship of the voices in the text.

Each of the voices described above has its own opinion as to what constitutes the essential material of history, and its own mode of narration. Drawing on our analysis, we can now summarize in tabular form the salient qualities of each of the voices in the text:

	Fictional	Historical	Metahistorical
Time	Now	Then	Eternal
Place	Here, inside	There, outside	Archimedean point, above
Trope	Metonym	Rhetorical question	Metaphor
Person	First person singular	First person plural	Impersonal/ universal

Laying out our observations in this way allows us to appreciate the balance *War and Peace* achieves. Of course, although we have separated the three narrative voices of *War and Peace* for analytic purposes, they do not live in their own narrative worlds in the text. No matter how monologic or monolithic one of them may seem at a given moment, it is always in actual or potential dialogue with the others. Thus, despite the seemingly dominant presence of one or another of the voices at certain points in the narrative, none of them can be seen as primary in *War and Peace* as a whole. The work succeeds because of the lines of tension this interaction engenders. Thus, to anticipate the argument that will be made more explicitly later on: the fact that Tolstoy's philosopher of history believes individuals are unimportant for the historical process, while his fictional narrator is concerned only with individuals, is not an example of muddled thinking, nor does a recognition of this contradiction lead to a "deconstruction" of *War and Peace*. Rather, it points to the fact that fiction and historical narrative are not the same thing, that each must take its own stance. Within the structure of the book their coexistence leads to mutual understanding, not mutual annihilation. Obviously, on this reading it is futile to attempt to derive Tolstoy's "philosophy of history" from any of the separate voices: any voice taken individually leads to a narrative dead end. But taken together they lead to a productive narrative equilibrium. How then does this intratextual dialogue function? What narrative tasks does it accomplish? Does it always work in the same way throughout the book? And what, ultimately, does it tell us about history and narration?

My insistence on a dialogic relationship in Tolstoy's text puts me at odds with most of those who have written on *War and Peace*. First and foremost, it is diametrically opposed to the position of the "father" of the study of dialogue, Mikhail Bakhtin. Bakhtin saw dialogue everywhere in Dostoevsky, but, he claimed, "A second autonomous voice (alongside the author's voice) does not appear in Tolstoy's world. . . . For that reason, there is no problem of linking voices, and no problem of special positioning for the author's point of view. Tolstoy's discourse and his monologically naive point of view permeate everywhere." [15] This is certainly not the place for a lengthy dispute with Bakhtin's approach to Tolstoy. [16] However, I would merely like to question whether the presence of a strong authorial voice must inevitably lead to authorial domination over a text. It has always struck me that despite the lack of an overt authorial voice in Dostoevsky's novels, I can tell what he wants me to believe, while despite the frequent intrusions of the Tolstoyan absolute voice, I am not so sure what to believe when I finish *War and Peace*.

My position is also different from those taken by more recent interpreters of *War and Peace*. If early reviewers were too quick to conclude that Tolstoy had simply written two irreconcilable narratives, a more recent tendency is to minimize narrative contradictions, to monologize the trialogue of Tolstoy's text by various unifying strategies. Edward Wasiolek, for example, tries to harmonize the views of the fictional narrator and the philosopher of history by claiming that "the point of the long theoretical discussion of history that dominates the later portions of *War and Peace* is to prove that necessity and freedom are resolved in the concrete historical act—the same point that Tolstoy had dramatized in the best moments of the domestic portion of the novel." [17] In *Hidden in Plain View*, Saul Morson brilliantly shows how Tolstoy creates extratextual dialogue with the novel genre and with his historical sources. In order to do so, however, Morson feels the need to work from a coherent whole, and so he tends to collapse all the internal lines of argument into what I have called the perspective of the fictional voice, eliding those moments within the text in which that perspective is not dominant.

It seems to me that in his justly celebrated essay, Isaiah Berlin lays the foundation for a dialogic reading of *War and Peace* when he notes aphoristically that Tolstoy was "by nature a fox, but [he] believed in being a hedgehog." [18] That is, in Berlin's view, Tolstoy was capable as no other writer before or since of noticing and capturing the multiplicity that surrounded him, but at the same time he had an irresistible desire to reduce that multiplicity to a single, overarching system. Nevertheless, in his actual reading of *War and Peace* Berlin attempts to derive a Tolstoyan philosophy of history almost exclusively from the comments of the voice of the philosopher of history.

In opposition to all of these readings, I would like to concentrate on those passages of the text in which more than one potential way of viewing historical events or history itself is present. As I pointed out in earlier chapters, the type of intergeneric dialogue that Russian authors favored for the presentation of historical material was precisely one in which separate monologic points of view (usually two of them) do not take each other's positions into account. The result is not a novel whose polyphony is part of the narrative discourse, but rather two or more separate monologic texts which are dialogized in the mind of the reader who knows them both. Ultimately, a reading of *War and Peace* in this context derives its authority from Tolstoy's own idea of his narrative method. In his drafts for the depiction of the battle of Austerlitz, he spoke of his need to portray the battle "from the point of view of military history [the historian's voice], from the point of view of epic poetry [the fictional voice], and from our point of view [the voice of the philosopher of history]." [19]

There are two main types of dialogue present in the final text of *War and Peace*. The first is the kind that Tolstoy mentions above, that is, the presentation of the same scene from the viewpoints of more than one narrative voice. An example that will be analyzed in detail later in this chapter is Tolstoy's descriptions of the Battle of Borodino. This is most like the type of intergeneric dialogue that had existed previously in the Russian tradition—what seem to be mutually incompatible views of the same events are juxtaposed, and the reader must understand why each one is a truthful representation within the limits and interests of its genre. A second type of intergeneric dialogue exploited by Tolstoy, one that had not, in the main, been possible for his predecessors, is generated by the deliberate use of a narrative voice in an "inappropriate" context. Terms appropriated from musical composition can help elucidate this phenomenon.

Let us say that a passage in *War and Peace* exhibits narrative harmony when the narrative voice of the passage is in accord with its normal function (normal here being what the reader has come to expect within the text). That is, when the fictional narrator relates fictional events (or the conversations of fictional characters devoted to historical events) from what seems to be the inside in the historical present, the passage is harmonic. The same is true when the historical narrator presents past-tense nonfictional material from the outside without an admixture of obviously fictional elements. Harmonic passages make up the vast majority of *War and Peace*, and this is necessary, for if the reader did not have a strong sense of the "normal," Tolstoy's various genres would not have been sufficiently differentiated to produce dialogue.[20] We might have had a truly polyphonic text, but intergeneric dialogue would not have been achieved.

Narrative dissonance results from an asymmetry between a textual voice and its expected function. Various types of narrative dissonance appear throughout *War and Peace*. The most obvious, of course, are those scenes that are the stock-in-trade of all historical novelists—scenes involving historical personages or events told through the eyes of a fictional character. As a rule, authors treat such scenes in one of two ways: either they choose moments in history that are well described in a history source and rewrite the source onto the perspective of a fictional character or narrator, or they make up an undocumented and undocumentable "historical" moment and place the characters in it. These textual moments are so common in historical novels and represent such mild forms of narrative dissonance that they are probably not even recognized.

More interesting, perhaps, are the moments of dissonance produced when Tolstoy allows his historical voice to narrate what are very obviously fictional passages.[21] In *Hidden in Plain View*, Morson analyzes carefully the passage in which Niko-lai Rostov's orderly Lavrusha meets Napoleon. Morson con-centrates on elucidating the extratextual dialogue with Louis Thiers's history of the campaign of 1812, which underpins this scene. This concern with extratextual dialogue, however, ob-scures the subtle internal dissonance of *War and Peace*. Tolstoy starts his description of the meeting by quoting Thiers's account of an encounter between Napoleon and a Cossack. He then interjects, "In reality, Lavrushka, after having gotten drunk and left his master without dinner . . . was captured by the French. . . . Finding himself in the company of Napoleon, whose identity he recognized easily and well, Lavrushka was not at all nonplussed, and simply tried with all his heart to serve his new masters" (11, 133). Morson glides over the "in reality" here, claiming that it would be a mistake to "suppose that he gives his version of the story as an attempt to describe what really happened."[22] But I do not think this "in reality," which is clearly a key to the presence of what readers have come to know as the historical voice, can be skipped over so lightly.

The whole passage after the "in reality" is told from the final-ized perspective of the historical voice, which knows exactly what happened and is going to tell the readers about it. The degree of narrative assurance is no different from that present when the historical narrator tells us what "actually happened" at any one of a number of "real" historical events described in the book. At the same time, Morson is surely right in saying that no reader really believes that Tolstoy is presenting histori-cal fact here. We realize quickly that this passage is as fictional as any between Pierre and Andrei. But there is a moment of hesitation, and that hesitation is induced by the narrative dissonance that results from the use of the historical voice to narrate a fictional scene.

The uneasy interaction of the fictional and historical narrators is exploited by Tolstoy even in the very earliest section of *War and Peace*. Indeed, this is what makes the opening of the book so effective.

"Eh bien, mon prince. Gênes et Lucques ne sont plus que des apanages, des private estates de la famille Buonaparte. Non, je vous préviens que si vous vous permettez encore de pallier toutes les infamies, toutes les atrocités de cet Antichrist (ma parole, j'y crois)—je ne vous connais plus, vous n'êtes plus my faithful slave, comme vous dites. Well hello, hello. Je vois que je vous fais peur, sit down and talk to me."

Thus, in July 1805, the well-known Anna Pavlovna Scherer, a maid of honor and confidante of the Empress Mar'ia Fedorovna, greeted Prince Vasily, a man of importance and high rank, who was the first to arrive at her soirée. (9, 3)

As this is the very beginning of the story, we do not yet know what kind of narrator is presenting information here. Eventually, we come to realize that the scene is fictional, although the tone of the first paragraphs is closer to historical than to fictional narration. The specific date attached to the evening, the wealth of potential interaction between the people described and the "real world," the references to specific historical events, even the work's original title (*The Year 1805*) would have all conspired to lead initial readers to suspect that they were reading a history.

It is important to recognize that the difference between fictional and historical narrator is not simply a function of the truth value of their statements. Tolstoy is well beyond the Aristotelian distinction of what happened versus what might have happened. The difference lies more in tone and position. While the fictional narrator is, as it were, within the scene and contemporaneous with it, the historical narrator is outside, a bit above, and narrates post factum. That this usually happens to coincide with a division between what can simplistically be called history and fiction is not entirely an accident. As we have seen, in Tolstoy's view the historian and the writer had entirely different tasks, so a basic difference in narrative approach was probably inevitable.

It is when the tasks of both historian and writer must be accomplished in one work that things get interesting. In this opening passage, for instance, the desire is to hold the reader in suspense for a certain amount of time, to make it difficult to tell what kind of text this is. And indeed, it takes the reader a number of pages to realize that the characters here are fictional, because they are being presented, at least initially, as if they were part of a historical narrative. The result of this blurring of generic lines is a singularly effective intergeneric dialogue, something Tolstoy worked hard to achieve. We can perhaps appreciate the balance between literature and history in *War and Peace* by comparing the ultimate beginning of the book with some of Tolstoy's earlier drafts of it.

As those who have studied *War and Peace* know, the book went through multiple configurations before Tolstoy found the approach and tone that satisfied him. What interests me is how he came to work out the techniques of dialogue between fiction and nonfiction that make this work so unusual. Two discarded openings hint at the opposite poles that Tolstoy eventually managed to reconcile. The first opens with a totally conventionalized narrator who would, presumably, have provided a kind of overview completely separate from the fictional text to follow:

It was between Tilsit and the fire of Moscow, at a time when all of Europe thought, spoke, and felt only Napoleon, when here in Russia families boasted of their French gouverneurs, when Petersburg women chased the functionaries of the French embassy, when everyone spoke French better than the French themselves, when everyone envied, feared, and quarreled about the French and Napoleon. It was at the time when the map of Europe was redrawn bimonthly in various colors. It was at the time that Napoleon had already been convinced that one did not need brains, constancy, or logic to succeed. (13, 58)

While this introduction is presented as if to give the facts, readers would have immediately recognized it as a standard ploy used by historical novelists to set the stage for their costume dramas. In particular, they would have heard the echoes of Dickens's celebrated opening to *A Tale of Two Cities*, which this draft closely resembles in diction and tone.

A different version of the opening attempted to avoid the artificial separation between historical overview and fictional narrative by starting right in with the introduction of a fictional character:

For those who knew Prince Petr Kirilovich B. at the beginning of Alexander II's reign in the 1850's, when Petr Kirilovich had been returned from Siberia an old man, white as a loon, it was difficult to imagine him as the insouciant, unaspiring, wild youth he had been at the start of Alexander I's reign, when he had just returned from abroad after having finished his education there at his father's desire. (13, 184)

From too much concern with the big historical picture we move to too little. The withholding of the hero's last name, the lack of topical detail point immediately to the fictiveness of the narrative. To say that in his final version Tolstoy introduces a tension between the presence of historical and fictional narrative is, of course, not to claim that Tolstoy attempts all the way through *War and Peace* to meld the two. What it does do is set up the possibility for their interaction at those moments when Tolstoy wants or needs to bring them into dialogue.

The Battle of Borodino: Intergeneric Dialogue at Work

By far the most successful and sustained example of the intergeneric dialogue between Tolstoy's historical and fictional narrators appears in the lengthy presentation of the Battle of Borodino. By the 1920's the Formalists, Viktor Shklovsky in particular, had already commented extensively on the device of montage and Tolstoy's masterful use of it in his presentation of battle scenes from multiple perspectives. For Shklovsky, each cut helped build up the perspective of the harmonious whole that Tolstoy was able to achieve. While not exactly disagreeing with Shklovsky, I would like to suggest a different line of approach, emphasizing the incompatibility of the fictional and historical narratives and the clash of their perspectives, rather than their ultimate melding. That is, rather than a whole, I believe that Tolstoy succeeds in creating two equally compelling parts, each with its own truth in creative dialogue.

Tolstoy begins his description of the battle firmly in the voice of his historical narrator. Book 3, part II, chapter 19 opens: "On the 24th was the battle at the Shevardino redoubt; on the 25th not a shot was fired from one side or the other; on the 26th the Battle of Borodino was fought" (11, 184). The rest of the chapter consists of a fairly straightforward presentation of "facts" by the historical narrator and some general commentary on these facts in the absolute voice. The tone is clearly polemical; Tolstoy is strongly disagreeing with the presentation of the historical event as proposed by other historians. He is particularly interested in proving that the Shevardino redoubt was a fortified point on the Russian left flank, rather than an advance post. The assumption here is that on the level of generality that interests the historian, the truth can be discovered. Phrases like "what happened, obviously, was this" (11, 187) make this clear.

The historian's position is outside and a bit above the events he is considering, after them in time. Nowhere is this made more apparent than in the map of the battlefield that the historian includes in chapter 19. The very existence of this map should be enough to convince us that the position of the historical narrator vis-à-vis the fictional is that of dialogic opposition rather than complementarity. For indeed, what the chapters that follow in the fictional voice seem designed to show is precisely the impossibility of a position anything like the one provided in chapter 19. The contrast is starkest when we juxtapose the map with Pierre's observations:

Everything Pierre saw to his right and left was so indefinite that neither the right or left side of the field completely satisfied his preconceptions. Wherever he looked he could see no field of battle as he had expected to see it, but rather fields, dells, troops, woods, smoking camp fires, villages, mounds, and creeks. No matter how hard he tried, Pierre could not make out a military position in the living landscape. He could not even distinguish between our troops and the enemy's. (II, 194)

Thus, the perspectives of chapters 19 and 20 could not be further apart. No mental operation will allow us to combine these pictures into one. We must instead realize that fictional and historical narration present different perspectives and different truths—equal perhaps, but separate, and presented here in dialogical contrast.

Chapters 20–23 give us Pierre's view of the battle as it unfolds, while chapters 24 and 25 show us Andrei's. As opposed to the historical narrator, who looks back on the whole knowing the outcome, the fictional narrator presents characters who know neither how the battle will end nor their own fate. In one sense, of course, Tolstoy cannot re-create the feeling of open-endedness that the participants experienced because he and his readers are constrained by the knowledge of what really happened (in the general way available to a historian, of course). For the actual participants all sorts of outcomes were imaginable, including routs of either the French or the Russians, the capture of Kutuzov or Napoleon, and so forth. Tolstoy cannot recapture this kind of suspense, so in the fictional chapters he concentrates instead on individuals, and it is here that he can take full advantage of the relative freedom of the fictional perspective. As readers (and especially as first-time readers), we stop caring about the outcome of the battle as a whole (which we know anyway), and we are caught up in the local drama of Andrei and Pierre. Thus, while there is certainly a sense in which Andrei represents metonymically the Russian army as a whole, this sense is less important during our reading than is his individuality.

Having moved from historical to fictional narration, Tolstoy now reverses direction. This time, however, he makes the transition gradual, creating in chapter 26 a kind of bridge between the two. This chapter describes Napoleon's preparations on the eve of the Battle of Borodino. The chapter is curious, because although it contains historical figures, it is narrated by the fictional narrator. There are a number of such chapters scattered through the work; they are actually among the few times that Tolstoy makes use of the standard conventions of the historical novel, which consciously tries to level the difference between fictional and historical narration by fictionalizing everything. In scenes like these, so standard in Walter Scott, the historical figure acts unconstrainedly because the situation in which he is placed has no historical significance. The historical personage becomes, momentarily at least, unbound, for his actions fall out of the teleological path that the backward-looking historian sees. Indeed, in most historical novels these are the only kind of passages in which world-historical individuals appear.[23]

The difference between the Napoleon presented by the fictional narrator and the Napoleon of the historical narrator becomes obvious when we compare chapter 26 with chapter 27. Much as Tolstoy might have disliked Napoleon, his fictional narrator nevertheless could and did imagine the French emperor acting more or less spontaneously upon seeing the portrait of his son. In chapter 27, however, when presented by the historical narrator Napoleon is once again a distanced figure on the battlefield, capable of nothing more than giving orders that are destined to be ignored. This is not to say, it should be emphasized, that the fictional narrator is more successful in his presentation: the two narrators simply have different interests, different perspectives, and different purposes.

The rest of the battle is presented in the same kind of dialogue. After chapters 27 and 28, which are narrated by the historian (with some admixture of the absolute voice), we are given another transitional chapter. Chapter 29 signals a move from history to fiction, again organized around the compositional technique of presenting Napoleon through the eyes of the fictional narrator. Chapters 30–32 are in the voice of the fictional narrator, 33 and 34 from the perspective of the historian.

Chapter 35 is transitional, but this time the historical figure of Kutuzov is fictionalized. Chapters 36 and 37 return us to the fictional narrator, and 38 and 39 close out the battle description with a summary from the historian's point of view.

In order to appreciate how unusual the Russian tradition of intergeneric dialogue is, it is instructive to compare Tolstoy's treatment of the Battle of Borodino with two great descriptions of the Battle of Waterloo from the French literary tradition. In *The Charterhouse of Parma* (1839), Stendhal depicts Waterloo from the completely confused perspective of his main character, Fabrice del Dongo. Fabrice's inability to understand what is taking place on the battlefield has frequently been pointed to as a source of influence for Tolstoy's battle descriptions. This may well be true on the level of fictional narration, but what *War and Peace* has and Stendhal's text lacks is dialogue between a single character's perspective and that of some kind of historical narrator.

In Victor Hugo's *Les misérables* (1862), the situation is reversed; in his 60-page digression devoted to the battle, Hugo depicts Waterloo solely from a historian's perspective, specifically denying, in fact, the possibility of capturing a battle in what I have called the fictional voice: "There is always a certain moment when the battle degenerates into a combat, particularises itself, scatters into innumerable details. . . . The historian, in this case, evidently has the right of abridgment. He can only seize upon the principal outlines of the struggle, and it is given to no narrator, however conscientious he may be, to fix absolutely the form of this horrible cloud which is called a battle." [24] And in keeping with this maxim, Hugo avoids placing any of his fictional characters (with their particular perspectives) on the battlefield. True, the historical voice that narrates the Waterloo digression is quite different from the voice that narrates the novel's fictional sections. But, as is also the case with Stendhal, and in opposition to the Russian tradition, there is no interaction here between historical and fictional voices, no intergeneric dialogue on the same historical events.

Intratextual Dialogue

In certain crucial cases, central ideas are illustrated on several levels simultaneously, and it is their combination in the reader's mind that leads to their full explication. Let us take as an example Tolstoy's complicated views on freedom and determinacy in history. The philosopher of history in *War and Peace* is obsessed with the question of how to reconcile human beings' belief that they can make free choices with the seemingly logical impossibility of this belief. "For history the admission that the free wills of men are forces capable of influencing historical events, that is, not subject to laws, is the same as would be to astronomy the admission of free will in the movements of heavenly bodies" (12, 338).

Thus we reach an impasse. The philosopher of history realizes that in theory there must be laws governing history. (Whether they are discoverable or not is a different question.) At the same time, no individual could live thinking that life lacked any degree of free will. This impasse cannot be resolved by Tolstoy on the level of philosophy. It can, however be thematized on the level of narrative through the interaction of the historical and fictional voices in the text. The historian's problem in dealing with past events is that he must always describe things that have already happened. For the historian it is true that "whatever we know we call the laws of necessity; that which is unknown is freedom" (12, 337–38). According to Tolstoy, if the historian were to reach or even approach his goal of knowing everything about a past event, he would reach the limit of total necessity. This is true because the historian is looking at events through time. They appear to have been absolutely necessary because their occurrence has conditioned the configuration of the present-day world. The reader of a history feels this too. Even as he reads about past actions unfolding in the historical narrative, he knows that they have already taken place, and this leads to an impression of their inevitability. This is particularly true of well-known historical events. Beginning a history of the War of 1812, the reader knows that the French will take Moscow and that they will eventually retreat and be destroyed. No matter how exciting a historian makes his narrative, there is nothing that can be done to make the events turn out differently.

In the reading and writing of a novel, however, none of these strictures applies. Readers who reach the scenes in which Natasha falls to Anatole's wiles have the illusion that these events are taking place in the present. We instinctively feel that Natasha has a choice. Perhaps even on the second reading, but certainly on the first, we hope she will not abandon Prince Andrei for the rake. We watch helplessly as she chooses, and while she is choosing, we are convinced she is free in a way that the generals debating strategy before the Battle of Borodino cannot possibly be.

The novelist must sense the same power of the moment. In some of the draft versions of *War and Peace*, Petia Rostov takes part in the attack on the French baggage train but is not killed. Later, for various reasons, Tolstoy decided to kill him off. This possibility—for a created character to get in the way of a stray bullet or not—represents fictionally the moment of freedom, that instant outside of time in which a person (or an author) is free to act as he wishes. Of course, once the choice has been made and is looked at from a distance of time and space, or over a narrative distance, it seems obvious that for the overall structure of the novel Natasha had to fall and Petia had to die.

Perhaps the most convincing evocation of the interplay of free will and determinism in *War and Peace* comes in the first epilogue when Nikolai Rostov, now a poor civil servant, pays a social call on Princess Mar'ia. Throughout the scene, in which both characters are trying to be formal and unconcerned, the reader, who has been set up to believe that there is a secret bond between them, wishes that they would drop their masks and acknowledge their love. Tolstoy draws the scene out, playing with the reader's expectations. The choice, it seems, is free; the decision could go one way or the other. However, once the choice is made, once the instant of narrative free will has passed, we are reminded that things had to happen this way. Tolstoy closes the chapter with the sentence, "For several seconds they stared silently into each other's eyes, and the distant and impossible suddenly became near, possible, and unavoidable" (12, 254). Tolstoy evidently liked to use scenes of this sort to demonstrate the potential of fictional discourse to generate an illusion of freedom. In *Anna Karenina*, for example, the scene in which Sergei Koznyshev fails to propose to Varen'ka is a replay of this one between Nikolai and Mar'ia, but the outcome is the opposite.

It is the interaction between the inevitable forward momentum of the historical portion of Tolstoy's narrative and the open-ended, unfinalizable fictional portion that embodies the tension between free will and determinism that the philosopher of history tries to express. Ultimately, historical truth must encompass both sides of this equation, but neither historical nor fictional narrative alone can capture it. Only intergeneric dialogue, which presents both viewpoints in an entirely convincing way and then juxtaposes them, can allow the reader to see what the philosopher of history can only hint at.

The same kind of dialogue is at work in Tolstoy's attempts to grapple with the problem of the role of the individual in history. Tolstoy's philosopher of history goes on lengthy tirades in an attempt to prove that the very idea of a single great man having the power to make history is ridiculous. On the level of his historical narration, he tries to show that Napoleon did not, in fact, have much to do with the outcome of various battles in the Russian campaign, that the strategic planning of individual generals was unimportant, and so forth. Yet it is obvious to any reader that while Napoleon, famous generals, and other "historical figures" may be unimportant for history, they are crucial for Tolstoy's historical narrative. To prove their unimportance, Tolstoy must focus on them constantly, and this focus undercuts the very point that the historical philosopher is trying to make.

The only truly effective way for Tolstoy's historical narrator to undercut Napoleon is by raising Kutuzov to the level of historical hero. Much has been written about Tolstoy's cavalier treatment of the historical figure of Kutuzov. It has less frequently been asked why this treatment was necessary. In part the answer has to do with the difficulty of producing historical narrative without a hero.[25] For all of the philosopher of history's insistence on integrating the infinite number of differentials that make up history, Tolstoy's historical narrator found it inconceivable to proceed without the presence of a central human figure. True, he attempted to create of Kutuzov a passive agent, one whose main quality was the experience and patience to do nothing. Nevertheless, Kutuzov's presence dominates the landscape of the historical narrative in Tolstoy's history, just as Napoleon had dominated the works of his predecessors.

The only level on which world-historical individuals can be safely ignored, or at least seen in a different perspective, is the fictional. It is only here that we as readers begin to understand that for Tolstoy's characters in the here and now of fiction (and presumably they are metonymically connected to other human actors), there are thousands of things that are more important than the historical events going on around them.

Those scenes in which Prince Andrei observes Napoleon exemplify how, from a perspective inside of and during events, the personal overrides what is generally seen as the historical. Having been wounded at Austerlitz, Prince Andrei looks up and sees, as if for the first time, the sky arching above him. At this moment he thinks, "How could it be that I never saw this high sky before? And how happy I am that I have finally discovered it. Yes! everything is empty, everything is deception, except that infinite sky. There is nothing, nothing aside from it" (9, 344). Against the background of this epiphany Andrei sees Napoleon, once when the latter is examining the field of victory, and a second time in the hospital. Both times Andrei is struck by the insignificance of his former hero in comparison with the immeasurability of the eternal as he has just experienced it.

Everything seemed so useless and insignificant in comparison with that stern and majestic flow of thought that had been called up within him by his weakness due to loss of blood, suffering, and the nearness of death. Looking into Napoleon's eyes Prince Andrei thought of the insignificance of greatness, about the insignificance of life whose meaning no one could understand, and of the even greater insignificance of death, whose sense no living being could understand or explain. (9, 359)

But this revelation is true only for Andrei, not for *War and Peace*, for Napoleon continues to play a central role in the book's historical narrative, even after Andrei's epiphany. And this is only natural, because the fictional and historical narrators have rather different narrative objectives. Andrei must experience life in all its vicissitudes and in all its unpredictable turnings until death. For him Napoleon is of only marginal importance. But the historical narrator has a different story to tell, one in which, despite all narrative protestations, Napoleon has a central role to play.

In the end, the kinds of questions that Pierre Bezukhov asks himself after his first separation from Helene are the only truly important ones for Tolstoy's fictional narrator: "What is the good? what should I love, what should I hate? what should I live for and who am I? what is life, what is death? what force governs all?" (10, 65). Clearly, history cannot reply to these questions, although it is only through his contact with the people and events of the French invasion that Pierre discovers answers. He is led to the solution by Platon Karataev, the Russian peasant whose very name is connected to the search for ultimate metaphysical truth. Karataev is also linked to "Russianness," which symbolizes the good on both the fictional and historical levels of the book. But while Karataev leads Pierre to an understanding of the eternal, the actual moment of revelation is, as it always must be, a purely personal one. It comes when Pierre is resting overnight with the other prisoners at the beginning of the retreat from Moscow. Trying to visit Karataev, he is turned back by a French guard. He sits down by himself and suddenly begins to roar with laughter. "The soldier did not let me pass. They've caught me, locked me up. They're holding me prisoner. Who, me? Me?—Me! My immortal soul! Ha, ha, ha!" (12, 105–6). As was the case with Andrei, Pierre comes to the revelation that the eternal exists apart from the historical process. It is precisely the importance of this eternal core, as opposed to the historical exterior, that Tolstoy's fictional narrator tries to express throughout *War and Peace*. What Napoleon and others like him (including historians and Tolstoy's historical narrator) consider important has nothing to do with questions of individual life, death, birth, and happiness. In the face of these questions the discussions of history are subsumed into the novel's narrative framework. In the final analysis, all the differentials of history that Tolstoy's philosopher of history discusses and that his historical narrator mostly ignores find full expression in the voice of the fictional narrator.

War and Peace is a culminating moment in the Russian literary tradition. Tolstoy brought the principles of intergeneric dialogue, developed by Russian writers in the first half of the nineteenth century in their quest to show how the past of the nation should be narrated, to an unprecedented level of complexity. In this respect *War and Peace* is, to borrow a phrase from Viktor Shklovsky, "the most typical" work on history by a Russian author. Tolstoy succeeded as none of his predecessors had in forcing readers to confront the implications of sustained intergeneric dialogue. Readers of Karamzin could (and usually did) ignore the footnotes in the *History of the Russian State*. Most editions of Pushkin do not include *The History of Pugachev*. But Tolstoy's version of dialogue was impossible to ignore. Each of Tolstoy's three narrative voices has its own historical interests and point of view, and each is allowed to present itself in its characteristic style. The enormous richness of *War and Peace* arises not so much from any one of its parts, brilliant as they may sometimes be, but from the narrative tension generated by their clashing viewpoints. *War and Peace* thus read is not primarily about the lives of Pierre, Natasha, Andrei, and the others, nor is it primarily about the Napoleonic invasion of Russia. Instead, it is about how histories can be narrated, and the answers it provides issue directly from the interaction of the three narrative voices.

Chapter Six

Utopian Historiography: *The Brothers Karamazov* as Historical Allegory

One can express incomparably more about our history through fidelity to poetic truth than through fidelity merely to history.

Feodor Dostoevsky [1]

While the assertion that *War and Peace* is about history is unlikely to surprise scholars or general readers, the same assertion made about *The Brothers Karamazov* is sure to raise eyebrows. After all, what does history have to do with a novel that is set in Dostoevsky's own time and deals with what seem to be universal questions of faith, good and evil, family relations, and so forth? Nevertheless, in this chapter I will argue that if *The Brothers Karamazov* is read together with Dostoevsky's heterogeneous *Diary of a Writer*, the novel can be understood as an allegorical expression of Dostoevsky's utopian philosophy of history. That is, I will claim that in his final two works Dostoevsky modified but continued the tradition of intergeneric dialogue on historical themes that had been used by some of his most illustrious predecessors. What is more, the dialogic relationship between the prophetic narrative voice that appears frequently in the *Diary* when historical questions are broached and the fictional narrative of *The Brothers Karamazov* is remarkably similar to the relationship between absolute and fictional voices in *War and Peace.*

That the *Diary of a Writer* and *The Brothers Karamazov* are related to each other is hardly a secret. Elucidations of these relationships are fairly common in the critical literature.[2] In his biography of Dostoevsky, Konstantin Mochulsky provides a typical assessment: "Dostoevsky too was an artist who, in the pages of *The Diary* was preparing his last, greatest work. *The Diary* is the laboratory of *The Brothers Karamazov*."[3] Mochulsky then goes on to list a number of themes shared by the *Diary* and *The Brothers Karamazov*, including observations on children, the relationship of fathers to sons, the collapse of the family, and so on.[4] Following Mochulsky's lead, most critics tend to use the laboratory model to interpret the relationship between these works. In this view the *Diary* was at best a preparatory step in the writing of the novel, a locus for trying out themes and ideas that receive powerful artistic treatment in the fictional work. Such an approach rules out a priori the possibility of dialogue, since it assumes a hierarchical relationship between the two texts with interpretive priority given to the ultimate expression of an idea in the fiction.

This view is particularly appealing because many critics, understandably enough, find the anti-Semitic and jingoistic ardor of the *Diary* distasteful, and it allows them to claim implicitly that Dostoevsky outgrew these unpalatable ideas by the time he wrote his novel. Embarrassed by the Dostoevsky who appears in the *Diary*, many critics probably see the work simply as one more example of a phenomenon of Russian cultural life that Dostoevsky himself had noted in a *Diary* entry: "It got to the point that people who seemed to have an occupation (some professor, for example, or a litterateur, a poet, even a great poet) did not value their professions . . . and almost all of them had a tendency to see in themselves the buds of another task, in their view a higher, more important, more civically useful one."[5] But there are a number of problems with this interpretive model.

First, there is a serious flaw in the assumption that fiction writing was automatically more important than journalism for Dostoevsky and that, therefore, the latter leads to the former but not vice versa. This notion is understandable, given the fact that for critics and readers of the twentieth century Dostoevsky the novelist has completely eclipsed all other aspects of his creative personality. But in Dostoevsky's own day, and perhaps in his own mind, his journalism was at least as important as his fiction. It should be recalled that the *Diary* was hardly Dostoevsky's first foray into journalism. He started his career writing feuilletons and continued to produce journalistic pieces throughout his creative life. He was editor and publisher of the journals *Time* (*Vremia*, 1861–63) and *Epoch* (*Epokha*, 1864–65), and editor in chief of *Citizen* (*Grazhdanin*, 1873–74). In addition, the *Diary of a Writer* was a huge success, both critically and financially, and Dostoevsky, as his letters show, was at least as proud of it as he was of anything else that he wrote.[6] This alone should give us pause before assuming a hierarchical or straightforward relationship between the *Diary* and *The Brothers Karamazov*.

The second problem with the hierarchical approach is that it leads to a major underestimation of the *Diary* itself. The foundations for a wholly different approach to the *Diary* were laid, quite ingeniously, by Saul Morson, who chose to treat it as an unusual but nevertheless coherent artistic work in its own right, one that combines heterogeneous genres and fuses them into a work of "threshold art."[7] Most important, Morson provides a Bakhtinian framework that allows for an appreciation of the complicated dialogue between the fictional works that appear from time to time in the *Diary* and the more straightforward journalism there. I am quite sympathetic to this method, and I think that it has produced great insight into reading a work that was habitually relegated to secondary status in Dostoevsky criticism. Indeed, this chapter is, in some respects, an extension of Morson's approach. I will read *The Brothers Karamazov* as if it were one more fiction within the *Diary*, and I will interpret the whole as an ambitious intergeneric dialogue on the topic of utopian historiography.

Perhaps the most important clue that *The Diary of a Writer* and *The Brothers Karamazov* should be read as engaged in active dialogue can be found in their compositional history. When this history is examined closely, it turns out that *The Brothers Karamazov* may be an integral part of the *Diary*. The *Diary* was published more or less monthly throughout 1876 and 1877. It was then broken off and not resumed until a single volume appeared in August 1880. Dostoevsky planned to continue it as a monthly in 1881, but had time to bring out only the January edition before illness and death intervened.[8] It was precisely during the hiatus in the appearance of the *Diary* that Dostoevsky wrote and published his final novel, which appeared serially from January 1879 until October 1880 (although the basic outline of the final chapter was already clear by the beginning of August 1880).[9] Thus, the question arises, if the *Diary* was merely the laboratory for the novel, why should Dostoevsky have returned to it when the novel was finished? If we see the two as being in dialogue, however, the return makes much more sense.

It is important in this regard to note that the tone of the *Diary* does not change substantially when it is resumed, leading one to suspect that Dostoevsky did not break off the *Diary* because he had said everything that he wanted to say in that medium, but rather because he needed to recast his thoughts and ideas in large-scale fictional form, as a supplement to the primarily nonfictional form of the *Diary*, before continuing.[10] This suspicion is borne out in a curious letter that Dostoevsky wrote to S. D. Ianovsky in December 1877. The letter provides perhaps the most convincing evidence for considering *The Brothers Karamazov* as a part of the *Diary*:

I will not be sending you my *Diary* for next year because I have decided to stop it for a while (one year). There are a number of reasons: I'm tired, my epilepsy has worsened (due to the *Diary*), and finally, I want to be freer next year, although I won't go more than a month or two without working. There is a novel in my brain and my heart demanding expression. And there are other reasons, and I expect that in a year it will be just the right time: I want to try a new publication in which the *Diary* would be just a part of the publication. In this way I would broaden my form of activity. The *Diary* has worked out in such a way that it is impossible to change its form even slightly.[11]

The novel that Dostoevsky refers to in this letter is obviously *The Brothers Karamazov*, for which he had already started preliminary sketches. The bigger project, of which the *Diary* was to be only one part, has remained mysterious. But whatever Dostoevsky had in mind in 1877, the need for this broader work was evidently satisfied by the finished novel together with the continuation of the *Diary*, since no other synthetic work was ever begun or even sketched out. Of course, Dostoevsky could not have known this in 1877 because he did not yet know what form the novel would take. Ultimately though, the novel clearly did allow Dostoevsky temporary freedom from the constraint of the diary form, and when he had finished it he was able to return to that form, thus completing the literary sandwich hinted at in the letter.

Another key piece of evidence for considering *The Brothers Karamazov* and the *Diary of a Writer* as a dialogic unit is formal. The monthly *Diary* is characterized by short chapters of heterogeneous nature, each bearing a pithy title. The structure of *The Brothers Karamazov*, with its interpolated portions, including the hagiographical vita of Father Zosima and the "Legend of the Grand Inquisitor," echoes that of the *Diary*, as do the frequently opaque designations of the novel's brief chapters. Thus, I would suggest that *The Brothers Karamazov* may be regarded as the *Diary*'s most extensive embedded piece of fiction, far longer but not qualitatively different from fictional works like "A Boy at Christ's Christmas Tree Party" ("Mal'chik u Khrista na elke"), "The Meek One" ("Krotkaia"), or "Dream of a Ridiculous Man" ("Son smeshnogo cheloveka").

A central objection to reading these two works dialogically is that there is no overt evidence that Dostoevsky, as opposed to Pushkin, for example, envisioned such an approach. To this, I would answer with an appeal to the Russian tradition that has been sketched thus far in this book, a tradition of which Dostoevsky was certainly well aware. When major Russian writers turned to producing history, they always envisioned this nonfictional work in dialogue with their own fiction on the same topic. By the time Dostoevsky was writing, I would argue, this method was so well ingrained in the tradition that there was no need to point it out overtly. In the final analysis, however, the proof will be in the pudding. To justify a dialogic treatment of *The Diary of a Writer* and *The Brothers Karamazov*, I will have to produce a convincing reading of the texts.

Of course, since my concern throughout this book has been with Russian writers' obsession with history, I will focus primarily on nonfictional/fictional dialogue on that topic. And immediately, such a focus leads to a paradox. While there can be no question that Russia's historical destiny is one of the central philosophical questions of the *Diary*, none of the critics who have studied the relationships between the *Diary* and *The Brothers Karamazov* discuss the possibility that Dostoevsky's historical philosophy plays a role in the novel. The reason, I suspect, is because of their discomfort with Dostoevsky's obsessively violent and jingoistic historical worldview (which will be discussed in more detail later in this chapter). While his views on the family, society, and the law are reconcilable with the image of Dostoevsky the great writer and thinker, his strange and abhorrent historical views may not be. This reading, however, will attempt to show just how central Dostoevsky's historical philosophy is to *The Brothers Karamazov* and to indicate how, on this level, the dialogue between the *Diary* and *The Brothers Karamazov* operates.

I believe that the overt historiographical philosophy expressed in the *Diary* stands in the same relationship to *The Brothers Karamazov* as the voice of the historical philosopher stands to the fictional and historical voices in *War and Peace*. The main formal difference is that Tolstoy followed the Karamzinian model of including both kinds of texts in a single book, whereas Dostoevsky used the Pushkinian method of splitting them. In the previous chapter I asserted that the role of the Tolstoyan philosopher of history is primarily to bring to the reader's consciousness problems that receive subtler and more complex treatment on other levels of discourse in the work. As a result, it is useless to search for Tolstoy's solutions to crucial problems like free will versus determinism, the great man in history, and so on in the pronouncements of the philosopher of history. Rather, one should realize that the role of this voice is to constitute and mediate the dialogue between the fictional and historical narratives that make up *War and Peace*.

It is a critical commonplace to note that one of Dostoevsky's chief concerns, at least from the end of the 1860's, was the creation of a fictional version of the "wholly beautiful individual," the fictional equivalent of Christ, or at least the novelistic proof of his existence. Dostoevsky evidently used the phrase for the first time as he was preparing to write the novel that was to become *The Idiot*.[12] It is also a commonplace, even for critics who find *The Idiot* to be on balance a successful novel, to note that in the character of Myshkin Dostoevsky fails to create such an individual. Few readers would, I believe, argue with Mochulsky's statement: "The image of 'the positively beautiful individual' did not attain its complete embodiment in the novel *The Idiot*. But Dostoevsky did not renounce the 'immeasurable' task. The pilgrim Makar Dolgoruky in *A Raw Youth*, Bishop Tikhon in *The Devils*, the Elder Zosima and Alyosha in *Brothers Karamazov*—all bear witness to the author's incessant efforts to achieve 'the miracle of embodying beauty.'"[13]

The question remains, however: why was Dostoevsky unable to fulfill his program for Myshkin, and how might *The Diary of a Writer* have helped him realize this ideal more completely? It seems to me that the answer, at least in part, lies in Myshkin's ahistoricism and in Dostoevsky's recognition that it would have to be overcome if he were to complete his project successfully. In *The Idiot*, Myshkin simply appears in the world, without any warning or preparation. He has no relevant history—his past is the blank from which he awoke in Switzerland. What is more, there is no clear reason why a Christ figure should appear in Russia at just this place and time, nothing that would make such an appearance seem inevitable or even plausible. These problems arise, I would argue, because Dostoevsky had not yet thought the question through completely. That is, he had the desire to create his modern Christ, he already had the millenarian vision, but he had not yet worked out a conceptual historical framework in which this idea could be realized.

Ultimately, as we will see, the historiography of *The Diary of a Writer* provided this conceptual framework, and *The Brothers Karamazov*, if read in dialogue with the *Diary*, can be seen as Dostoevsky's most complete instantiation of the task he had set for himself as early as the 1860's. But to see how this process came to be, and to appreciate the dialogue, I must define Dostoevsky's historiography and show how it differs from what had preceded it.

The first four chapters of this book have surveyed the development of the Russian tradition of intergeneric dialogue for the presentation of historical material and have analyzed the complexities of this dialogue as manifested in a few key works by major writers. To this point, questions of motivation have not been of central concern. This is by no means to say that writers' stated reasons for using history are or should necessarily be privileged for the purposes of analysis. Still, by examining these overt motivations I think we will be able to appreciate the ways in which Dostoevsky's brand of historiography differs from those of his predecessors even as it operates within the same basic intergeneric paradigm.

For the initiators of the Russian tradition of intergeneric historiography, the reasons for studying history can be summarized with three *p*'s: pedagogy, patriotism, and pleasure. It was assumed that a knowledge of history would, by making Russians aware of the nation's glorious past, instill in them patriotic pride and thereby counter certain negative impressions that were circulating in Europe. As I noted earlier, Catherine the Great claimed to have written her *Notes Concerning Russian History* specifically for patriotic purposes: "These notes concerning Russian history are composed for our youth at a time when books calling themselves histories of Russia have been appearing in foreign languages. But these books should really be called biased creations, since every page bears witness to the hatred with which they were written."[14] The "unbiased" account written by a German woman occupying the Russian throne was presumably meant to be an antidote to negative publicity in Europe.

Karamzin's understanding of the nature and value of historical knowledge is, in most crucial respects, not that different from Catherine's. But by emphasizing analogies between the past and the present, he places greater stock in the overtly pedagogic nature of the project: "History is, in a sense, the holy book of peoples: a central and necessary one; it is a reflection of their essence and activity; the tablet of their discoveries and riches; the legacy of ancestors to future generations; a supplement to or an explanation of the present and an example for the future. Leaders and legislators act according to the suggestions of history and look on her pages as navigators study charts of the sea." [15] The focus, clearly, is on what we can learn from the past, on its pedagogic value for the here and now.

Karamzin strengthened this claim for the value of history further, by asserting in the dedication to the *History* that the credit for Russia's recent triumph over Napoleon could have been due, in part at least, to Alexander's recognition of certain historical parallels, parallels that had been pointed out by the historian himself: "In 1811, at one of the happiest and most unforgettable moments of my life, I read several chapters of this History to YOU, O Sovereign, about the horrors of Batu's invasion; about the feats of the hero Dmitry Donskoi. At that moment, when a thick cloud of trouble hung over Europe threatening our dear fatherland as well, YOU listened with an attention that thrilled me; you compared the distant past with the present and did not envy the glorious dangers of Dmitry because you foresaw even more glory for yourself." [16]

Simultaneously, Karamzin emphasizes the sheer aesthetic pleasure to be derived from a contemplation of history, an emphasis one does not find in Catherine's work, but one that is not surprising in a writer of Karamzin's stature. History "raises the dead, putting life in their hearts and words on their lips . . . and in presenting a series of ages with their various passions, mores, and actions to the mind, it broadens the borders of our own existence." [17] Such a dramatic resurrection of the past obviously stimulates our imagination and adds pleasure to pedagogy and patriotism.

This triad remains the dominant motivating force for most of the historical and literary researches that followed in the first half of the nineteenth century. One could adduce numerous quotes to show the centrality of these attitudes across a broad spectrum of Russian writers, but I will limit myself to a few. Ryleev, for example, is clearly interested primarily in patriotism, with a secondary focus on pedagogy. He introduces his *Dumy* as follows:

To remind our youth of the feats of their ancestors, to acquaint them with the brightest epochs in the people's history, and to link love for the fatherland with the earliest recollections of memory—that is the surest way to inculcate a love for the homeland in a people. Later on, nothing can efface these first recollections, these earliest ideas. They strengthen with time and create brave warriors and brilliant statesmen. That is what Niemcewicz says about the sacred goal of his historical songs (*Spiewy Historiczne*); I had the same goal in writing my dumy. [18]

Khomiakov, however, as befitted an ardent Slavophile who wanted Russia to recall her pre-Petrine past and to draw up plans for present action based on it, is far more concerned with the pedagogic potential of historiography: "The science of the past equals knowledge of the present, and in submerging ourselves in the past and getting to know it we come to understand the present and come to coexist with it body and soul." [19]

In the cases of Pushkin and Tolstoy, of course, the reasons for their turn to history are complex. As I tried to show earlier, Pushkin had a general tendency to produce works in more than one genre on the same theme, and his appreciation of the possibilities inherent in intergeneric dialogue was primarily aesthetic. Pushkin also adds another p to our equation—parody—both in *The Captain's Daughter* and even more overtly in *The History of the Village of Goriukhino* (*Istoriia sela Goriukhina*). [20]

At the same time, Pushkin's desire to treat the events of the Pugachev uprising was also related to his attempt to explore history as a means for understanding contemporary Russia. One sees this goal not only in the pair of texts discussed here, but also in *The Bronze Horseman* (*Mednyi vsadnik*), where Eugene's plight is linked directly to the history of St. Petersburg. The same theme is apparent on the personal level in the unfinished story *The Moor of Peter the Great* (*Arap Petra Velikogo*) and in some references in the unfinished long poem "Ezhersky." Moreover, at least in relation to *The History of Pugachev*, pedagogy is also present. Pushkin's "Notes on the Rebellion" ("Zamechaniia o bunte"), which were given to the tsar separately, were meant to acquaint him with material that for various reasons could not be published, but they also contain hints that could be construed as pedagogical.[21]

Finally, in the case of Tolstoy, the turn to history was, at least initially, motivated by a felt need for historical grounding in order to understand the present. Tolstoy claimed that the work that was eventually to become *War and Peace* grew out of a plan to write a story about a Decembrist who returns to Russia in Tolstoy's own day.[22] But Tolstoy found himself unable to present the life of his character without showing how the present grew out of the past, and so he hit upon a new, historicized plan, manifested in a draft version dating from 1863, entitled *Three Epochs*: "And so, having gone back from 1856 to 1805, I now intend to guide not one but many of my heroes and heroines through the historical events of 1805, 1807, 1812, 1825, and 1856."[23]

But in the final version of *War and Peace*, we might say that all three *p*'s are present, each one primarily the property of one voice. Patriotism is clearly central to the historical narrator—the frequent use of the first-person plural pronoun, the obvious attempts to glorify the feats of the Russian people, and so on, attest to this. The philosopher of history is more concerned with pedagogy: what lessons (laws) might we learn from history that could be useful to us in the present as we plan for the future? Finally, the fictional voice allows for and encourages straightforward sybaritic pleasure in the text, an invitation that most Tolstoyan readers have experienced and continue to experience.

When we turn to Dostoevsky, however, the motive for a concern with history seems different. As opposed to his literary/ historical predecessors, for whom history was primarily a problem of the interaction of the past with the present, Dostoevsky stressed the relationship between the past and the *future*. As he asserts in a typical passage of *Diary of a Writer*: "I dare to state that the fact that Russia will be able to say the word of living life to humankind in the future lies in the foundations of the Russian nation and in her Orthodoxy."[24] It is not simply that knowledge of the past will help Russians make decisions in the present (although Dostoevsky thinks it might do this too); Russian history, properly understood, contains the guarantee of Russia's future preeminence, even if mistakes are made in the present. An understanding of the past is important because history has become a means for prophecy.

Prophecy, particularly near-term prophecy, is omnipresent in the *Diary*. In this respect, the monthly format of the work proved advantageous. Dostoevsky was able to remind his readers that predictions he had made just months earlier had now come true. Successful short-term predictions were, of course, significant in and of themselves, but they were even more important as a means for lending credibility to Dostoevsky's long-term, messianic prophecies. "Yes, gigantic transformations await Europe, of a kind that the human mind refuses to believe. It considers their fulfillment somehow fantastic. Nevertheless, much that seemed fantastic, impossible, and exaggerated only this summer has literally come to pass in Europe toward the end of the year. . . . We note this merely in order that our readers believe our present 'predictions.'"[25] Naturally, like most journalistic prophets, Dostoevsky simply ignored those predictions that failed to become reality.

Thus far in this chapter I seem to be claiming that Dostoevsky's vision of history as prophecy marks a new departure for Russian historiography. But this is true only if we are speaking of those writers who were working in the intergeneric tradition. If we cast our net a bit wider, we can find many precursors, although it will be seen that Dostoevsky's historiography is not merely epigonic. As I noted in the introduction, the notion that the glorious millenial future will eventually issue forth from Russia goes back at least to early sixteenth-century ideas of Russia as the third Rome. According to a certain strand of Orthodox doctrine, after the fall of Constantinople (the second Rome) in 1453, Russia became the last truly Christian kingdom on earth. Its church, "like the sun, was to illumine the entire world—furthermore, after two Romes had fallen, Moscow the third Rome would stand permanently, for there was to be no fourth." [26] As historians have pointed out, however, this doctrine was entirely religious and had no direct political implications, nor was it ever explicitly endorsed by the Russian state. Nevertheless, the idea that Russia had a messianic role to play in the world was evidently lodged quite deeply in the Russian cultural mind, and it was to be resurrected by a number of thinkers in the first half of the nineteenth century, albeit in rather different form.

In his "First Philosophical Letter," Petr Chaadaev announced that Russia "had no history." This was seen as the great stumbling block to her further development. But in his "Apology of a Madman," Chaadaev reinterpreted the implications of his conclusion from negative to positive. Russia's lack of history, Chaadaev concluded in his recantation, was the guarantee of unique future possibilities: "He [Peter the Great] saw that a historical foundation was wholly lacking to us, that consequently we could not rest our future on such an empty ground; he understood that, confronted by the ancient civilization of Europe, . . . we could not afford to drown ourselves in our own history . . . we had to seize our promised destiny by a spontaneous leap. . . . And so he freed us from all those precedents that clutter historical societies." [27] Under the influence of

German thought, this kind of thinking, what Morson has described as "interpreting every void as a potentiality," became quite widespread.[28]

Isaiah Berlin sums up the reasoning underlying this approach with the wit that is his trademark:

The German romantic historians were particularly zealous in preaching the view that, if the west was declining because of its scepticism, its rationalism, its materialism, and its abandonment of its own spiritual tradition, then the Germans, who had not suffered this melancholy fate, should be viewed as a fresh and youthful nation, with habits uncontaminated by the corruption of Rome in decay, barbarous indeed, but full of violent energy, about to come into the inheritance falling from the feeble hands of the French. The Russians merely took this process of reasoning one step further. They rightly judged that if youth, barbarism, and lack of education were criteria of a glorious future, they had an even more powerful hope of it than the Germans.[29]

It will be noticed, however, that this kind of thinking is historical only in a very curious way, for it takes no real interest in the past. Russia is a void, a tabula rasa, and so her own history cannot be important. All that matters is the future, which does not so much grow out of the past as spring fully formed from the head of the utopian thinker. Thus, while thinkers of this ilk were much interested in Russia's future, they had little interest in exploring the history of a blank spot, and this may explain why they did not become involved in the tradition formed by Catherine, Karamzin, Pushkin, Tolstoy, and others. They did not write historical works; for the most part, they spun myths. Nonetheless, Dostoevsky's prophetic inclination clearly issues from this utopian strain of Russian thinking, even as his historical interests transcend it.

At the same time, there was at least one significant group of thinkers in the first half of the nineteenth century who were fascinated with Russia's past, and Dostoevsky's understanding of Russia's history owes a great deal to them. I have in mind, of course, the Slavophiles. This group was heterogeneous and their views evolved over the course of a couple of decades, so it would be foolhardy to pretend that they possessed a monolithic doctrine. Nevertheless, they had in common the conviction that there was something valuable in Russia's past, and therefore that the nation's history was worthy of careful consideration.

What most of them lacked, however, was a developed mechanism for connecting the past to the future. This is perhaps not surprising, for the Slavophile position developed, in the words of Abbott Gleason, "in argument and talk, in relatively restricted groups of beleaguered intellectuals, whose feelings about their present position underlay a great deal of what was being said."[30] The Slavophiles were primarily interested in history as patriotism and pedagogy; they wanted Russians to take pride in their past, to appreciate its uniqueness, and to use principles exhumed from the past for the reconstruction of contemporary society. Unquestionably, many Slavophiles believed that Russian civilization was superior to that of the West, but their thought was generally free of the messianic element so strongly felt in Dostoevsky's historiography. As Andrzej Walicki puts it, "It is possible to call Slavophile philosophy conservative utopianism: *utopianism* because it was a comprehensive and detailed vision of a social ideal, sharply contrasted to existing realities; and *conservative* or even reactionary because it was an ideal located in the past."[31]

It was left to the so-called Pan-Slavists, Nikolai Danilevsky and Dostoevsky in particular, to synthesize explicitly the historiography of the Slavophiles with millenarian and messianic views of Russia's destiny.[32] In certain respects, Danilevsky and Dostoevsky had a great deal in common. Both were members of the ill-fated Petrashevsky circle in the late 1840's, and both were found guilty and punished (Dostoevsky more seriously) for their part in the "conspiracy." In the 1850's and 1860's both seemed to turn away from their youthful follies, Danilevsky by becoming a respected scientist and Dostoevsky a writer and journalist. At the same time, although by separate routes, they transformed their youthful fascination with Fourier into a Pan-

Slavic messianism. This is not the place for a full-scale comparison of the two, because our concern is with the interrelationship of history and literature (for which topic Dostoevsky is crucial), rather than with the intricacies of Pan-Slavic historiography per se. Suffice it to say, however, that many of Dostoevsky's historiographical concerns and interests were doubled by Danilevsky, although the two men also differed in many ways.[33]

In *Diary of a Writer*, Dostoevsky is concerned with two central and related historical questions: the development of European civilization, and Slavdom's (read Russia's) relation to that development in the past, the present, and (most importantly) the future. Both of these problems are discussed within a millenarian framework. As Morson puts it:

The central—and certainly the most frequently repeated—theme of the monthly *Diary* [is], namely, that the apocalypse is literally imminent. In countless articles, the author argues that social "fragmentation," "dissociation," and "isolation" have reached such an extreme that the "final battle" is almost certainly near. And as promised in the Revelation to St. John, he contends, that battle will be followed by the millennium—which, for him, means a worldwide utopia headed by Russia and based on the Russian Orthodox faith.[34]

The millennium is not merely a miraculous promise to be accepted on faith, however; it is fully historicized and will issue forth directly and logically from the nation's past.

According to Dostoevsky (and here he draws primarily on German idealist notions while giving them a Russian spin), various nations or groups of nations take their turn as leading actors on the world-historical stage.

If it wants to live for a long time, every great nation believes and must believe that the salvation of the world lies in it and only in it, that it exists solely in order to stand at the head of the peoples in order to join them all to itself and lead them in harmonious accord to the final goal for which they have all been created. I assert that this has been so for all great nations of the world, from ancient times to the most recent, and that only this belief elevated each of them in its proper time to the possibility of having its gigantic world-historical influence over the fate of humankind.[35]

Contemporary Europe, in Dostoevsky's view, was on the verge of collapse. Of course, this had been the contention of the Slavophiles as early as the 1830's. But Ivan Kireevsky, Khomiakov, and the Aksakov brothers, for all their idealization of the Russian past and Russia's potential, realized that Russia had a great deal of internal work to do before it could even think about a place on the world-historical stage. As a result, their discussions of Europe's senescence were meant primarily as warnings to Russians against following a bankrupt European-style path of development, rather than as clarion calls for national glory in the here and now. As far as Dostoevsky was concerned, however, the Russians were ready to take the leading world-historical role from a faltering Europe in his own day.

And what is this "word" that the Russians are preparing to say to Europe and the rest of the world? "Our mission and our role are not at all like those of other nations, for there each separate people lives exclusively for itself and in itself, while we will begin, now that the time has come, precisely by becoming the servants of all for universal peacemaking. And this is in no way something to be ashamed of; on the contrary, this constitutes our greatness because it all leads to the ultimate unity of humankind."[36] Here Dostoevsky's historical system takes a definite turn toward millenarianism; for if the meaning of history is the harmonious union of all humankind, and if the Russian Orthodox ideal (which is about to be realized) is identical to it, then it follows that history is about to come to an end.

Necessarily, Dostoevsky follows two strategies to convince himself and his readers of the soundness of his views. On the one hand, he eagerly scans the periodical press for signs of Europe's imminent demise. On the other, he looks for evidence in Russia of the ripening of the Russian ideal. Evidence for the demise of Europe seemed abundant:

The fourth estate is coming, it is knocking and banging on the door, and if the door is not opened, it will break it down. It does not want the former ideals and rejects all previously existing law. It will not make compromises or concessions, and buttresses will not save the building. Concessions only make them more fired up and they want everything. Something is coming that no one can imagine. All their parliamentarism, all the governmental theories now professed, all the riches that have been accumulated, the banks, science, the yids—all of this will crash irreversibly in a moment.[37]

Here Dostoevsky sounds suspiciously like his character Shigalev in *The Devils* (*Besy*), who "looked as though he expected the destruction of the world, and not as if at some time in the future, according to a prophecy that might or might not come true, but quite concretely, tomorrow morning, say, at precisely ten twenty-five."[38]

On the positive side, Dostoevsky finds his strongest evidence for his claim of Russia's universality in what might seem at first to be an unlikely place—literary history. But then again, when we recall the intimate connection between Russian writers of belles lettres and historiography, this source may seem less surprising. In any case, it is in the works of Pushkin (and to a lesser extent Tolstoy) that Dostoevsky finds the Russian ideal expressed most strongly.

There are two main ideas in Pushkin and both of them contain within themselves the prototype of our entire future mission and of Russia's entire future goal; that is, of our entire future fate. The first idea is that of Russia's *universality*, her sympathy for and the real, unquestionable, and deep kinship of her genius with the geniuses of all times and all the world's peoples. . . . Pushkin's other idea is in his turn to the people and his trust in their strength alone, the testament of the fact that in the people and only in the people do we find in toto our Russian genius and the recognition of its mission.[39]

And as is the case throughout the *Diary*, Dostoevsky insists that the future can be predicted directly from a knowledge of past and present phenomena. Literary history becomes a basis for general historical prophecy: "If we have literary works characterized by such ideational power and such mastery [Dostoevsky is referring here to *Anna Karenina*], then why is it impossible for us to have *later* our *own* science, and our own economic and social solutions, and why does Europe deny our independence, deny that we have *our own separate* word." [40]

In sum, the *Diary* brings to the surface and systematizes the conditions for the appearance of and describes the characteristics of the end of history, not merely as a vision but in real (as far as Dostoevsky is concerned) historical time and space. The historical voice of the *Diary* asserts that Europe and European ideals are on the verge of collapse and that this collapse will come in the immediate future. Furthermore, it claims that the Russian word, characterized by the universal sympathy of Orthodoxy, nourished by contact with the Russian people, and broadened by Russia's knowledge of the West from the time of Peter the Great, is about to be spoken. This was the historiographical conception that had been lacking when Dostoevsky was writing *The Idiot*. For Christ appears in time, Dostoevsky realized; therefore, he may have reasoned, the plausibility of a work that describes his reappearance depends on a convincing presentation of an appropriate concrete historical moment. [41] The elaboration of this moment in the 1876 and 1877 issues of the *Diary* allowed for, and indeed necessitated, a new attempt at the novelistic depiction of the perfect individual.

As we turn to *The Brothers Karamazov*, then, we will be looking at how Dostoevsky constructs a novel on the base of the historiographical framework elaborated in the *Diary*. This framework does not appear overtly, but if we read the novel as historical allegory—the fictional incarnation of the utopian, millenarian ideal presented as prediction in *The Diary of a Writer*—its presence becomes obvious. Such a reading does not, of course, preclude many other possible approaches to the novel. It even ignores many central aspects of *The Brothers Karamazov* entirely. Nevertheless, the historical philosophy that Dostoevsky worked out in *The Diary of a Writer* is crucial to an understanding of the basic architectonics of the novel. Ultimately then, in this reading, *The Brothers Karamazov* is no less a historical fiction than is *War and Peace*. It is simply a work in which historical interest has been shifted from the past to the future, and one in which the dialogic interpretive framework is external to the text rather than internal.

In order to read *The Brothers Karamazov* as historical allegory, it is necessary to understand that its constellation of fictional characters is representative of the world political/historical situation at the moment just before the millennium— that same moment in which Dostoevsky felt that he himself lived, and the moment whose existence is the sine qua non for the *Diary*. The Karamazov family is not merely a family: their interrelationships are a microcosm of the development of world history.

It is a basic tenet of Dostoevsky's historical conception that the millennium is to be ushered in by the self-destruction of Europe. In the novel, Ivan Karamazov, with his highly developed sense of the rational and, particularly, his attempts to solve problems of faith and doubt through reason alone, is the primary carrier of European ideas. As Mochulsky puts it, "In Ivan we find completed the age-old development of the *philosophy of reason* from Plato to Kant. . . . 'Man is a rational being'— this axiom has entered his flesh and blood." [42] Ivan, however, is not simply an admirer of European civilization and mores. He is the paradoxical type of Russian westernizer Dostoevsky had described in the *Diary*: "Precisely our most fervent westernizers, precisely the fighters for reform became, at the same time, the negaters of Europe." [43] And indeed, in Dostoevsky's ambiguous presentation of Ivan we see all of Russia's complicated love/hate relationship to European civilization. "I want to go to Europe and I'll be going off there from here, even though I know that I am going to a graveyard," Ivan tells Alesha. [44] For whatever Europe had given the world and Russia, it was, in Dostoevsky's view, doomed to imminent destruction as a condition for Russia's ascendancy, and in Ivan's ultimate feverish collapse into incoherency toward the end of the novel, it is not hard to recognize the fictional equivalent of Europe's demise. True, Dmitry is convinced that Ivan will recover, but there is nothing in the text to confirm this assertion.

According to *The Diary of a Writer*, the destruction of Europe should be a cause for rejoicing rather than for grief, because it is precisely in this context that the Russian word—the message of universal service under the banner of Russian Orthodoxy—will be spoken. The carrier of this Russian word in the novel is clearly Alesha. And here I must disagree with many readers of the novel who criticize Alesha as at best an unsatisfactory hero. Alesha is unsatisfactory because he is a postmillennial character living in a premillennial world. The Russian word, according to Dostoevsky's historiographical framework, is about to be spoken, but until that time, the future speaker of the word cannot be known in all his glory. Just as the Russia of Dostoevsky's day is not quite ready to lead the world's civilization and therefore must seem imperfect in the *Diary*, so must Alesha still prepare himself for the task that lies in the near future.

In this respect it is interesting to note the similarity between Dostoevsky's presentation of the near-term millennium and that of Nikolai Chernyshevsky. In *What Is to be Done?* (*Chto delat'?*), Chernyshevsky hints that the revolution will be coming in 1865, two years after the date of the novel's composition. In the preface to *The Brothers Karamazov*, Dostoevsky tells his readers that the story told in the novel took place thirteen years prior, and that "the crucial novel is a second one—that is, the actions of my hero at our present moment."[45] This clearly implies that what was then present in Alesha only in embryonic form is now in the process of being realized, just as the messianic prophecy for Russia is about to be fulfilled. Had the sequel actually been written it would, presumably, have had to depict postmillennial Russia, so it is probably just as well for Dostoevsky that he died when he did.[46]

In Alesha's psychological makeup are traits exactly analogous to Russia's as described in the *Diary*. Alesha's version of Christianity is exactly that of Russian Orthodoxy as Dostoevsky described it in *The Diary of a Writer*. In the September 1876 issue, Dostoevsky claims that "in reality, in Russian Christianity, there is not even any mysticism; there is merely love of humanity and the image of Christ—that's the most important thing, at the very least."[47] Compare this with the narrator's careful characterization of Alesha when he first appears in the novel: "First of all I would like to announce that this youth, Alesha, was not at all a fanatic, and, in my opinion at least, *not even a mystic* at all: he was simply a precocious *lover of humanity*" (14, 17, emphasis mine). In the novel we also find the ideal of universal service, even at the cost of personal suffering. This is precisely the task Father Zosima gives Alesha when he tells him to "go from these walls and be a monk in the world," and it is what he predicts when he says, "Life will bring you much unhappiness, but it will be your happiness" (14, 259).

Father Zosima is, of course, the bearer of the ancient Orthodox idea in all its purity.[48] But in Dostoevsky's historical conception the Orthodox idea cannot be hoarded by Russia alone. It must go out into the currently imperfect world. And so Alesha will take the "final mortal word" (14, 155) of Father Zosima as his legacy and bring that word into the world. Just as Russia will serve all the world's nations, so will Alesha serve first his own family, then his adopted family of children. When Alesha unites the boys at the very end of the novel, he is on his way to fulfilling his task, a task that will be completed only in the future, but one which is historically inevitable.

The transmission of the true Orthodox "word" of universal service from the pure but limited Zosima to the more worldly Alesha is analogous to Dostoevsky's vision of the Russian word's historical development as described in *Diary of a Writer*. In this regard it is necessary to recall that for Dostoevsky, in sharp contrast to most of his Slavophile predecessors, Peter the Great was a positive figure because he broke down Russia's isolation from the West, thereby creating the possibility for the Russian word to break free from the confines of its country.[49] Zosima, for all his saintliness, cannot be the speaker of the Russian word to the world (even though Alesha thinks he will be [14, 29]). Like the grain of Dostoevsky's biblical epigraph that must die in order to bear fruit, Zosima must die to pass on his word to Alesha, the avatar not of Orthodoxy in its traditional, insular mode, but rather of a new universal variety, one that has come in contact with Europe and can live and serve as an example in the world. Zosima has passed on that word in all its purity to Alesha, and Alesha, through his contact with, understanding of, and ultimately successful resistance to the West (in the person of Ivan), is a worthy symbol of Russia as Dostoevsky saw her in his day.

But in addition to contact with the West, which has supplemented but not modified it, the pure Orthodox word is also nourished, in Dostoevsky's utopian historiographical scenario, by contact with the people. In the novel, the symbolic representative of the Russian people is Alesha's eldest brother, Dmitry. There is no need for a comprehensive enumeration of those character traits that make this identification obvious—suffice it to mention the stereotypical images of unbridled passion, drunkenness, and so on, combined with sentimentality, generosity, and willingness to suffer. As the Prosecutor says: "He [Dmitry] seems to represent unmediated Russia—oh, not all of her, not all of her, God forbid that it should be all of her. Still, nevertheless, here she is, Mother Russia; you can smell her, sense her." [50] Yet Dmitry will ultimately be saved, precisely because Dostoevsky equates his character with that of the Russian people. This is pointed out by Robert Louis Jackson with reference to Dostoevsky's admonition in the February 1876 *Diary*, "Judge the Russian people not by those abominations which it so often commits, but by those great and sacred things for which even in its abominations it constantly yearns." [51] It is, of course, a mark of Alesha's universal sympathy, another trait Dostoevsky finds essential to the Russian ideal, that he is able to love and be loved both by Dmitry and by Ivan.

But, we may ask, why did Dostoevsky need fiction if he was able to express his central philosophical and historical concerns in *The Diary of a Writer*? The answer, I think, lies in Dostoevsky's appreciation of the different possibilities inherent in fictional and nonfictional writing—that is, in his appreciation of the strength of the Russian intergeneric tradition. Just as a novel lacking in proper historical/philosophical grounding, like the *Idiot*, could not fully succeed, so the pronouncements of the authorial voice in the *Diary* were too skeletal on their own, too lacking in the flesh and blood detail so central to Dostoevsky's fictional realism. In order to be made fully convincing, these concepts had to be embodied in fictional characters, moved into fictional space and allowed to play out the conflicts that so obsessed Dostoevsky. Tolstoy had faced the identical problem in *War and Peace*. Although the voice of the philosopher of history could bring the central problems to consciousness, their full articulation could only occur on the level of fictional and historical narrative.

Let us take as an example the analysis of the European political situation that Dostoevsky provides in the January 1877 *Diary*. In an article entitled "Three Ideas" ("Tri idei"), he lays out the historical positions of Catholicism, Protestantism (which he identifies as well with paganism), and Orthodoxy. He concludes his thoughts with the assertion that "all three of these gigantic global ideas have come together in their denouement almost at the same time. All this is no caprice, of course, no war over some kind of inheritance, nor is it the result of a spat between a couple of high-placed women, as in the previous century. This is something universal and final, and although it will not decide the entire fate of mankind, it unquestionably carries within it the beginning of the end of the whole previous history of Europe."[52] We see here, in outline form, the entire germ of *The Brothers Karamazov*. It is not a novel about "some kind of inheritance," despite the fact that Fedor Pavlovich's money plays a central role (and despite Freudian readings of the novel since Freud's own). It is not about the quarrel between "a couple of women," although the rivalry between Grushenka and Katerina Ivanovna is central to the plot. Instead, it is a novel about the beginning of the end of history, as the three fraternal branches of the Christian faith—the Catholic ideal (Ivan), the Protestant/pagan ideal (Dmitry), and the Orthodox ideal (Alesha)—enact the final denouement of civilization as Dostoevsky knew it.

The drama that plays itself out in the novel is the fictional equivalent of the apocalypse that Dostoevsky had predicted so frequently in the *Diary*. *The Brothers Karamazov* is infused with a future-oriented historiographical scenario that was fated to play a central role in Russian culture in the decades that followed. If pedagogy, patriotism, and pleasure had been the prime movers of intergeneric historiographical work before the 1870's, prophecy took center stage for the next forty years. Vladimir Solov'ev, the Russian symbolists, and some of the most important Russian Futurists (discussed in the next chapter) all developed historiographical schemes in which, as was the case with Dostoevsky, the past was of central importance neither for its own sake nor for its utility in the present, but rather for the insights it could give for future (usually utopian) development.

Chapter Seven

Futurist Historians?

*We must learn to read the signs inscribed on the pages
of the past in order to free ourselves from the fatal line
between the past and the future.*
                    Velimir Khlebnikov [1]

To most casual students of Futurism, the title of this chapter
should sound like an oxymoron. If there is any single ideological plank that seems to unite disparate Futurist groups, it is
the desire to erase the past in the name of the future, "to toss
Pushkin, Dostoevsky, Tolstoy, etc., etc., from the steamship
of modernity." [2] And, it is usually claimed, what was rejected
in the ubiquitous manifestos was rejected in artistic practice as
well. As Marjorie Perloff sums up: "Narrative, in other words,
does not and cannot recount 'what happened,' for the past, as
the Futurists repeatedly insist, does not exist." [3] Clearly then, if
my chapter title is to be more than a joke, and if this section is
to fit into this book, my task is to demonstrate that the Futurist
break with history was neither as decisive nor as complete as the
Futurists would have had their readers believe.

I should point out that the Futurist historians were exclusively Russian. As far as I have been able to ascertain, it seems
that an almost complete rejection of the importance of the historical past in favor of the dynamic present and eagerly antici-
pated future was in fact characteristic of the European branches
of Futurism. This, I believe, helps strengthen the central argument of this book: that the attitude displayed by Russian writers
of belles lettres toward history was highly unusual. For if historians were harbored even among the Russian Futurists, then

surely this is strong evidence that the tug of history and the traditions of treating it artistically must be extremely powerful in Russian literary culture.

Of course, the fact that some of the Russian Futurists had a keen interest in history does not mean that all of them did. Such figures as Vladimir Maiakovsky (in his Futurist period) and Aleksei Kruchenykh in poetry, Kazimir Malevich in painting, and Mikhail Matiushin in music were, like their European counterparts, either uninterested in or directly hostile to the past, both within their chosen artistic fields and in general. Nevertheless, at least two writers of crucial importance to Russian Futurism were unquestionably obsessed with history, and an analysis of some works by Velimir Khlebnikov and Vasily Kamensky will illustrate that despite their abundant use of certain kinds of innovations, both writers incorporated historical material into their artistic systems in a surprisingly conservative manner—combining fictional and nonfictional writing and preserving and extending the principles of intergeneric dialogue that had been used by the Pushkins, Tolstoys, and Dostoevskys, "etc., etc.," throughout the nineteenth century.

Probably the key factor that allowed history to remain a central category for at least some Futurists in Russia was the influence of primitivism on Russian culture immediately before and during the Futurist period. As opposed to most of the bewildering array of artistic "isms" that appeared in Russia in the first two decades of the twentieth century, primitivism was not the exclusive property of any one cultural group: there were primitivists amongst the Symbolists, there were primitivists in Sergei Diagilev's circle, and there were primitivists among the Futurists. What is more, primitivism spread easily across media boundaries, into Igor Stravinsky's score for *The Rite of Spring*, the visual art of Mikhail Larionov, Natal'ia Goncharova, David Burliuk, and Nikolai Rerikh, and the writing of Sergei Gorodetsky, Aleksei Remizov, Nikolai Kliuev, Khlebnikov, Kruchenykh, and Kamensky.[4] In part, primitivism was so pervasive because it meant different things to different people.

In his discussion of the origins of the first important Russian Futurist grouping, Hylaea, Vladimir Markov mentions among primitivist-inspired interests Slavic mythology, folk and naïf art, children's art and writing, and prehistoric art.[5]

The one thing that unifies this group of disparate interests is their radical break with the kinds of historical sources and events that had been of central concern for the artists and historians of the nineteenth century. The main focus of nineteenth-century historiography had been the collection, analysis, and interpretation of written documents. In the absence of documents, or as a supplement to them, fictional writing in Russia frequently took the form of missing documents, which filled in the holes of an otherwise coherently narrated text while engaging that text in intergeneric dialogue. The early-twentieth-century primitivists, however, were attracted primarily to events that had fallen outside the purview of nineteenth-century historiography— either because they had literally occurred in prehistoric periods, or because they had seemed too insignificant or too poorly documented to draw the attention of historians. Like their late-eighteenth-century counterparts, the primitivists preferred to work with historical periods on which less information was available, and they employed a highly volatile and fluid genre system to express their discoveries. Eschewing the relatively straightforward nineteenth-century choice of either historical or fictional prose, they presented historical material through imitations of folk tales, in verse cycles, dialogues, ballet, and supersagas.[6]

Nevertheless, in the cases of Khlebnikov and Kamensky at least, two solid principles inherited from the Russian tradition were never abandoned. One was intergeneric dialogue; as we have seen, the strategy of inscribing the same history in multiple genres, both fictional and nonfictional, was the most enduring and unusual aspect of the Russian literary obsession with history. Khlebnikov and Kamensky brought this technique to new degrees of virtuosity. The other was the belief that an understanding of the past could allow for predictions of the future, and in particular, that events in Russia's past, properly interpreted, would reveal Russia's peculiar, probably messianic, role in world history.

In *Svoiiasi* (written in 1919), Khlebnikov claims that what stimulated him to understand history was the Russian defeat in the 1905 Russo-Japanese War: "The laws of time, which I wrote a promise to discover (on a birch tree in the village of Burmakin, Iaroslavl Guberniia) after having heard the news about Tsushima, were collected over ten years."[7] However, the earliest extant text of Khlebnikov's in which he discusses his search for the laws of time is the dialogue "Teacher and Student" ("Uchitel' i uchenik"), published in 1912. From the very subtitle of the work, "About Words, Cities, and Peoples," we can see the dual engine that will drive Khlebnikov's musings on history in a wide variety of genres over the course of the next decade: the direct (usually metonymic) equation linking the history and future prospects of language with those of human civilization. Khlebnikov's tireless linguistic experiments and his historical researches grow out of the same impulse; to find in the past the path to a utopian future in the short term. And, as we will see, complications and failures in one field inevitably had repercussions in the other.

Language and History

"Teacher and Student" is couched in the somewhat unusual literary form of the dialogue. As with many of Khlebnikov's works, it is difficult to classify this piece on the fiction/nonfiction curve, and indeed, there is probably no point in doing so. Henryk Baran discusses the originality of Khlebnikov's revival of the dialogue in his article "The Problem of Composition in Velimir Chlebnikov's Texts."[8] However, Baran does not mention one seemingly obvious immediate Russian predecessor to "Teacher and Student." I have in mind Vladimir Solov'ev's "Three Conversations About War, Progress, and the End of Universal History" ("Tri razgovora o voine, progresse i kontse

vsemirnoi istorii"). Not only is the form of Solov'ev's work similar to that of Khlebnikov's, but they share the central element
of prophecy.[9]

"Teacher and Student" opens with the teacher's request that
the student show his discoveries. This the student proceeds to
do in four separate parts. It is worth noting at the outset that
the expected roles of student and teacher are reversed in this
dialogue, symbolic, presumably, of the fact that the student
represents a new kind of thinking, and that his discoveries are
the wave of the future. In any case, the student begins by de-
tailing his discovery of the laws of the internal declension of
Russian words.

Have you heard, by the way, about the internal declension of words?
. . . If the genitive case answers the question "whence," and the accusative and dative answer the questions "whither" and "where," then
the declension of a root in those cases should produce words with
opposite meanings. These fraternal words should have great significance. And this is the case. Thus, бобр [the root for beaver] and бабр
[the root for tiger], which define a harmless rodent and a frightening carnivore, and which are formed from the accusative and genitive
cases of the root бо [which does not exist], by their very structure
indicate that you should trail a beaver and hunt it as prey, while you
should fear a tiger, since in this case you could become the prey of
the tiger.[10]

Building on this "insight," the student then tries to identify and
categorize the simplest patterns of internal phonemically significant relations that have survived in modern Russian. But it
is not much of a step, and one that Khlebnikov would soon take,
from here to the attempt at the re-creation of a protolanguage
constituted on the basis of these same correspondences.

   Nevertheless, what is important here is not merely that this
scientifically spurious (albeit ingenious) act of finding meaning
in unetymologically derived "relationships" will eventually lead
to Khlebnikov's version of *zaum* or "beyondsense" language.
Even more significant is the general notion that the outer shell
of language hides deep truths which it is the task of the in-

vestigator to discover. The idea that there exists a historically grounded but now hidden internal logic (a deep structure, as it were) linking what seem, on the surface, to be unrelated phenomena motivates the connection of the student's linguistic "research" to his quest for the meaning hidden in geography, history, and literature. After the linguistic section, the student discourses on and provides mathematical formulas for calculating the distances that must separate important cities and the time spans that govern the fates of nations. Far from seeming to be the work of a committed Futurist, these tables, obsessively filled with the dates of historically significant events, seem more the work of a nineteenth-century positivist gone slightly insane. The group of calculations pertaining to the fate of nations is of particular interest. After presenting a long series of dates concerning the rise and fall of past empires, and in response to the teacher's ironic question "Don't you want to compile a list of everything that will happen in the next 1,000 years?" the student replies that his "teaching does not deny predictions of the future." [11] And then, in what became Khlebnikov's most celebrated prediction, the student asks, "Should we not expect the fall of a state in 1917?" [12]

For the remaining decade of his life, Khlebnikov wrote actively in many genres and on many subjects, but he continually returned to his theoretical/mathematical work in the areas of linguistics and history, repeating, developing, and refining the concepts he had first broached in "Teacher and Student." This process would reach its apotheosis in *Zangezi*, probably Khlebnikov's greatest work, but there are a number of intermediate steps that must be considered before we examine the approach to history embodied there, for without an appreciation of some of these the intertextual dialogue that gives *Zangezi* its artistic coherence is incomprehensible.

In the area of linguistic theorizing, Khlebnikov's 1919 declaration "To the Artists of the World!" ("Khudozhniki mira!") is worthy of attention, because in this manifesto-like work the combination of primitivism and utopianism so characteristic for Khlebnikov's thought becomes clear. At the beginning of "To the Artists of the World!" Khlebnikov announces that his long-sought (and now achieved) goal has been the creation of "a common written language . . . that can be understood and accepted by our entire star." It turns out, however, that this language is not so much a creation as a rediscovery. There was once a time, in the prehistoric past, when "words served to dispel enmity and make the future transparent and peaceful, and when languages, proceeding in stages, united the people of (1) a cave, (2) a settlement, (3) a tribe or kinship group, (4) a state, into a single rational world. . . . One savage caveman understood another and laid his blind weapon aside."[13] The goal of poetic creation and historical/linguistic research is to rediscover this original human protolanguage.[14] The poet, therefore, must abandon linguistic history in favor of linguistic prehistory; the historian of language becomes an archaeologist. Poetic creation in this new/old language will lead to universal understanding and the re-creation of paradise lost. "Mute graphic marks will reconcile the cacophony of languages,"[15] and humankind in general.

Of course, many ancient peoples believed that their history had contained a golden age in the deep and almost forgotten past. Khlebnikov was well aware of this myth, and one sees in his poetic vision, as one scholar has put it, a tendency "to counterpose a contemporary reality, treated at best with irony and more frequently with explicit hostility, to an idealized Slavic past, a Golden Age of uncomplicated direct feelings and heroic patriotic behavior."[16] Khlebnikov's methodology and assumptions were certainly influenced by such mythological constructs, and there can be no doubt that his strong Russian nationalism,[17] especially in the early part of his career, initially stimulated his interest in history.

At the same time, an analysis of Khlebnikov's thought solely in terms of its connection with primitive myths of the golden age fails to take into account the essentially utopian mode of Khlebnikov's thinking. What is clear from "To the Artists of the World!" is that Khlebnikov was fascinated by history not merely as a counterweight to an unacceptable present, but because he felt that historical knowledge was a tool for action in the present and could lead directly and quickly to a utopian future. This attitude can hardly be ascribed solely to Khlebnikov's knowledge of ancient mythology, for as we have seen elsewhere in this book, a desire to find somewhere in Russia's past a point from which a program for action in the present can be derived and a departure for the future can be made is one of the engines that drives the Russian obsession with history. This was particularly the case for Slavophile-inspired thinkers, to which camp the early Khlebnikov, at least, belonged.[18] True, Khlebnikov delves further back into history than had any of his predecessors and makes use of a wider variety of historical data, but the basic impulse remains the same. And although later in life Khlebnikov's utopia became far more internationalist, the word was still to emanate from Russia, if only because Khlebnikov himself was to be the first "President of the Globe."[19]

The rest of Khlebnikov's manifesto is devoted to a presentation of what he believes to be the inherent meaning of each letter of the alphabet. The specifics of his claim are not really of interest to us here, but the main thrust is to discover a connection between the shape of the signs for Russian consonants (vowels play no role in the theory) and the types of words they begin. Thus, for example, because of its shape the grapheme x is seen naturally to begin words that define things that "protect the point of man from the hostile point of bad weather, cold, or enemies."[20] The fact that twenty such words in Russian do in fact begin with x is taken as proof of the theory's validity. It is curious to recognize that Khlebnikov's theory implies the priority of written over oral language, or at least their simultaneity, making him something of a precursor to Derrida. On a more serious note, we should point out the obvious Russocentric bias of this supposedly universal theory of language. But the fact that Russian serves as the basis for universal language seems not to have bothered Khlebnikov. The theory is also synesthetic; that is, sounds, the hieroglyphs that should be used to represent them, and appropriate colors are linked, thus paving the way for works of art that would easily be able to transcend media boundaries.[21]

At the end of the manifesto, Khlebnikov presents his own version of a sentence in Russian "translated" into his proposed universal *zaum* language. The sentence he chose to translate is in itself extremely suggestive, because it illustrates the close ties between the types of historical events that interested the poet and the language proper for describing them. As we will see in our analysis of *Zangezi*, the connection will only become more intimate later in Khlebnikov's life. Of all possible sentences, Khlebnikov provides the following for the purposes of illustration:

Соединившись вместе, орды гуннов и готов, собравшись кругом Аттилы, полны боевого воодушевления, двинулись далее вместе, но, встреченные и отраженные Аэцием, защитником Рима, рассеялись на множество шаек и остановились и успокоились на своей земле, разлившись в степях, заполняя их пустоту.[22]

Having linked up and gathered around Attila, the hordes of Huns and Goths, filled with martial enthusiasm, moved forward together. But having been engaged and repulsed by Aetius, the defender of Rome, they scattered into a multitude of bands. They halted and settled down peacefully on their own land, spilling out into the steppes and filling their emptiness.

Next, Khlebnikov gives two *zaum* versions of the sentence, which are presumably meant to be synonymous:

Ша + со (гуннов и готов), *вэ* Аттилы, *ча по, со до,* но *бо + зо* Аэция, *хо* Рима, *со мо вэ + ка со, ло ша* степей *+ ча*

or, alternatively,

Вэ со человеческого рода *бэ го* языков, *пэ* умов *вэ со ша* языков, *бо мо* слов *мо ка* разума *ча* звуков *по со до лу* земли *мо со* языков *вэ* земли.

It will be noted, of course, that the "universal" *zaum* text is written in Cyrillic letters, and that in addition to monosyllables it contains recognizable Russian words.

Then, and this is far more surprising and significant, Khlebnikov provides what a professional would call a "back translation" from *zaum* into Russian. While this new sentence does not much resemble the original on the surface, we are evidently meant to perceive that their semantic deep structures are identical. Far from being a random nonsense language, *zaum*, it turns out, allows the poet to decode the true meaning hidden in ordinary linguistic signs:

Думая о соединении человеческого рода, но столкнувшись с горами языков, бурный огонь наших умов, вращаясь около соединенного заумного языка, достигая распылением слов на единицы мысли в оболочке звуков, бурно и вместе идет к признанию на всей земле единого заумного языка.

Thinking about the unification of humankind but running up against the mountains of languages, the energetic flame of our minds turns to the unity of beyondsense language, achieving the scattering of words into thought units cloaked in sound, and energetically and in concert moves toward the acceptance of a single beyondsense language for the entire world.

The wars between Rome and the barbarians, the conflicts between East and West, turn out to have been signs of humankind's ultimate desire for unity. A historical event may have hidden within itself the seeds of utopia, but these deeper meanings can only be divined by the poet through his "translation" of the words used to describe them. As a thinker, Khlebnikov claims to have apprehended the hidden meaning of history, while as a poet he is creating the conditions for mutual understanding, paradise on earth, and the end of history. The only thing lacking in order to unlock fully the potentials hidden in history and language is a mechanism for recognizing essential analogies between events in the past and present: understanding must somehow be linked to prediction. For this, Khlebnikov turns from linguistics to mathematics.

Mathematics and History

Ten men, battalions, or divisions, fighting against fifteen men,
batallions, or divisions, overcame the fifteen. That is, they
killed them all or took them prisoner, and they lost only four
men; therefore, on one side four were lost and on the other fifteen.
Consequently, four were equal to fifteen, and consequently,
$4x = 15y$. *Consequently*, $x:y = 15:4$. *This equation does not*
give the value of the variables, but it gives the ratio between the
two variables. And by treating various historical units (battles,
campaigns, periods of war) in such equations, we get a series of
numbers in which laws must exist and can be discovered.

                              Lev Tolstoy, War and Peace

I discovered the pure Laws of Time in 1920 in Baku. . . . First
I discovered the characteristic reversibility of events after 3[5]
days, 243 days. Then I continued to increase the powers and
extents of the time periods I had discovered, and began to apply
them to the past of humanity. The past suddenly became
transparently clear; the simple laws of time suddenly illuminated
it in its entirety.

                    Velimir Khlebnikov, The Tables of Destiny

Khlebnikov eventually came to believe that he had discovered the very mathematical laws of history whose existence was posited by the philosopher of history in *War and Peace*. Of course, Khlebnikov does not mention Tolstoy very frequently, and I would not be so rash as to attempt to descry any kind of direct influence here.[23] Nevertheless, the convergence of their interests here is indeed striking. And as we examine Khlebnikov's theories more closely, we will see a number of other convergences that point to the existence of at least an unconscious dialogue with the nineteenth-century tradition I have been explicating in this book.

It has already been noted that Khlebnikov first attempted to formulate mathematical laws of history in his dialogue "Teacher and Student" (1912). Over the next decade, these laws were further developed and refined in a whole series of semiartistic prose pieces.[24] Among them are "Argument About Priority" ("Spor o pervenstve," 1914); "The Battles of 1915–17: New Teachings About War" ("Bitvy 1915–17 gg. Novoe uchenie o voine," 1915); "Time, the Measure of the World" ("Vremia mera mira," 1916); "V. Khlebnikov's Colloquy Concerning States" ("Razgovor, vziraiushchii na gosudarstva V. Khlebnikova," 1917); "Duel with Hammurabi" ("Poedinok s Khamuraby," 1918); "In the World of Numbers" ("V mire tsifr," 1920); and *Tables of Destiny* (*Doski sud'by*, 1922–23). This is not the appropriate place for a detailed analysis of Khlebnikov's mathematical theories of history, for I am interested in them not in their own right, but because of the role they play in *Zangezi*. I cite these titles merely to illustrate the obsessive manner in which Khlebnikov returned to his mathematical/historical researches.

Despite the complicated development Khlebnikov's theories underwent between 1912 and 1922, there are a certain number of constants that need to be emphasized. The first is the focus of the poet's attention: the primary type of historical action that interests Khlebnikov throughout his career is the battle. In particular, he was obsessed with discovering the laws of time governing not just any battle, but those that marked a shift in historical momentum from East to West or vice versa. This concern is expressed most succinctly in a chart that appeared in the first part of the *Tables of Destiny* under the heading "Waves of two worlds, the alternating spears of East and West, clashing through the centuries."[25] As examples Khlebnikov mentions six pairs of battles separated by the appropriate number of years (a power of three, since powers of three are said to separate movements of opposite direction).[26]

For all their seeming strangeness, these theories play a role in Khlebnikov's artistic worldview analogous to the musings of Tolstoy's philosopher of history in *War and Peace* or Pushkin's historical persona in *The History of Pugachev*. That is, for Khlebnikov, the historical mathematician expresses a point of view that seems to be objective and nonfictional, but this perspective is unable to present historical truth in its totality. For that, it must be brought into dialogue with the very different perspectives provided by linguistics and embodied in literary texts. The main difference is that Khlebnikov believes the truths provided by language and by mathematics to be, ultimately, synonymous. Thus, the dialogue he proposes is not, as it was for Karamzin, Tolstoy, or Pushkin, between alternative world-views; rather, as was the case with Dostoevsky, the perspectives of the two genres (here, linguistics and mathematics) are meant to reinforce each other.

Khlebnikov's particular concern with conflicts of East and West is, on the surface, related to the fact that one such shift, the Japanese defeat of the Russians during the war of 1904–5 was, as we have seen, the stimulus that motivated him to begin his search for the laws of time in the first place. Eventually Khlebnikov decided that the "war of 1904 was a compressed and reversed repetition of the conquest of Siberia." [27] At the same time, it is important to remember that this concern was by no means unique to Khlebnikov: an obsession with reversals of historical motion between East and West had been a com-monplace in Russian literary/historical thought at least since Tolstoy described the process in *War and Peace*. [28]

By the end of the century, however, Russia's place in the East/West equation had changed. From Tolstoy's Eurocentric perspective, Russia was the East. But starting with Solov'ev, Russia began to shift camps as more and more attention was focused on the nations of Asia. Thus, in the "Three Conversa-tions" of 1899, one of Solov'ev's characters predicts that "the center of gravity of universal history is, evidently, moving to the Far East." [29] In the "Short Tale About the Antichrist" ("Kratkaia povest' ob Antikhriste") appended, we read that events leading up to the apocalypse are to be touched off by a Japanese-led conquest of the entire world by the Asian peoples. And, as if to prove that these thoughts are not merely those of his characters, the philosopher says in the introduction: "It was important for me to define more realistically the coming horrible conflict of two worlds." [30] After the appearance of Solov'ev's influential work, and even more so after the loss of the Russo-Japanese War, the "yellow peril" became an obsession in Russian culture. By the turn of the century, Russia, which had been viewed (whether positively or negatively) through most of the nineteenth century as part of the East, had now firmly become part of the Western camp, liable to be overrun at any moment by the Asian hordes.

Not that everyone thought the specter of destruction from the East was necessarily a bad thing.[31] Valery Briusov, interpreting the results of the Russo-Japanese War in the light of Solov'ev's prophecy, welcomed the "Approaching Huns" ("Griadushchie Gunny"), seeing in the defeat of the West (Russia) by the East (Japan) both a cyclical repetition of the conquest of Rome by the barbarians and a promise of positive revolutionary energy:

> Где вы, грядущие гунны,
> Что тучей нависли над миром!
> Слышу ваш топот чугунный
> По еще не открытым Памирам.

> Where are you Huns who are coming,
> Who cloud the wide world with your spears?
> I hear your pig iron tramping
> On the still-undiscovered Pamirs.

> На нас ордой опьянелой
> Рухните с темных становий—
> Оживить одряхлевшее тело
> Волной пылающей крови.

> Like a drunken horde from dark field-camps
> Fall on us in a clamoring flood—
> To revive our too-soon-grown-old bodies
> With a fresh surge of blood.[32]

Thus, by the time Khlebnikov took up an interest in the issue of East versus West it had practically become a cultural cliché.

Prophecy and History

Before turning to *Zangezi*, it remains only to ask what the committed Futurist poet thought a knowledge of history was for: that is, how did Khlebnikov envision the connection between the past and the future? The most obvious answer is that an understanding of the mathematical laws underpinning history would allow for prediction; prophecy, a goal that was so often part of the Russian writer's agenda, would become scientific and exact. As Khlebnikov baldly put it in his 1914 "Argument About Priority": "The equation of mores derived from the study of the stories of the distant past—of Pushkin, Chebyshev, and Chaadaev—allows us to make judgments about future generations."[33]

With understanding, however, came new problems. Perhaps not surprisingly, the central one was exactly the same as that which had bothered Tolstoy when he had contemplated historical laws: that is, the existence of historical laws seemed to eliminate the possibility of free will. At first, this prospect did not bother Khlebnikov. In 1914, he announced without commentary that "the law of 28 years shakes the concept of free will."[34] Later in life, however, Khlebnikov modified his position. He began to think that an intimate understanding of history would do no more than give humankind the knowledge necessary for making informed choices about the future. Prediction would not be absolute. Presumably, historical laws would function as a more exact Futurist version of, say, entrail reading. Instead of knowing exactly what would happen at a given time, future generations would know what general kinds of things to expect, and, within the constraints of the possible, they could decide what to do accordingly. "One could also make measurements of the flow of time, constructing the laws of tomorrow by studying the patterns of future times that grow out of the lessons of past centuries. . . . It has long been a commonplace that knowledge is a form of power; so predicting events is equivalent to controlling them."[35] Thus, as was true for Dostoevsky, the patterns of the past allow not for perfect knowledge, but merely for prophecy. Still, Khlebnikov's mathematical historiography claims to be far more "scientific" than Dostoevsky's apocalyptic impressionism.

In the main then, despite the shockingly innovative nature of his poetic language, in his choice of historical problems and in his treatment of them through a dialogue engendered by works on the same theme in heterogeneous genres, Khlebnikov was essentially a conservative. His desperate attempts to formulate laws of history can be seen in the context of the general Russian literary obsession with history merely as an extension of a common cultural trend.

Zangezi

By all accounts, *Zangezi* is the magnum opus of Khlebnikov's last period, although there seems to be little agreement among scholars as to even its most basic meaning.[36] I will not attempt an exhaustive analysis of it here. Instead, I will provide a reading of *Zangezi* that concentrates on the role of intergeneric dialogue and of history in the text. From the outset, it should be said that *Zangezi* seems almost to have been written specifically for the student of intergeneric dialogue. While the other authors discussed heretofore used versions of the technique, and some even provided hints as to what they thought it meant, in his "Introduction" Khlebnikov talks quite openly about how a work like this is organized. "A superstory, or supersaga, is made up out of independent sections, each with its own special god, its special faith, and its special rule. To the old Muscovite question about one's orthodoxy, 'How dost thou believe?', each section must answer independently of its neighbor."[37] If we are to make sense of the whole of a supersaga, to appreciate its artistic message, we must perceive the internal dialogue that is implied by the very structure of the work. At the same time, we must be aware that *Zangezi* is constructed like an iceberg. Each separate section represents a poetic distillation of ideas that the poet initially developed elsewhere, and this means that *Zangezi* makes sense only if we recognize its implied dialogue with most of Khlebnikov's earlier work.

After the theoretical "Introduction," *Zangezi* begins with what might be called stage directions: the description is of a natural setting, empty for the moment of human or animal life, but implying their existence. For, we are informed, it is in this setting that Zangezi "reads his sermons to the people" (192). The stage directions are followed by twenty or so sections called "planes." The first two, both written in *zaum*, contain conversations of birds and gods respectively. We recall, of course, that *zaum* is supposed to be a re-creation of universal speech, and thus realize that the dialogue in these scenes, although incomprehensible to us, represents coherent conversation for its participants. The universality of the language is emphasized by its being used by gods of wildly differing traditions (Roman, pagan Russian, and, perhaps, Finnic).[38] That the *zaum* lines represent coherent conversation and not nonsense is buttressed by the fact that the section after Eros's first "speech" is marked "The gods respond." What we do not know, however, is the time frame of this conversation: is it taking place in the distant past, when language was still universal, the future, when it will be again, or is it outside of human time altogether?

The third plane helps clear up some of the mystery. Passersby appear and, in fairly standard colloquial Russian, discuss Zangezi himself. We are, it would seem, still in the interregnum after the loss of universal language and before its reinstitution. The attitude of the passersby to Zangezi is curious. In public, they appear to be sympathetic, but in private they seem to think him a sort of village idiot. Most confusing is the first passerby, who in one and the same line calls the absent Zangezi "teacher" (perhaps a reference to the dialogue "Teacher and Student") and "forest fool" (196). The people call out for Zangezi, but they find instead a piece of paper in his handwriting entitled "The Tables of Destiny."

The reference to Khlebnikov's own theoretical work on history is quite significant, both because it encourages us to see Zangezi as an autobiographical character and because it points to a dialogue between the supersaga and Khlebnikov's quasi-literary work. The excerpt itself does not correspond directly to any section of the published versions of the *Tables of Destiny*,

but considering Khlebnikov's penchant for obsessively reworking his texts this is hardly surprising.[39] In any case, the basic
content of this section, which concerns mathematical equations
for the fall of empires, is familiar. But the context in which
this excerpt appears changes its meaning significantly. Read by
themselves, the *Tables of Destiny* seem entirely serious. Here,
however, the equations are read not only by an implied reader
outside the text, but by specific readers inside it. Their observations lend a note of irony, even levity to the presentation. We
begin to suspect that Khlebnikov might have been aware of just
how crazy his theories seemed to most people. "Obscure. None
too comprehensible, either. And yet—the lion's claw is visible
in all of this!" (197) says the second passerby after the fragment
is read.

When Zangezi finally appears in plane six, he comes not
as the confident prophet, the implied author of the "Tables of
Destiny," but rather as a tired preacher unsure of his place in
the world.

> I have come like a butterfly
> Into the hall of human life
> And must spatter my dusty coat
> As signature across its bleak windows . . .
> Already I have worn away
> My bright blue glow, my pointillated patterns,
> My wing's blue windstorm. The bright notes
> Of my first freshness are gone, my wings waver,
> Colorless and stiff, I droop despairing
> At the windows of the human world.
> Numbers, eternal numbers, sound in the beyond;
> I hear their distant conversation. Number
> Calls to number; number calls me home. (198)

Particularly important here is the expression of the desire to escape the world of humankind, and presumably to join with that
one in which the universal language is spoken; to escape history
for the infinite. In great measure, this is the central theme of
Khlebnikov's poem. What is the place of the poet/prophet in

an uncomprehending world? Is it enough to have discovered the laws of time, history, and language? Or is the prophet simply doomed in this world?

Inspired momentarily by the requests of the humans to "describe the horrors of our age in the words of the Alphabet! So that never again will we have to see war between peoples or the sabres of the Alphabet; instead, let us hear the crash of Alphabet's long spears" (198), Zangezi launches into a virtuosic and untranslatable poem in which elements of contemporary Russian history are narrated through the interaction of words containing letters of the alphabet which have, as was predicted as early as "Teacher and Student," inherent meaning. The importance of intergeneric dialogue is clear once again. However, if the reader is not aware of Khlebnikov's theories on these subjects, this section of *Zangezi*, which in any case is fairly opaque, simply makes no sense at all. What is unexpected here is the attempt to describe almost exclusively events of recent Russian history, a subject that is clearly now of greater concern to Zangezi/Khlebnikov than is universal history. Instead of creating a universal *zaum* language to express world history, in the seventh plane Zangezi plays with the internal "meaning" of the Russian language in order to make sense of purely Russian history to Russian speakers. The question is, can the poet's linguistic virtuosity rescue Russia from the chaotic violence it had known without cease from 1914 until 1922, when this poem was being written? Can poetry usher in utopia not in principle but in fact, despite what Zangezi says in the course of his poem: "Рог! Рог!/Бог Руси, бог руха" (Horn! Horn!/God of Russia, god of ruin)?[40]

Building on his accomplishments of the seventh plane, in the eighth plane Zangezi attempts again to construct a universal language, one that would presumably allow his human listeners to communicate with the gods and birds of planes one and two and that would lead to a utopia on earth. As he says when he finishes, "Someday this language will unite us all, and that day may come soon" (204).

Zangezi follows up this first experiment in *zaum* with two more. Plane nine is constructed by adding various prefixes to the root for "mind" (*um*). They are first recited mantra-like, and then provided with commentary.[41] The *zaum* of the tenth plane is built by replacing various letters of the alphabet in a series of words with the letter *m*; Zangezi promises that this linguistic tactic will "wake the sleeping gods of speech" (210), probably those same gods who already speak the universal language. This he succeeds in doing, for in the eleventh plane the gods, crying out in their own *zaum*, fly away. It is noteworthy, though, that the *zaum* spoken by the gods (and the birds) is different from Zangezi's. While his *zaum* is clearly based on Russian, theirs is not, and this forces the reader (but evidently not Zangezi) to question the likelihood of the realization of the utopian dream of unfettered communication. Additionally, the fact that the gods have flown away in response to Zangezi's recitation seems to undercut the universal appeal of his approach, something his human listeners evidently understand: "The power of our voices has terrified the gods! Is that good or bad?" (211). Rather than ushering in a new era of universal understanding, Zangezi seems to have created a tower of Babel in reverse. As humans rediscover a single language, it serves not as a link to the gods, but as a means to exile them, leaving the gap between human-kind and the divine intact. Still, this might seem a small price to pay for the institution of utopia on earth.

That the gods have in fact been exiled by Zangezi's prophetic power appears to be confirmed in plane thirteen. I say appears to be because this plane is hardly transparent and is, I imag-ine, open to various readings. Nevertheless, the opening line, "Летуры летят в собеса толпою ночей исчезаев," which Paul Schmidt translates as "Ledglings in flight, seeking their self and, / Flocking through darkness to vanishment,"[42] seems to me a pretty clear reference to the disappearing gods. What remains after their flight is simply the earth in the present, and now Zangezi, having banished the gods, must order the world entirely by his own powers: "And I am the God-Maker,

Divicator, / Left all alone" (214). At the end of plane thirteen
the poet/prophet Zangezi reaches his apotheosis. He has eliminated the gods, formulated the laws of history, and reinvented
the universal language. But to do so, he has had to become the
ultimate solipsist. The universe is defined by what he sees and
says, and nothing outside of him can exist. Zangezi thinks the
problems of history and language are solved because they, like
everything else, have been internalized.

> Move ever onward, Planets of Earth!
> Thus by plural number does my greatness cast its spell.
> I am the Many-Maker, Multiplicator of Planet Earth:
> Wobble yourself into hordes of earths,
> Spin yourself, Earth, into swarms of mosquitos:
> I sit alone, with folded arms,
> Singer of the grave-ground
>
> I am what is not.
>
> I am the only son of who I am. (215)

From this point on, however, it is all downhill. Zangezi's solip-
sistic world building is intruded on by forces that turn out to
be beyond his control. His listeners revolt: "All right! That's
enough! Please! Go suck a sour pickle, Zangezi! Give us something with substance! Something with guts" (216). Considering
that Zangezi thought he was giving them nothing less than the
entire universe, this response cannot be very encouraging.

Things get worse when, in plane sixteen, one of his listeners
has a fit and in its throes begins to recite a poem/dialogue that
sounds a great deal like Khlebnikov's long violent poem about
the Russian civil war, "Night Search" ("Nochnoi obysk").[43] This
has the obvious result of calling attention away from Zangezi's
universal but artificial utopia and toward the less-than-perfect
present. The passersby note in horror:

> He's having a seizure. This is the falling sickness:
> War-fear has wounded his soul.
> War cuts our days like a throat.
> This man has been seized—and he shows us
> That war exists, that it still exists (218)

Despite his best efforts to escape history by literally having its number, the poet/prophet is part of this world and he cannot replace the gods he has exiled. Zangezi is dismissed and derided by a trio who proceed to quote almost verbatim a section from "Night Search."[44] Here the intergeneric dialogue becomes quite complicated. By interpolating a poem steeped in the bloody realia of the civil war into the universalist idyll that Zangezi has constructed, the trio assert the power of history and memory over universality and the creative imagination. Zangezi's portentous "Tables of Destiny" are reduced even by himself to "matches of destiny" (219).

Stunned by the incursion of reality into his universe, Zangezi makes a final desperate attempt to overpower the present with his historical/utopian theories. This time, however, the cycles of violence that are his concern are not brought to resolution. This is the most significant change wrought in Zangezi's world by the intrusion of the person suffering a fit. The quotation from "Night Search" links the world of the supersaga with Khlebnikov's own, and it goes a long way toward explaining the despair of one who thought that his theories of history and language would liberate humankind but who now fears that they merely provide a blueprint for continued suffering. The utopian future that would re-create an idealized primitive past has been overwhelmed by the crushing weight of a history that appears to alternate between repetition and reversal. Zangezi is unable to control the situation, and there remains nothing for him to do other than to ride off into the sunset, which he does at the end of plane nineteen. By this point, it is clear that the author Khlebnikov knows and understands more than his character Zangezi, for the author recognizes the failure of the project whose goal it is to escape history, while Zangezi does not. Indeed, we may perhaps see Zangezi as a self-portrait of the Khlebnikov of the late 1910's.

Plane twenty, although more comprehensible, from a linguistic point of view, than many of the preceding sections, is quite difficult to interpret. According to the editors of the most recent edition of Khlebnikov, it was written before the rest of the supersaga,[45] and this may help explain its distant and at best metonymical connection with the rest of the work. It consists of a conversation between Woe and Laughter that has been likened to "some fantastic medieval mystery play."[46] I will not attempt even a partial interpretation of this section here, but will turn instead to its finale. Laughter concludes his final monologue with the lines: "The movement of Time undoes us all; / Oh, what a fall!"[47] As I see it, this comment serves as a fitting epigraph to the work as a whole, and to Khlebnikov's utopian project. The goal of Khlebnikov the poet, prophet, and historian was to conquer time. The distant past was to be measured, understood, and interpreted to create the utopian future. Unfortunately both for Khlebnikov and his autobiographical hero, real historical time proved unstoppable. *Zangezi*'s story is one of the triumph of time and disorder over the heroic attempts of the poet/prophet to find unity and organization; it is about the incompatibility of the world of "Night Search" with that of the *Tables of Destiny*.

The ending of *Zangezi* is one of irony rather than transcendence. Felled by time, Laughter drops dead. This is followed by the news that Zangezi too has died, a suicide. However, just at this moment Zangezi strides onstage, announcing that "Zangezi lives. It was all just a stupid joke" (235), and the supersaga ends with the parenthetic "A sequel will follow."[48] But the resurrected Zangezi is at best a shell of his former self, stripped of prophetic power or knowledge of a beyondsense language. The promised sequel by Zangezi's creator never appeared, because real historical time did indeed catch up with the first "President of the Globe," only months after he finished this first part.

Futurist Historians: Part II

Isn't it time just to jump into Razin's boats? Everything is ready. We'll form a Government of the Presidents of the Globe.
                                                      Velimir Khlebnikov

Khlebnikov had one other historical obsession that does not exactly fit into any of the categories described thus far. This one is with a specific period of Russian history—the seventeenth-century Cossack rebellion led by the colorful Sten'ka Razin. I have not discussed this theme earlier because it lies a bit outside the center of Khlebnikov's major historical concerns, and because it has been treated extensively in the scholarly literature on the poet.[49] Interestingly, however, Khlebnikov's obsession with Razin was shared by one of his fellow Hylaeans, the aviator, poet, and prose writer Vasily Kamensky. I will focus on Kamensky's treatments of the Razin theme because they provide a contrasting case of the working methods of a Futurist historian, and because they have not yet been adequately studied.

Kamensky's Razin appeared in many works and in various genres. In addition, a number of the individual works are characterized by the kind of intergeneric dialogue we have come to expect from Russian writers with an interest in history. Finally, Kamensky was well aware of the changing ideological climate in which his Razins appeared. As a result, his work provides an unusual example of dialogue between pre-Soviet and Soviet literary treatments of history by the same author.

A glance at Kamensky's bibliography reveals the depth of his obsession with the Razin theme. His novel *Sten'ka Razin* appeared in 1916, followed by the poem cycle *The People's Heart: Sten'ka Razin* (*Serdtse narodnoe—Sten'ka Razin*) in 1918. To these were added a play, also entitled *Sten'ka Razin* (1919), and, finally, two more revisions in 1928: the novel *Stepan Razin* and the long poem *Sten'ka Razin*.

Kamensky evidently began work on the first version of his novel in the summer of 1914. In an autobiography written long after the fact, he recalled: "Swept by enthusiasm, I wished to build a bridge from the village to Futurism, and from Stepan Timofeevich Razin to my contemporaries . . . and that summer when world war flamed, when all of Russia's life suddenly bubbled, when an elemental shaking of hearts and minds began—my assurance about my work on Razin doubled, as if on a wave of momentous premonitions."[50]

The reader is thus prepared for an energetic and perhaps anarchic text. Both qualities are abundantly present. What one is not prepared for, however, are the ardent lyricism and even more ardent nationalism that pervade *Sten'ka Razin*. The novel begins first with a dedication to and then a hymn in praise of the "heroic Russian people." The tone and language of the novel are as far from the difficult and complicated primitivistic linguistic experiments of Khlebnikov as could possibly be. Kamensky's novel is, of course, primitivist as well, but his version is naïf rather than prehistoric, drawn primarily from the rhythms of Russian folk poetry. What links Khlebnikov's searches to Kamensky's is their common desire to find in the historical past a basis and a pattern for predicting the future. While Khlebnikov sought to do this by collecting more and more facts and assembling them into more and more complicated schemata, Kamensky concentrated on one story, attempting to squeeze out everything it contained. Still, Khlebnikov must certainly have approved of the end of Kamensky's introduction: "I sense, I believe, I await—soon the hour of victory will arrive—and a great miracle will occur: the heroic Russian people in Easter-ringing, seven-hued rainbows will cover the Russian land with their freewheeling days and will create a life full of miracles such as never before seen or heard of. I wait and prepare."[51] Future utopia in the near term is predicted by a proper understanding of the past.

The novel that follows presents a lyrical portrait of the life and times of the famous Cossack rebel. No attempt is made to provide historical background or detail, and Razin is presented as larger than life, an epic figure emblematic of all Russian people, whose virtues are extolled at the novel's outset. The following excerpt both characterizes the hero and gives an idea of Kamensky's rhythmic lyrical prose:

> Like the Russian people themselves, Stepan was gigantic, strong, talented, unexpected.
> Like the Russian people themselves, Stepan was always disorganized, always rebellious, always disheveled.
> Like the Russian people themselves, Stepan was either wildly out of control or tranquil and majestic in his light blue wisdom.

Like the Russian people themselves, Stepan believed in God, made pilgrimages to monasteries, prayed fiery prayers, repented his sins, and was tortured by lonesomeness while wandering the unknown orphaned roads.

Or suddenly, like the Russian people themselves, uncontrollably, unexpectedly, in an energetic whirlwind outburst, Stepan, forgetting God, monasteries, prayers, repentance, and languor, would give in to his burbling youthful will.[52]

Vladimir Markov is undoubtedly right when he says that "the novel's lyric, rhythmic prose . . . soon wears thin. . . . The book has too much lilt and garish folkloric color."[53] Nevertheless, there are a number of things of interest here. The first is that the anarchistic Stepan is primarily portrayed not as a Cossack ataman or as a revolutionary, but as a singer of songs. This, of course, encourages us to identify Stepan with Kamensky himself, an identification parallel to that between Zangezi and Khlebnikov, and it helps to explain both poets' enthusiasm for Razin.[54]

The second notable feature, one which will become important when we look at Kamensky's later revision of his work, is the novel's celebration of wild anarchy. Neither Razin nor the Russian people are presented as having a coherent agenda. They simply follow the dictates of their collective will, which for all its potential for violence, is considered to be basically child-like and good. Whatever Kamensky's ideas about the coming revolution were in 1914, they were bereft of any kind of organized political or ideological component. His is a lyrical, almost romantic anarchism, a view of revolution as the release of spiritual and national energy.

Finally, the most interesting feature of Kamensky's work, from the point of view of narrative technique, is his free mixture of lyric ornamental prose and folk-inflected poetry. That is, *Sten'ka Razin* is structured around an internal intergeneric dialogue. There are basically two kinds of lyrics in the novel. The most common are folk-style episodes that serve to create atmosphere and to break up the monotony of the lyrical prose. Included here are a number of poems written in what is claimed to be Persian (at one point in his colorful career, Stepan spent some time living in Persia). Although they do contain some distorted Persian and Tatar words, they serve primarily as *zaum* interludes within the all-too-transparent texture of the novel.

The other poetry in the text is used at moments of high tension, particularly battle scenes, and is extremely effective in capturing the energy and heat of situations that were beyond the capabilities of Kamensky's flabby prose. These volatile passages are among the best moments in the book. As opposed to the lyrical, flowing, nostalgic view of the past provided by the prose narrator, these poetic sections attempt to re-create history in its immediacy and confusion, a division of labor not unlike that between Tolstoy's historical and fictional narrators. Naturally, *Sten'ka Razin* is no *War and Peace*, but it is nevertheless a further experiment in intergeneric dialogue on historical themes. Poetry and prose are combined to produce a portrait of an anarchic poet/rebel and an allegorical rendering of Kamensky's view of the situation in Russia at the beginning of the First World War.

Had he dropped the subject here, Kamensky's work would have merely merited a footnote in the annals of Russian literary history, but by following his novel with many more versions of the Razin story, each "with its own God," as Khlebnikov might have put it, Kamensky created a potentially very interesting dialogue on the Razin theme. In 1918, Kamensky published what would ultimately be his most successful Razin-inspired work: a cycle of 60 short (4- to 31-line) poems. They are almost all in the style of folk poetry, clearly a direct imitation of the collections of folk poems on historical subjects that had been published by nineteenth-century folklorists. Some had appeared in either identical or similar form in the 1916 novel, and their repetition signals an invitation to dialogue between the two works. This dialogue, however, does not tell us very much, for the poem cycle far outshines the novel. Separated from the overly flamboyant lyrical prose of the novel, the poems are far more effective, and what is lost in narrative coherency is more than made up for in the understatedly energetic verse.

But dialogue becomes of central importance when we compare this 1918 cycle with the long poem *Sten'ka Razin* and with the revised *Stepan Razin* novel, both published in 1928. What immediately strikes the reader is that the story has been provided with a completely new ideological underpinning, dictated presumably by a revisionist historical view. The Razin who was a harbinger of revolution was a poet, an anarchic, uncontrollable figure, on the side of the people (*narod*), of course, but without a political agenda. The new "Soviet" Razin, on the other hand, comes out from the very beginning with denunciations of "merchants, princes, and boyars."[55] Razin's banditry is no longer seen merely as energetic anarchism, but as a sign of his class consciousness.[56] In verse, the loose nonnarrative structure of the poem cycle, a form that appropriately echoed Stepan's character, has been replaced by the tighter narrative of the long poem. In prose, the lyric effusions that characterized the 1916 novel have been toned down and a more or less traditional historical narrator has been introduced. In both cases, the story starts with Stepan's "Bolshevik" revolt and ends with his execution. Razin's life has been turned into an object lesson in pre-Soviet history.

In twelve years Kamensky transformed himself from Futurist bad boy to Soviet writer, and we can see the progress of that transformation in the tortuous revisions of his Razin. Thus, the evolution of Kamensky's work shows us, in microcosm, the passing of an epoch in the use of history in Russian literature, and illustrates one of the most problematic aspects of early Soviet historiography. Immediately before and just after the 1917 Revolution, many competing ideas about the direction of Russian historical development were in competition. Universalist utopian conceptions like Khlebnikov's (which could have been identified with, although they were not directly related to, Trotsky's picture of "permanent" revolution) and anarcho-peasant views like Kamensky's (which had their political equivalent in the platform of the anarchists and some of the left SRs) could be found cheek by jowl with more orthodox Marxist positions.

By the mid-1920's, however, after a decade of almost constant turmoil, the new U.S.S.R. entered a period of consolidation. In the political arena, this was signaled by the gradual triumph of Stalin's vision of building socialism in one country. The state began to make more and more insistent claims to possess absolute knowledge of the direction of Russia's future development, and this made the production of millenarian predictions of Russia's future based on the course of its history increasingly problematic. Khlebnikov had announced the need "to read the signs inscribed on the pages of the past in order to free ourselves from the fatal line between the past and the future,"[57] but for most of Russia's leading writers the future had become less interesting by the mid-1920's. The prophetic line in Russian literary treatments of history, initiated by Dostoevsky and continued by the Futurists, came to an end, at least for the moment.

At the same time, the burst of experimental cultural energy in the first quarter of the twentieth century, which had produced what seemed a sharp break with nineteenth-century literary traditions, began to wane. More traditional prose genres (the short story and the novel, in particular) made a comeback after having been eclipsed by poetry, drama, and experimental hybrids. In the theater, Anatoly Lunacharsky proclaimed a return to Ostrovsky, and although modernist productions by no means disappeared, the most radical period of theatrical experimentation had ended by 1925. It was in this climate that the work of the next major Russian writer to take up the intergeneric tradition appeared. Like Tolstoy, Iury Tynianov was fascinated by the challenge of discovering what had really happened in the past, and he saw historical knowledge not as a means to predict the future but as a way to understand the present.

≈✿≋

Chapter Eight

Literary History, Criticism, and Fiction:
The Case of Tynianov

I have no religious awe toward the document in
general. . . . I begin where the document leaves off.
Iury Tynianov [1]

In the West, Iury Tynianov is known primarily to a scholarly audience as a literary theorist and literary historian, one of the most influential of the so-called Formalist critics. In Russia, by contrast, he is known to a much broader public as a fiction writer, the author of a series of biographical and historical novels and stories. Various reasons could be cited for this divergence of reception, but from my point of view, the divergence is far less significant than is the fact that the bulk of Tynianov's work, scholarly and fictional, concentrates on a single period of Russian history—roughly the first third of the nineteenth century. As has been the case throughout this book, I am interested in the intergeneric dialogue that results from a simultaneous reading of works by a single author on the same theme in radically different genres. In particular, I will attempt to define Tynianov's reasons for combining the writing of "scientific" scholarship with the writing of belles lettres, and I will try to show that some of the reasons for Tynianov's turn toward this tradition grew out of his theoretical concerns.

Even before beginning a discussion of the dialogic relationship between Tynianov's criticism and his fiction, we must deal with one argument that, were it true, would threaten to vitiate the project at the outset: that Tynianov turned to writing fiction because of the impossibility of writing literary criticism in the Marxist-dominated Soviet Union of the late 1920's and beyond. This argument rests on a belief in a simple cause and effect relationship between the vicious criticism launched at the Formalist school by "Marxist/Leninists" starting in about 1926 and the disintegration of the school by 1930. As Victor Erlich puts it: "The extinction of the Formalist school did not result in the disappearance from the literary scene of its chief spokesmen. However, the latter were apparently compelled to forgo literary theorizing, from now on an exclusive domain of 'Marxism-Leninism,' and turn toward safer modes of expression. Thus Tynianov virtually relinquished literary scholarship to devote himself to historical fiction—a genre at which he had first tried his hand in the mid-twenties."[2] In this view, there was no dialogue between criticism and fiction. Fiction was instead merely a substitute (presumably a poor one), and there would therefore be no reason to expect anything other than an accidental relationship between the two.

This is not the place to dispute Erlich's opinion relating to the demise of Formalism in general (to be fair, it should be pointed out that later in his book Erlich does discuss the importance of internal development and crisis for the dissolution of the school[3]), but he certainly exaggerates the chronological split between Tynianov's scholarship and fiction, and he seems to underestimate the quality of the latter. Tynianov's first historical novella, *Kiukhlia*, was not at all the trifle Erlich's "tried his hand" might lead one to believe. Rather, this fictionalized biography of the poet Vil'gel'm Kiukhel'beker is as successful and original a biographical novel as one is likely to find. Furthermore, it was written well before outside pressure could have forced Tynianov away from literary theorizing. The same can be said for his novel based on the life of Griboedov, *The Death of Vazir-Mukhtar* (*Smert' Vazir-Mukhtara*), which began to appear in 1927, the same year in which Tynianov wrote his celebrated theoretical article, "On Literary Evolution" ("O literaturnoi evoliutsii"). And even after 1930, when he wrote mostly fiction, Tynianov still remained active as a critic, publishing his famous article on Pushkin's *Journey to Arzrum* (*Puteshestvie v Arzrum*) in 1936 and his scholarly edition of and essay on Kiukhel'beker as late as 1939. Indeed, just the fact that he produced his most significant scholarly work on Kiukhel'beker after he had written *Kiukhlia*, while with Pushkin it was the other way around, must complicate any picture of the relationship between criticism and fiction in Tynianov's oeuvre. Thus, as opposed to those who view Tynianov's fiction as a poor cousin of his scholarship, I believe we must see him as working consciously within a very definite Russian tradition, which held that neither fiction nor nonfiction alone was sufficient for a full representation of crucial moments in the nation's past, but rather that a full picture could only come from the dialogic interaction of fictional and nonfictional forms.

It may, of course, seem strange to focus on a writer whose concerns were entirely with literary, rather than with political or military, history. It is important to keep in mind, however, that our concern here is far less with the content of the works in question than with the tendency of Russian writers to suspect that neither fiction nor history alone is adequate to narrate the past. For the modernist writer (and Tynianov was a modernist in many respects), the portrait of the artist himself frequently takes center stage. It is perhaps not surprising, then, that his historiographical position was elaborated through a consideration of literary material—for him, history collapses almost entirely into cultural history, and fiction becomes not a version of the traditional historical novel, but rather the biographical novel devoted to cultural figures. It would be wrong, therefore, to think that this exclusive concern with the literary process means Tynianov was interested "merely" in cultural history. As we will see, his novels and articles are undergirded by a general theory of historical development that he worked out in his theoretical essays of the 1920's. I do not think it difficult to see how the intergeneric dialogue between Tynianov's literary history and his fiction can be translated into terms that the writers whom we have discussed already might have recognized. What does make his case both tricky and unusual, however, is that Tynianov, a spectacularly well educated literary and cultural critic, was aware of the operative traditions, and this awareness allowed him to exploit them in ways different from those chosen by his predecessors.

Tynianov's 1928 article on Khlebnikov, which appeared in the famous collection *Archaists and Innovators* (*Arkhaisty i novatory*, 1929), is as close as he ever came in print to commenting directly on the relationship between artistic and scientific work.[4] Praising Khlebnikov's mathematical experiments, Tynianov notes, "The chasm separating the methods of science and art is really not very wide. It's only that what is sufficient in and of itself for science provides art with its reservoir of energy. Khlebnikov was able to produce a revolution in literature because his mind-set was not simply literary. He created from the language of verse and the language of numbers, accidental street conversations and world-historical events, because for him the methods of literary revolution and historical revolutions were similar."[5] In understanding this passage it should be recalled that in Russian the word *nauka* (science) is used more broadly than in English and could be construed to cover both Khlebnikov's mathematical experiments and the Formalist study of literature. It is also worthwhile to note here Tynianov's explicit endorsement of a view in which literary and political history are, for all intents and purposes, methodologically equivalent.

Although Tynianov never directly said so in print, there is abundant reliable evidence that for him, literary history and fiction filled separate but complementary slots. Kornei Chukovsky, in his memoir devoted to Tynianov, notes that even before he began to write fiction, the critic was known for his oral ability to re-create historical figures (usually writers) in all their vividness. Indeed, Chukovsky claims that before Tynianov began writing fiction, the relationship between the artistic and scholarly sides of his personality was almost like that between Dr. Jekyll and Mr. Hyde: "For some incomprehensible reason, Tynianov the scholar disliked Tynianov the artist and

kept him hidden away for private use. He gave him his freedom only in merry company, on holidays, when he wanted a
break from serious work."[6] As an illustration, Chukovsky goes
on to relate that in 1924, he heard Tynianov give a lecture on
Kiukhel'beker's style, a lecture that was poorly received by a
tired audience. But on the way home, says Chukovsky, "Iury
Nikolaevich spoke with such artistry, told me about the tragic
life of the poet with such an abundance of picturesque detail,
and so vividly depicted his relationships with Pushkin, Ryleev,
Griboedov, and Pushchin that I cried out, rather naively and,
I admit, tactlessly, 'Why didn't you say all this about Kiukhlia
there in the club, to the audience?'"[7] A year later, Chukovsky, as a member of an editorial board, commissioned a short
biographical novel about Kiukhel'beker from Tynianov. And
while Chukovsky claims that Tynianov accepted solely because
of his dire financial condition, the fact that the novel ultimately
produced was three times the length of the one commissioned
leads one to believe that whatever his initial doubts, Tynianov
came to find the potentials inherent in fiction writing congenial.
Indeed, if Chukovsky's initial impression of a split between the
scholarly and artistic sides of the young Tynianov's personality
was accurate, it may be that fiction writing ultimately proved
personally therapeutic, allowing for the possibility of internal
as well as intergeneric dialogue. Whatever the case, from this
point on, the writing of fiction and literary history proceeded in
tandem for Tynianov.

It has already been noted that Tynianov's major concern both
in his fiction and in his literary/historical work was the first
third of the nineteenth century, a time that has frequently, if
a bit inaccurately, been called the "Pushkin period." As with
Khlebnikov's attraction to the deepest recesses of the Slavic
past, which as we have seen was connected to a general interest in primitivism in the first decade of the twentieth century,
Tynianov's turn to the "Pushkin period" reflected not an idio-
syncratic preference, but rather a general Russian cultural fascination of the 1910's and 1920's. Although primitivism and

Pushkinism did overlap temporally to a certain extent, there was a clear refocusing of historical concern among Russian writers through the 1910's, and by the 1920's primitivism had mostly disappeared. Instead, as Boris Gasparov has said, for the Russian modernists

Pushkin and his age occupy a central place in the ramified system of cultural myths created by the Modernist era. The Modernist self-consciousness—indeed, all of the era's creative activity—was marked by Pushkin's mythological presence and by a general fascination with a "Pushkin essence" as manifested in the poet's imagery, poetics and symbolically interpreted biography. "The Pushkin myth" served as a constant symbolic background against which the age of Modernism saw itself, tested its ideas and aspirations, and recognized and comprehended its ideal transcendent essence and destiny.[8]

Despite his academic career and scholarly reputation, Tynianov was no exception to the general rule formulated by Gasparov. Indeed, as Monika Frenkel Greenleaf has noted, in Tynianov's explication, "repeatedly, Pushkin's poetic practice reveals structural principles homologous with Tynianov's theoretical discoveries of 1924–1927"; and furthermore, "his [Tynianov's] portrait of the late Pushkin bears a curious resemblance to himself: the writer with an antipathy to literature, who retreats to a position of selecting and splicing, editing and recombining documents."[9]

At least once in his fiction as well, in the following depiction from *Kiukhlia* of St. Petersburg during the Decembrist uprising, Tynianov overtly emphasizes the parallels between his own period and the first decades of the nineteenth century. In this passage, the rivers and squares of the city take on allegorical significance in the wider revolutionary paradigm.

The unit of Petersburg is the square. The river flows through it separately, like an independent aquatic prospect. Today, just like one hundred years ago, the inhabitants of Petersburg know no other rivers besides the Neva, although the Neva's tributaries are also in Petersburg. The tributaries go by the name Neva, too. The river's independence rouses it at least once in a century to rebellion. The revolutions in Petersburg took place on the squares; that of December 1825 and that of February 1917 occurred on different squares. And both in December 1825 and in October 1917 the Neva took part in the rebellions: in December the rebels ran across the ice, and in October the battleship Aurora threatened the palace from the Neva.[10]

To a Russian reader this section does far more than point out overt historical parallels. The reference to the hundred-year time gap and to the rebellious Neva is an unmistakable allusion to Pushkin's long poem *The Bronze Horseman*. That poem, which begins with a prologue describing the founding of St. Petersburg in 1703, introduces the "modern" city with a reference to the time that has passed since then—"One hundred years have passed"—and goes on to describe events constructed around a literal rebellion of the Neva, the great flood of 1824. Thus, in this passage Tynianov not only marks an overt parallel between his age and the first decades of the nineteenth century, he also draws a parallel between himself and Pushkin as writers describing "rebellions" in Petersburg in literary form.[11]

Before continuing to explore the ways in which Tynianov's belief in the connection of his own age to that of Pushkin is expressed in his literary/historical and fictional writings, we must first pause to examine the theoretical underpinnings of the historiographical model that motivated this perceived connection. For as opposed to most other Russian modernist writers, who accepted the mythological connection of the two ages without elaborating a theory to explain them, Tynianov the Formalist attempted to construct a "scientific" theory of literary/historical evolution to account for the parallels. That is, it appears that Tynianov's theory of literary evolution served to justify a preexisting cultural/mythological paradigm.

Among the central principles shared by the early Formalists was the idea that the role of art was to renew perception: to struggle against automatization. As first formulated in the early articles of Viktor Shklovsky: "It is this inexorable pull of routine, of habit, that the artist is called upon to counteract. By tearing the object out of its habitual context, by bringing together disparate notions, the poet gives a *coup de grace* to the verbal cliché and to the stock responses attendant upon it and forces us into heightened awareness of things and their sensory texture. The act of creative deformation restores sharpness to our perception." [12]

The implications of such a view of artistic creativity for literary history were elaborated by Tynianov in a series of articles, including "The Literary Fact" ("Literaturnyi fakt"), "Dostoevsky and Gogol: Toward a Theory of Parody" ("Dostoevsky i Gogol: k teorii parodii"), and "On Literary Evolution," all of which appeared in *Archaists and Innovators*. First and foremost, Tynianov recognized that the Formalist canonization of struggle with the automatized past is fundamentally opposed to the basic assumptions of most nineteenth-century historiography (both literary and general). Where his predecessors had seen measured, gradual, and progressive development, Tynianov and the other Formalists found constant conflict. As he notes in "The Literary Fact":

In constructing a "solid" "ontological" definition of literature as "essence," literary historians had to understand historical shifts as peaceful successions, the peaceful and smooth unfolding of this "essence." . . . What escaped attention was that each new phenomenon displaced an old one, and that each such displacement was a complicated process; we can only speak about succession within a school or through epigonism, but not when discussing literary evolution, whose central principle is struggle and displacement. [13]

Literary history, therefore, is seen as a series of cataclysmic changes, as one school or writer struggles to overcome the ossified legacy of his predecessors. "Every literary sucession is first of all a struggle; the destruction of an old whole and a new construction from old elements." [14] It is not surprising, perhaps, that such a theory should have occurred to men barely out of their twenties, whose formative years were spent in Russia from 1905 through the Revolution. To a certain extent, in its canonization of violent struggle and in its basically dialectic structure

Formalist historiographical theory resembles that of Marxism/ Leninism. But these similarities are quite superficial. Most important, as opposed to their Marxist contemporaries, the Formalists do not perceive a telos, an ultimate goal, toward which the literary system is heading. Consequently, the question of progress becomes moot for them. In addition, they reject the claim that economic factors are of prime importance for historical development (except, presumably for economic history, which is not their central concern), claiming instead that internal factors are of paramount importance for understanding the evolution of any system.

At first glance this theory of "permanent revolution" might be expected to imply unidirectional motion and to exclude cyclical tendencies, but this is not the case. According to Jurij Striedter, all of the Formalists, Tynianov included, agreed with the following formula put forth by Viktor Shklovsky: "Every new school of literature is a kind of revolution, something like the appearance of a new class. But of course, this is only an analogy. The conquered line is not destroyed; it does not cease to exist. It is simply driven from the crest and dives under; it can reemerge at any time, for it remains a pretender to the crown." [15] Unlike in biological evolution, therefore, displacement from a niche does not lead to extinction. The conquered generation's "genes" remain a potential source for later inspiration, and indeed, as Tynianov puts it, in the struggle against their literary fathers, sons often turn out to look a lot like their grandfathers.[16] Of course, they do not simply borrow directly from these ancestors, for much new material is introduced into the world and into the literary system in the course of two generations. But they are similar enough to make the resulting view of history more or less spiral. And now we can begin to see how Tynianov's "scientific" theory of literary evolution provides a mechanism to support what for other writers of his generation had been a merely instinctual connection to the first decades of the nineteenth century. In some respects (and we will examine Tynianov's views on this subject more closely a bit later) it seems that the writers of the early twentieth century are the grandsons of the writers of the Pushkin period.

Tynianov's choice of the fathers and sons metaphor is one more invitation to extend his approach from a theory of literary history to a general historical theory. After all, Turgenev's *Fathers and Sons* (*Otsy i deti*) describes, in fictional form to be sure, a case of generational conflict that became legendary in Russia—the clash of the so-called men of the forties with the men of the sixties. Indeed, it would not be an exaggeration to say that Russians came to recognize and understand the nature of their historical development through the text of Turgenev's novel. In choosing generational conflict as the engine of change, Tynianov is linking his literary history with a preexisting and strongly held Russian view of social/historical change. And the fact that generational conflict as a mechanism for social change in Russia was first articulated in novels (in Turgenev's and in Dostoevsky's *The Devils*) only makes the potential analogy between literary history and all other kinds of history stronger. As a result, even though Tynianov chose literary history as his topic while the other writers we have treated in this book chose social and political topics, his attempt to understand the past was no less global. He instinctively seems to have understood what was articulated only in the 1960's by Iury Lotman and his followers—for most educated Russians, life and literature were inseparable, and therefore to discuss literary history *was* to discuss history in general.

Before turning to the specifics of Tynianov's intergeneric approach to history, it remains to discuss the relationship between his more or less cyclical vision of history and those others that were circulating at about the same time. The most obvious candidate for comparison with Tynianov is Oswald Spengler, whose *Decline of the West* appeared in German in 1918. By 1922, this book was already a subject of serious debate in the Soviet Union.[17] Certain aspects of Spengler's "morphological" system do seem analogous to Tynianov's ideas. There is first of all the idea that cultures do not simply succeed each other in a progressive fashion. Instead, successive cultures are incompatible and young cultures must struggle with their predecessors until they manage to displace the older rival. At the same time, because in Spengler's view all cultures must pass through the same stages, different cultures at analogous stages exhibit similarities. Thus, like Tynianov's system, Spengler's contains both conflict and repetition.

But the differences between the two systems are far more crucial than their similarities. As opposed to Spengler's cultures which must inevitably pass through certain stages from birth to death, Tynianov's cultural spirals could, theoretically, continue indefinitely. More important, while for Spengler cyclicity is intercultural (i.e., each culture passes through the same succession of stages, but movement within a culture is teleological), for Tynianov the cycles are intracultural, with returns (returns with a difference, of course) occurring potentially every other generation. Finally, Spengler's theory lacks any kind of internal motivation. He sees cultures as biological constructs but cannot say why this should necessarily be the case. He simply deduces a theory from observed patterns, with no concern for the mechanisms of the system's development. Tynianov, on the other hand, is not really concerned with large-scale patterns. True, cycles can emerge within his system, but they do not have to. Sons sometimes choose to emulate grandfathers, but nothing requires that they do so. The only ironclad law is generational conflict, but the system itself is not analogous to the biological life cycle (i.e., it does not have a childhood, maturity, old age, etc.). In the end, one can say that Tynianov's and Spengler's historiographies share a common dissatisfaction with standard nineteenth-century historicist views, but any similarities are more or less accidental.

Of course, Tynianov would not have had to look as far afield as Germany to find cyclical versions of history. As I noted above, he was an admirer of Khlebnikov, whose cyclical historical theories were discussed in the previous chapter. He would also have been familiar with Dmitry Merezhkovsky's version

of eternal return as expressed in the famous trilogy of historical novels *Julian the Apostate (Iulian otstupnik*, 1896), *Leonardo
da Vinci* (1901), and *Peter and Aleksei* (1905). But once again,
what sets Tynianov apart from his Russian predecessors are his
theoretical strivings to understand the mechanisms underlying
historical cycles, rather than merely to assert their existence.

Ultimately, to understand why Tynianov wrote the kind of
literary criticism and the kind of fiction he did, we must examine for a moment the work of his literary fathers as he might
have perceived it. For if the revolt of sons against fathers canonized by the Formalists reflects any literary/historical reality,
it must presumably also apply to their own productions vis-
à-vis those of their immediate predecessors. In the case of
Tynianov, the father figure in literary criticism was S. A.
Vengerov, in whose seminar at St. Petersburg (and then Petro-
grad) University the young scholar apprenticed from about 1913
to 1918. Vengerov was, notwithstanding Viktor Shklovsky's un-
kind memories, an extremely erudite Pushkinist, from whom
Tynianov learned a great deal.[18] At the same time, there were
a number of areas in which Tynianov's ideas about Pushkin
clashed significantly with those of his mentor. In particular,
one notices in Vengerov's work an almost hagiographical tone
toward Pushkin, the evident conviction that the poet's greatness lay entirely in his personal genius, and a belief that the
job of the critic was to emphasize Pushkin's unique status and
radical separation from his and all other ages. This mind-set was
accompanied by a positivist's love of facts and the confidence
that an accumulation of sufficient factual material would lead
to an understanding of the poet without any need for abstract
theorizing.

Unfortunately, we do not have the thesis-length article on
Pushkin and Kiukhel'beker that Tynianov produced as the cul-
mination of his work for Vengerov.[19] Nevertheless, the subject
matter and the consistency with which Tynianov developed this
theme in the course of his life (it is touched upon in *Kiukhlia*,
1925, treated extensively in "Pushkin and Kiukhel'beker,"

1934, and returned to in the essay that introduces the 1939 edition of Kiukhel'beker's works) allow us to reconstruct the main outlines of Tynianov's revolt against his literary/historical father.

The most immediate manifestation of this revolt is in the young scholar's choice of a theme. Evidently Tynianov's first serious work in Vengerov's seminar had been on Alexander Griboedov, from whom he turned to the then almost completely unknown Kiukhel'beker. It was known, of course, that Kiukhel'beker had been a close friend of Pushkin's and that Griboedov had crossed Pushkin's path, but neither belonged to Pushkin's immediate "pleiad." For Vengerov and other scholars of his generation, neither Kiukhel'beker (whose artistic work had been almost entirely forgotten) nor Griboedov (who was respected only for his play *Woe from Wit* [*Gore ot uma*]) was worthy of undivided scholarly attention. From Tynianov's perspective, however, it was precisely their marginality for previous criticism that made them attractive.

Indeed, in producing his work on Kiukhel'beker, Tynianov was probably not all that unlike the Dostoevsky he was soon to describe in his first published article, "Dostoevsky and Gogol: Toward a Theory of Parody" (1921). Like the young Dostoevsky, Tynianov borrowed a great deal from his master; in this case, Tynianov shared Vengerov's impressive command of the facts of literary life in the first decades of the nineteenth century and of the literature on Pushkin. But also like Dostoevsky, Tynianov borrowed, not to imitate, but to overcome.[20] Gone forever (from Tynianov's work anyway) was the pedestal Pushkin—he became just one poet in a milieu. By foregrounding the seemingly clumsy and unsuccessful verses of Pushkin's school chum, and by showing that certain central features of Pushkin's work developed out of their interaction, Tynianov disrupted the canonized unproblematic genealogy of Pushkin's development (from Karamzin, the "Arzamas" society, etc.). And finally, Tynianov chipped away at the teleological view that had held sway in Russian culture: that Pushkin and his poetry had triumphed and that all development had to proceed from that triumph. By treating one of the younger archaists (although he probably did not call them that yet) and his program seriously, Tynianov resuscitated noncanonized literary groupings as a source of inspiration for Russian poetry. That this theoretical insight coincided with a turn in contemporary Russian poetry (in the work of Maiakovsky in particular) toward the more "oratorical" poets of the eighteenth and early nineteenth centuries was probably not accidental.

In effect then, Tynianov produced a deadly serious parody (as he would later call it) of the Pushkin criticism of the previous generation. In article after article throughout the 1920's and 1930's, Tynianov continued his parodic critical and theoretical struggle with his fathers. Many of his articles continued to be about Pushkin, it is true, but in the majority of cases Pushkin appeared with the wrong cast of characters and without his halo, as in "Archaists and Pushkin" and "Pushkin and Tiutchev." A nonhagiographical approach dominates even the late and unfinished novel *Pushkin*.

Coupled with this somewhat irreverent attitude to the Pushkin period were the theoretical conclusions that Tynianov drew from his research. In general, abstract theorizing was anathema to scholars of Vengerov's generation, and another element of revolt can be seen in Tynianov's eagerness to engage in such activity. At the same time, Tynianov's personal revolt led him to take a position that meshed with that of many of his contemporaries. In particular, his conception of parody, developed as we suspect from the experience of Vengerov's seminar as much as from textual material, fit in nicely with Shklovsky's independently derived ideas on literature's role in deautomatizing perception, and allowed a place for Tynianov in a new generation of literary critics—the Formalists.

In the area of belles lettres, Tynianov had to struggle with a group of writers of an entirely different cast of mind from that of academics like Vengerov. His literary fathers were the Russian

Symbolists and the writers of the various schools that formed after the collapse of Symbolism, including Acmeism and Futurism. It is true, of course, that Tynianov's literary fathers were scarcely a decade older than he. But because they started writing young and their first poetry appeared almost twenty years before *Kiukhlia*, the generational gap was larger than birth dates indicate. What is more, the two generations were separated by something even more important than time—the Russian Revolution, which radically transformed the entire literary scene and formed a sharp divide between those writers who had appeared before it and those who had not.

For the previous generation the central genre was poetry, generally the short lyric. Prose, when it was written at all, tended to be ornamental and opaque, a far cry from the novels of the mid-nineteenth century, the generation of Tynianov's literary grandfathers. For Tynianov, the central father figure among poets was probably Velimir Khlebnikov. Of all the great poets of the twentieth century, Khlebnikov seems to have interested Tynianov the most.[21] In particular, as we noted earlier, Tynianov praised Khlebnikov's ability to combine art and "science." Nevertheless, the works of fiction Tynianov produced could not have been more unlike the work of his fathers. And here once again, as had been the case with Tynianov's revolt against the criticism of Vengerov's generation, his break with the literary traditions of his fathers coincided with a well-defined trend in Russian literature.

As a critic, Tynianov was highly attuned to this generational switch. He discussed it at length in the article "Interregnum" ("Promezhutok," 1924). "Three years ago prose definitively told poetry to clear out: prose writers occupied the places of poets, who retreated somewhat panic-stricken."[22] Even more to the point, Tynianov recognized just what sort of prose writing was coming to the fore in 1924: "Not long ago, readers began to skip poetry and prose. This kind of reader is still timid, still not willing to admit that he does so; nevertheless, this is just about the most interesting type—he goes straight to chronicles, reviews, polemics, to those journalistic back pages from which a new kind of journal is emerging." [23]

And it was precisely in the context of this current of writing, the so-called literature of fact, that Tynianov's biographical novels can be situated. Indeed, Tynianov can be said to have been one of the initiators of this trend, both through his theoretical articles (including "The Literary Fact," 1924) and his novels. [24] Because of Tynianov's interests and knowledge, his literature of fact did not deal with contemporary life, of course. Instead, his novels and stories are set in the same period toward which his scholarly attention was directed: the age of Pushkin. Still, as has been noted, Tynianov considered his own age and that of Pushkin to be functionally similar, so the time difference may have seemed irrelevant to him.

It remains finally to explore the dialogic relationship between Tynianov's critical articles and his novels. Why did he feel the need to produce both? How does reading them in tandem give his audience a truer picture of historical reality than either "scientific" criticism or fiction alone can provide? As an example of how Tynianov exploited the different possibilities of criticism and fiction, let us examine his presentation of one characteristic moment from the life of Kiukhel'beker.

In 1820, immediately after Pushkin's exile to the south, Kiukhel'beker read aloud and then published a poem entitled "Poets," which included obvious reference to his friend's ill-treatment at the hands of the authorities. [25] Realizing that nothing good could come of this, Kiukhel'beker decided to leave the capital. By chance, an opportunity to do so presented itself in the form of employment as private secretary to A. L. Naryshkin, a well-placed Russian nobleman who was about to go abroad. Kiukhel'beker left Russia with Naryshkin in September 1820, returning only in August 1821. The two traveled through Germany and southern France, and then stopped in Paris, where they spent most of 1821. While there, Kiukhel'beker presented a series of lectures on Russian literature, the political content of which was evidently radical enough to anger Naryshkin and cause him to dismiss his wayward employee.

Like any historian, literary or otherwise, Tynianov attempts to squeeze as much as possible from the few facts he has about Kiukhel'beker's adventures in Paris. Nevertheless, there are clear lines beyond which he is not willing to go. In the article "Kiukhel'beker's French Connections" ("Frantsuzskie otnosheniia Kiukhel'bekera"), Tynianov ends his discussion of the trip to Europe with the following cryptic but enticing remarks: "In addition, there is one fact pertaining to Kiukhel'beker's journey that has still not been explained."[26] It turns out, Tynianov goes on to say, that there were rumors circulating that Kiukhel'beker did not intend to return to Russia, but would instead go to Greece to fight in the War of Independence against the Turks. As circumstantial evidence to support the truth of these rumors, Tynianov mentions a classmate of Kiukhel'beker's, Sil'ver Broglio, who died fighting on the Greek side in 1821.

In his "Introduction" to the two-volume set of Kiukhel'beker's works, Tynianov presents a similar version of events, based again on little historical information and carefully qualified: "There is good reason to suppose that after this [his dismissal], Kiukhel'beker intended to go to Greece to fight for her independence (Sil'ver Broglio, one of his comrades from the Lycée, became a philhellene while abroad and died in battle). At the very least, Alexander I, who was well informed by his secret agents, knew about this intention."[27] Clearly then, this event in Kiukhel'beker's biography was important for Tynianov's understanding of him, presumably because it would be the first indication of Kiukhel'beker's willingness to take part, actively and physically, in a revolutionary movement, and would thus serve as the first link in a chain leading Kiukhel'beker to the Senate Square on December 14, 1825. But to Tynianov the historian, the paucity of facts available must have been extremely frustrating. His careful literary/historical researches opened up intriguing possibilities and gaps that those same researches were unable to fill. This was particularly true because his literary criticism, both in the Formalist period and later, lacked a psychological component. Tynianov never really broke with his mentor Vengerov in this respect—explanations had to proceed from hard facts. The novel, in contrast, must have seemed quite liberating. The gaps could be filled in by conjecture, and psychology was an accepted, almost required component. Here Tynianov could indeed begin where the documents left off.

When we turn to the novel *Kiukhlia*, written some fifteen years before Tynianov's scholarly articles on Kiukhel'beker (although it is possible that the question of Kiukhel'beker's role in the Greek uprising was treated in the earlier lost scholarly work), we see how Tynianov used his sparse factual material and his imagination to create a full-fledged portrait. Tynianov devotes a three-page section of the chapter about the European journey to a meeting of Kiukhel'beker and his classmate Broglio. Here, Broglio (who, as far as Tynianov's facts told him, was somewhere in Europe at the time, but not necessarily in Paris) tells Kiukhel'beker about the revolutionary ferment and encourages him to go to Greece. And in the novel, after Naryshkin fires him, Kiukhel'beker does indeed set off for Greece. Tynianov pays close attention to the details of his journey south, mentioning in particular the police agent shadowing his hero (the source for Alexander I's eventual knowledge, one presumes). But Tynianov does much more with this little story than flesh out the facts available to him: in the continuation, he provides another potential plan of interpretation by inventing an entirely imagined scene that is, in fact, an intertextual reference to a famous and potentially relevant nineteenth-century work.

Tynianov describes Kiukhel'beker's voyage in a gondola from Villefranche to Nice. Initially, the gondolier fears a storm and does not want to take him but, after a nod from the police spy, he agrees. They start off, but when they are part way there the gondolier suddenly attempts to kill his passenger.

Kiukhel'beker overpowers him, though, and manages to get back to shore. Later, he realizes that he was also robbed by his assailant.

At first glance, it is not entirely clear what this little story is doing here; it certainly lacks any basis in facts that were available to Tynianov. After thinking for a moment, however, one realizes that this incident has obvious structural parallels with the story "Taman" in Lermontov's *Hero of Our Time*. There, the first-person narrator writes of being stuck in a small seaside town. He gets involved with a mysterious group of people and one night ends up at sea in a rowboat, where he is attacked and almost drowned. The story ends when he realizes that although he saved his own life, he was robbed of his valuables.

There are several reasons Tynianov might have invoked this familiar story. A cynical reader might say that he could not help it: as a literary critic his head was filled with other people's narratives, and when it came time to write his own he was unable to avoid reusing someone else's plot.[28] More constructive criticism, however, might note that in using a plot his readers would recognize, Tynianov reminds readers of the fictional nature of a narrative that otherwise threatens to be confused with reportage or, worse yet, literary criticism. As Chukovsky pointed out, Tynianov was at pains to keep these identities separate, and obvious fictionality may have helped.

There may, however, be a deeper intertextual purpose to the appeal to Lermontov's novel, which may help interpret the character of Tynianov's hero. Lermontov, it will be remembered, keeps an ironic distance from his "hero," Pechorin. Kiukhel'beker, despite his quixotic traits, really does seem to have been a hero in Tynianov's eyes, and because of precisely those qualities most lacking in Pechorin: unselfishness, loyalty to friends or an ideal, and constancy.[29] Thus, in recollecting Lermontov's story, Tynianov may well have wanted to set his real hero of the early nineteenth century against a more famous but ironic one. Kiukhel'beker is a hero of his time, and, given the implicit connection between the 1820's and the 1920's (emphasized, it will be recalled, in the passage from the novel quoted earlier), a hero of Tynianov's time as well.

Be this as it may, the contrast between Tynianov's presentations of this minor incident from the life of Kiukhel'beker indicates the ways in which he managed to reconcile the Aristotelian historian with the poet. For those readers inclined to believe that the "poetic" version seems to have all the advantages and none of the disadvantages of the historical, do not forget that Tynianov felt the need to write history after he had already provided the fictional account. He clearly wanted interested readers to know what he had constructed his fiction from, just as much as he wanted the freedom to construct. This need to move back and forth from fiction to history and to fiction again, and to allow the reader to appreciate the relative merits of the two approaches, is, of course, a standard tactic among Russian authors. In connecting Tynianov with a tradition that stretches back into the eighteenth century, I can only hope that my analysis explicates the intuition of Tynianov's brother-in-law and closest friend Veniamin Kaverin, who insisted: "It is high time to put out a collection of his work that would unite his artistic prose with his scholarly work and diaries, because everything he created is intimately connected." [30]

Although Tynianov continued to write both biographical fiction and literary history in the 1930's, his brand of intergeneric dialogue belongs, for all intents and purposes, to the 1920's. And if for writers of the 1920's it was possible to escape worrying about the future by exploring the past, by the mid-1930's even the past was dangerous. If in the 1920's the state claimed to know only the path of Russia's future development, Stalinist culture asserted its infallible understanding of all past epochs as well. It could do so because, as the passage by Boris Groys cited in the Introduction explains: "Stalinist culture looks upon itself as postapocalyptic culture—the final verdict on all human culture has already been passed, and all that was once temporally distinct has become forever simultaneous in the blinding light of the Final Judgment and the ultimate truth revealed in Stalin's *Short Course* of party history. . . . Socialist realism, which regards historical time as ended and therefore occupies no particular place in it, looks upon history as the arena of struggle between active, demiurgic, creative, progressive art aspiring to build a new world in the interests of the oppressed classes and passive, contemplative art that does not believe in or desire change but accepts things as they are or dreams of the past."[31] There is obviously no room in this system for intergeneric or any other kind of dialogue on historical themes. God and the angels, in the person of Stalin and his cultural lieutenants, have spoken, and it is up to the writer to find the one proper way to treat his material. Dialogue implies at least two perspectives, one of which is invariably incorrect—and incorrect thinking was frequently a capital offense.

Thus, it is not surprising that the period of Stalinism marked an interregnum of sorts in the Russian tradition of intergeneric dialogue. Even in the darkest period of the Stalinist night, however, there were writers who continued to believe that it was their right and duty to interpret the nation's past. They published nothing on Russian history, however, preferring to wait for more propitious times, preserving the tradition in silence. And one might have thought that after the death of Stalin the tradition of intergeneric dialogue on historical themes could have been revived. When the first serious literary attempt to reinterpret Russia's relatively recent past appeared, however, it turned out that despite de-Stalinization, the Soviet Union was still very much a monologic state. The scandal surrounding even the relatively limited probing of *Doctor Zhivago*, a novel that treats the Revolutionary period both in narrative prose and lyrical poetry, indicated that Russia was not yet ready for a dialogue with her own past. As it turned out, a full-scale intergeneric treatment of twentieth-century Russian history could only be produced in emigration, by a Russian writer who very openly views himself as the heir to many of the central Russian literary traditions of the nineteenth century.

Chapter Nine

꙳ၵ⊛ၵ꙳

Back to the Chronicles:
Solzhenitsyn's *The Red Wheel*

The author would not have permitted himself such a
flagrant break of the novelistic form had Russian history
itself, her whole memory not been flagrantly broken up
previously, and her historians destroyed.
Alexander Solzhenitsyn [1]

Alexander Solzhenitsyn's 6,000-page cycle *The Red Wheel* (*Krasnoe koleso*) is so dense and so difficult that it is daunting even to contemplate saying anything coherent about it as a whole. In the time between the initial publication of *August 1914* (*Avgust chetyrnadtsatogo*, 1971) and the appearance of *April 1917* (*Aprel' semnadtsatogo*, 1991), Solzhenitsyn's understanding of his project inevitably evolved, as did many of his compositional devices. Thus, while the volumes of the series look almost identical (the same publisher, graphics, typefaces, basic format, etc.), there are significant differences that must be taken into account. Moreover, the world in which the author first envisioned his cycle and the one in which he completed it could not be more different. In the afterword to *August 1914* Solzhenitsyn claims to have had his first thoughts on this project in 1937, at the height of the Stalinist purges. But the majority of the work was completed in the 1960's and 1970's in the Soviet Union and, after the author's exile in 1974, in the West. By the time Solzhenitsyn was writing the last volumes, the U.S.S.R. was on the verge of collapse. And even if a recognition of the changes that were occurring in the outside world as he wrote the final sections of his narrative did not cause him to modify his plans, the death of the state whose birth Solzhenitsyn chronicles inevitably affects our perception of *The Red Wheel*.

Despite these obstacles, there are a number of things that can and should be said about Solzhenitsyn's cycle as a whole. The most obvious is that the author is quite consciously working within the tradition that has been the focus of this book. *The Red Wheel* cycle is certainly the most grandiose attempt to capture historical truth through the intergeneric dialogue of fictional and historical writing. Each of the four "knots" (as Solzhenitsyn dubs his sections) consists both of chapters devoted to the lives of fictional characters and of chapters featuring historical figures. However, as we will see in the course of our analysis of the cycle, Solzhenitsyn's method of integrating the two differs substantially from those of his predecessors. Indeed, Solzhenitsyn's radical innovativeness vis-à-vis the Russian tradition has not been sufficiently appreciated by critics, who have generally seen him either as nothing more than a twentieth-century Tolstoy imitator or as an anomalous and unique phenomenon.

What the critics have failed to recognize is that despite relatively frequent references to Tolstoy in *August 1914* (the first of the knots and the only one to have been translated in its entirety into English thus far), Solzhenitsyn's work is not all that close to Tolstoy's. For as we have seen, the uniqueness of Tolstoy's achievement in *War and Peace* does not lie in the mere compositional device of combining the writing of history and fiction. This is the normal mode in Russian culture, and in this regard Solzhenitsyn is no more like Tolstoy than he is like Karamzin or Pushkin or Khlebnikov, and he is certainly no anomaly. Like all of his illustrious predecessors, Solzhenitsyn believes that it is the duty of a Russian writer to tell the truth about the key moments of the nation's past. And to express that truth, neither fiction nor history alone is sufficient. Each major writer who inscribes himself into this tradition must rethink the relationship of fiction and history, as well as of past and present. That rethinking is what justifies the production of such works and, from the scholar's point of view, it is what makes their analysis worthwhile. Of course, there is no doubt that the anxiety of Tolstoy's influence is palpable in *The Red Wheel*, and Solzhenitsyn's attempts to escape this influence will be discussed. But because I expect that by this time my readers are attuned to the basic cultural paradigm, my analysis of *The Red Wheel* cycle will concentrate on the innovations Solzhenitsyn brings to the tradition, rather than on elements of continuity.

From the very beginning, *The Red Wheel* is provided with a confusing panoply of generic and descriptive terms. One suspects that this confusion is deliberate, an attempt to classify the work while avoiding generic tags too closely linked to defined genres, fictional or historical. The title page of the first volume of *August 1914* reads "*The Red Wheel*. A Narrative in Measured Periods. Knot I, August 1914." In Russian, narrative (*povestvovanie*) is not a traditional generic marker. What is more, the noun usually requires a qualifier—historical, fictional, first-person, and so on. Its use here signals first and foremost an absence—in this respect it reminds us of Tolstoy's negative characterization of *War and Peace*: "Not a novel, still less a poem, still less an historical chronicle."[2]

The "measured periods" and "knots" are also mysterious at first, although they are explained in an author's afterword at the close of *August 1914*: "The principle of knots . . . [is to give a] full and thick exposition of events in condensed chunks of time, but with total breaks between them."[3] Initially, there were to have been twenty such knots, but, according to Solzhenitsyn, a number of considerations, including his age, the quantity already written, and the internal logic of the events described, made publishing more than four unwise and unnecessary.[4] Instead, as an appendix to the final completed volume, the author provides a 150-page summary of what he would have written in the remaining knots.

August 1914 is provided with one more generic tag on the second title page: "Act One: Revolution." This theatrical term is important because it implies that in Solzhenitsyn's view historical events can be understood within an overarching dramatic structure. For the second act, however, readers had to wait almost two decades and five thousand pages. *April 1917* is sub-tagged "Act Two: People's Government." The remaining acts appear only in the final summary as "Act Three: The Coup," "Act Four: We Versus Us," and "Act Five: Forging the Paths." Thus, as it turns out, the structure is that of the five-act drama-seria (a tragedy, in fact), without, of course, the formal features of a play or any dramatic tautness. Still, the theatrical terminology does provide an interpretive framework for the cycle as a whole.

The subject of Solzhenitsyn's tragedy is the history of a people that could give itself freedom by overthrowing the tsar, but that could not defend its hard-won freedom and ended up in the clutches of an even more fearsome despotism. Although Solzhenitsyn does not mention the connection, the outline of this story sounds remarkably like the chronicle story of the accession of Riurik as Ryleev or Khomiakov might have interpreted it. But I am getting ahead of myself here; a consideration of *The Red Wheel* in the light of the Russian chronicle must wait until a bit later in the chapter. For now, I simply note that even from the title page, Solzhenitsyn's cycle invokes a competing field of generic terms, each calling up expectations but none defining in any clear way the text at hand.

Of course, *The Red Wheel* was hardly Solzhenitsyn's first attempt to avoid standard generic markers or to combine the writing of history and literature. *The Gulag Archipelago*, for example, which the author subtitled "An Experiment in Artistic Investigation," can be seen as a quasi-literary narrative in dialogue with *One Day in the Life of Ivan Denisovich*, the short novel that made Solzhenitsyn a household name. The generic similarities between *Gulag* and *The Red Wheel* are not accidental, for the five-act tragedy of the years 1914–22 can be viewed as a kind of prelude to the *Gulag*. Indeed, Solzhenitsyn himself said about *The Red Wheel* cycle (although without elaborating precisely what he meant): "I am writing a kind of 'Gulag Archipelago' of 1917."[5] One might say, in fact, that the raison d'être for *The Red Wheel* is to answer the question, how did the Gulag come to be? And certainly, by the end of *April 1917* the reader has absorbed sufficient descriptions of the Bolsheviks, their tactics, and their methods to understand how the prison camp system, to which Solzhenitsyn gave up fifteen years of his life and the Soviet Union millions of its citizens, could have come into existence.

Solzhenitsyn has frequently been seen as another in the line of Russia's writer/prophets, and indeed he is in his extraliterary pronouncements. One has only to read his Harvard commencement speech or his essay "How Can We Reconstruct Russia" ("Kak nam obustroit' Rossiiu") to be convinced of this. In his artistic work, however, this aspect is muted to the point of nonexistence. Like *War and Peace*, and unlike the explicitly prophetic works of Dostoevsky and Khlebnikov, *The Red Wheel* is a narrative devoted to the exposition of a multifaceted and multivoiced historical panorama, and to an exploration of how the author and his society got to be where they were at the time of its composition. The twist is that Russian historical reality of the twentieth century, as Solzhenitsyn sees it, is not glorious but horrifying. And this horror, which commenced when Russia went off the rails, must be fully presented in order to exorcise the suffering of Solzhenitsyn and his fellow inmates, to diagnose the disease from which Russia has been suffering, and to suggest a cure.[6] Instead of looking to a past moment of harmony that can serve as a model for future development, Solzhenitsyn explicates in *The Red Wheel* the roots of disaster.

It is only natural that any Russian writer intending to produce an epic-scale narrative centered around the responses of Russians to a major war would sense the long shadow of Tolstoy. Solzhenitsyn certainly did so, especially in the early stages of his project. And as is frequently the case with major writers, his response was twofold. On the one hand, he incorporated a number of Tolstoyan features directly into his book. On the other, he included both overt and covert attacks on his great predecessor, and he introduced cardinal changes in literary technique in an attempt to escape his influence.

A quick overview of the content and structure of the first

knot will help define its similarities to *War and Peace*. The book chronicles the reactions of a variety of individual Russians and of Russian society as a whole to the events of August 1914. Some of these personages are fictional and, as in Tolstoy's epic, a number of the central characters are based directly on the families of Solzhenitsyn's mother and father.[7] Solzhenitsyn's book is more "democratic" however, in that he draws on characters not just from a single class, as did Tolstoy, but from a wide spectrum of classes and locations. Like Tolstoy, only more frequently and to a much greater extent, Solzhenitsyn freely mixes chapters devoted to historical figures (treated novelistically) with those concerning invented characters, and he imports undigested contemporary documents directly into his text. From time to time he employs an absolute "authorial" voice that is made to seem privileged and outside the narrative stream, able to interpret the general course of history. Finally, he includes two long historical digressions—biographies of Stolypin and of Nicholas II—in order to provide the reader with sufficient historical background.

At the same time, Solzhenitsyn emphasizes his differences with Tolstoy in both subtle and not so subtle ways. In this regard a scene at the very beginning of the book, in which Sania Lazhenitsyn pays a visit to the sage of Iasnaia Poliana, is of crucial importance. Lazhenitsyn, who thinks of himself as a Tolstoyan, is a fictional character based, as we have noted earlier, on Solzhenitsyn's father. His pilgrimage is an act of homage to the master, but it does nothing to deepen his convictions. Instead, the unsatisfying answers Tolstoy gives to his questions lead Sania to take the first steps toward rejecting his idol. Ultimately, Sania's decision to volunteer for the Russian army at the beginning of the war marks his final break with Tolstoyism. It is easy, in retrospect, to read Sania's initial attraction to Tolstoy's philosophy and his ultimate break with Tolstoyan teaching as indicative of Solzhenitsyn's own attitude toward his predecessor. As Lazhenitsyn is attracted to Tolstoy but ultimately rejects him, so his "son," Solzhenitsyn, while irresistibly attracted to

Tolstoy's genre of national epic, eventually comes to reject most of its main constructive principles.

Indeed, there are indications that Solzhenitsyn holds Tolstoyism (or, better, a certain view of life that accords with Tolstoyan belief) responsible for the catastrophe that he is describing in *The Red Wheel*. Later in *August 1914*, Sania and his friend Kotia explain why Sania became disillusioned with Tolstoyism. They tell the story of Tolstoy's answer to a peasant's question: "Our country, he said, is like an overturned cart, and it is very heavy and inconvenient to drag it along—how long are the toiling masses supposed to drag it? Isn't it time to put wheels on it?"[8] And Tolstoy supposedly answered by saying that if you put wheels on it everyone will want to jump in and you'd have to drag them all along. Better just to forget about the cart and go your own way. This refusal to take responsibility for the general good, and the desire on all levels of Russian society to go one's own way is, in Solzhenitsyn's view, what led the country into chaos and anarchy and ultimately cleared the way for the Bolshevik takeover. All of Solzhenitsyn's heroes in *The Red Wheel*, both fictional and historical, are individuals who reject the twin Tolstoyan virtues of nonresistance to evil and lack of involvement with society at large.

Another way for Solzhenitsyn to distance himself from Tolstoy is by using a Tolstoyan "absolute voice" to make statements completely at odds with the views of Tolstoy's philosopher of history. For example, Solzhenitsyn disagrees with Tolstoy's contention that history is made by the everyday actions of ordinary individuals and, consequently, that those people who think they are making history are doing nothing of the kind. Instead, in *October 1916* (*Oktiabr' shestnadtsatogo*) we read the following: "And in general, each regiment occupies only one area, contains an inexpressive number, while wars are made—by the active ones, the scouts, the brave, the initial attackers. *Just as history is made—by a chosen minority*."[9]

In addition to his more or less subtle and ironic dialogue with Tolstoy and Tolstoyism, Solzhenitsyn scatters various specific references to *War and Peace* through *August 1914*. He is unimpressed, for example, with Tolstoy's ideas concerning what makes a good general. In chapter 58 of *August 1914*, he mercilessly skewers General Blagoveshchensky, who shirks his duty to act. "General Blagoveshchensky had read about Kutuzov in Lev Tolstoy, and as he was 60, greying, stout, and immobile he felt himself to be just like Kutuzov, only he had both eyes. Like Kutuzov he was watchful, cautious, and cunning. And like Tolstoy's Kutuzov he understood that he should never undertake any sharp, decisive actions of his own." [10] Here it is not merely Tolstoyan thinking that causes problems. The baneful influence of *War and Peace* itself is blamed for the collapse of the Russian offensive at the beginning of the First World War.

Or, while discussing the incompetence of most of the Russian officer corps, Solzhenitsyn adds parenthetically, "we would like to console ourselves here with Tolstoy's conviction that it is not generals who lead armies, not captains who lead ships and regiments, not presidents and leaders who govern states and parties—but the twentieth century has too frequently showed us that it is precisely they." [11] On the one hand, statements like these place the *Red Wheel* cycle firmly in the mode of *War and Peace*—a work that mixes the novelistic and historical freely in an attempt to reconstruct the underlying truth of a crucial period in the nation's history. On the other hand, and perhaps more importantly, they indicate that Solzhenitsyn radically disagrees with Tolstoy's concept of history. For Solzhenitsyn, the conscious actions of specific individuals make history, and for that reason *The Red Wheel* concentrates consistently on individuals, as many as possible, and emphasizes their personal role in and responsibility for the flow of history.

Nevertheless, despite all my references to Solzhenitsyn's debates with Tolstoy, it would be a mistake to imagine that *The Red Wheel* cycle is nothing more than a twentieth-century remake of *War and Peace*. Rather, I would say, for Solzhenitsyn Tolstoy's was a presence that had to be overcome, and the process of overcoming it was more or less complete by the time

August 1914 was finished. The remaining knots are noticeably less Tolstoyan than the first. After *August 1914* there are no more direct references to Tolstoy, and fewer open disagreements. Additionally, the use of the absolute voice becomes more sparing, and by *April 1917* it has disappeared altogether. Indeed, after having read the whole cycle, one gets the feeling that the prominent place afforded Tolstoy and *War and Peace* in the first knot was not so much an indication of dependence or influence per se, but merely a reminder to readers that Solzhenitsyn was reviving the intergeneric tradition epitomized in Russian culture by Tolstoy's masterpiece. Having accomplished this, Solzhenitsyn could get down to his real task: a complete revision of the traditional artistic treatment of historical material. *August 1914* then can be seen (to appropriate a military metaphor) as a rear-guard action. It combines elements of the past tradition with radical innovations. In the later knots, Solzhenitsyn's own voice comes through far more clearly, and I will therefore concentrate my analysis on the final knot, *April 1917*. Nevertheless, anyone who has read the earlier volumes carefully will see that practically everything that is fully developed in *April 1917* was present, albeit in attenuated form, in the earliest volumes as well.

What are the innovations that Solzhenitsyn brings to the Russian tradition of literary/historical writing? First and foremost is a reorientation of the spatio-temporal axes of narrative. Where a Tolstoy, a Pushkin, or a Tynianov was primarily interested in the interrelationships of one or a few characters over time, to each other and to the historical process, Solzhenitsyn wants to show how the actions and ideas of a large number of people shape the historical moment. Therefore, he presents a multitude of characters united only by their temporal coexistence. The effect is to shift concern from relatively long-term developmental processes to short-term atomized actions and reactions. One could say that Solzhenitsyn takes seriously the Tolstoyan philosopher of history's injunction: "Only by being willing to observe the infinitesimally small unit—the differential of history, that is, the uniform attractions of people, and by achieving the art of integrating them (taking the sum of all these infinitesimally small things), can we hope to grasp the laws of history." [12] *The Red Wheel* provides the differentials, as it were; the reader's job is to integrate them into a coherent picture.

Simultaneously, Solzhenitsyn shifts the emphasis from fictional characters to "real" historical actors, while at the same time refusing to make any narratological distinction between the two. As opposed to the clear divisions into historical and fictional voices that in one form or another marked the dialogically juxtaposed monologic texts of his predecessors, Solzhenitzyn makes no distinction in presenting the thoughts, dreams, and inner lives of his created characters and those of, say, Nicholas II or Lenin. The result is a text in which the fictional is thoroughly historicized and the historical is thoroughly fictionalized.

From the very beginning of the first knot, Solzhenitsyn strives to avoid making any kind of narrative distinction between fictional and historical characters. The first chapter opens in medias res with the thoughts of an unnamed character (who turns out to be Sania Lazhenitsyn). "They had left the village on a sharp, clear morning, when the mountains, shining whitely in their blue depths, seemed to stand practically within reach. Each sharp peak could be seen, and they looked so close that an outsider might have thought you could drive up to them in a couple of hours." [13] That this observation does not belong to an omniscient narrator, but rather is the point of view of a single character at a specific time, becomes clear only on the next page, through the frequent use of time markers ("today," "right now") and various other obvious indications of *style indirect libre*. [14]

Some 80 pages later, when the first "historical" character (General Samsonov) is introduced, the technique is identical. The chapter opens with a sentence that could be either the perspective of an omniscient third-person narrator or an individual's perception in *style indirect libre*: "It was getting dark, and the electric streetlights were turned on next to the stone two-story headquarters of the Second Army in Ostrolenk." [15] It turns out that we are seeing the world through the eyes of General Samsonov's adjutant, and from there we pass to the perspective of the general himself. At this stage, it is true, passages in *style indirect libre* are mixed with passages that seem to emanate from an external narrator; nevertheless, *style indirect libre* is clearly the dominant narrative mode throughout *The Red Wheel*.

There are four exceptions to this dominance. The first consists of what might be called nonnarrated passages (excerpts from newspapers, telegrams, etc.); the second includes the sections marked *ekran* (screen), which present a number of visually arresting scenes as if from the point of view of a movie camera with a wide-angle lens, and which are written out as screenplays; the third comprises incursions of the "absolute voice"; and the fourth consists of passages providing biographical and historical background. It is significant, however, that the absolute voice, any presentations of background material not through *style indirect libre*, and almost all hints of an external omniscient narrator disappear by early in *March 1917* (*Mart semnadtsatogo*). This is further evidence that, as I suggested earlier, in the process of writing Solzhenitsyn came to understand what was unique about his method of integrating history and literature, and gradually eliminated traditional methods as he pressed on. In my view, therefore, *The Red Wheel* takes on its true character (which was present but masked in the earlier knots) only in *March 1917*. This makes sense thematically; as Solzhenitsyn noted himself, "the center of gravity" of his narrative ultimately came to be the rise and collapse of the provisional government. [16] As a result, the first two knots turn out to have been the prehistory of the crucial events of March and April 1917. By the third knot, all of the necessary background has been provided, and Solzhenitsyn can get down to his main task: the fullest possible re-creation of the events of those two months from the largest possible number of points of view.

The result on the level of character is a dizzying series of narratives, each told from an individual point of view in the present tense with no overt narrative control or commentary. Within each chapter, the point of view of the central character is presented as if unmediated by any external consciousness, and, as a result, there is no way to separate an individual's truth from the Truth. The illusion is that we have direct access to his or her thoughts and visions, and there is no distinction between the thoughts and visions of historical and fictional characters.

Although it sometimes appears that broad statements or observations of the general situation are coming from an external narrator, in the last two knots they always turn out to be someone's personal view. Compare, for example, two passages, one from the point of view of the fictional Colonel Vorotyntsev, the other from that of Alexander Kerensky:

Two weeks had already passed since Vorotyntsev was at Headquarters, and he'd even gotten into the tactical division—lucky, Svechin had tried hard.

But this was not the same headquarters he had imagined from a distance: it had turned into something that looked like a retirement home for superannuated generals. At headquarters now generals and senior officers who had been sentenced to death by their divisions or simply kicked out by soldiers' committees were piling up.[17]

Revolution is a magical red whirlwind. And anyone who wants to soar within it without burning his wings (or breaking his legs) must have a natural ability (it can't be learned artificially) to fly over abysses acrobatically, or to balance on thin and flexible high balance beams with no railings. And everything is decided by boldness, self-assurance, sincerity, breadth of soul, and a sudden unerring impulse.

And Kerensky was ecstatic to discover all of these qualities in himself.[18]

Both of these passages are characterized by narration effectively in the present tense, as if drawn directly from the thoughts of the character. And this kind of narration (with only a handful of exceptions) is constant through the final two knots (approximately 3,500 pages) of *The Red Wheel*. The result is a sharp break with the traditions of dialogic interaction that characterized the work of Solzhenitsyn's predecessors. Whereas dialogue had previously been built on a careful separation of the fictional and the historical (which could be accomplished in various ways, of course), Solzhenitsyn has erased the line. On the level of characterization, Solzhenitsyn has completely outgrown the native tradition, which always recognized in principle the distinction between fiction and history, while demanding the right to produce both.[19] At first glance, it might seem that Solzhenitsyn has simply bypassed the Russian tradition and turned to that of Walter Scott. In fact, however, Solzhenitsyn's strategy is quite different: whereas Scott makes both historical and fictional material sound like fiction, Solzhenitsyn makes them both sound like history.

On the level of narrative structure, Solzhenitsyn is hardly less innovative. In standard fictional texts we expect that the created characters will interact even if, in some modern texts, the principles of interaction are sometimes hard to fathom. For example, in the first 50 pages of *War and Peace*, Tolstoy manages to include practically all of the important characters of his 1,000-page book. To do so, of course, he has to compress severely the space of the first chapters (Anna Pavlovna Scherer's St. Petersburg salon and the Rostovs' Moscow house). He also finds it necessary to make everyone related to everyone else (a technique that Tolstoy uses in practically all of his fiction), since blood ties help provide motivation for the close and constant personal contacts among the main characters. As the events of the Napoleonic wars begin to involve the novel's fictional characters, a space circumscribed by Moscow and St. Petersburg is no longer sufficient. Eventually Tolstoy's narrative space expands dramatically to cover most of the territory on which the Napoleonic campaign was fought. Nevertheless, the familial closeness that marked the novel's opening chapters is never abandoned: the Rostovs and their various present and future in-laws remain the axis around which all events revolve. The existence of this central nucleus is absolutely necessary for the poetic structure of the novel. Indeed, Tolstoy can cover such a large expanse of space and time only because of the interconnectedness of the actors who fill that expanse. In historiographical narratives, on the other hand, while we do not necessarily expect that all the figures discussed must meet or interact, we realize that they are all included because of their common connection to some central narrative line in whose development they play significant roles.

Solzhenitsyn's approach to his material is entirely different. He provides fifteen or twenty separate fictional narratives that are related to each other only insofar as they unfold in the same unit of time. The unit of narrative interest is neither the story (with its beginning, middle, and end) nor the event, but rather the month. In this respect, Solzhenitsyn is again building on Tolstoy; but while Tolstoy's war on standard narration remained incomplete, Solzhenitsyn takes it to its logical conclusion. This is not to assert, of course, that Solzhenitsyn has no overarching concept of Russian history or of the lives of his created characters; as we have indicated earlier, he most certainly does. It is just that traditional causal chains have no place in the narrative scheme of *The Red Wheel*. If the month is the only relevant unit of narrative concern, then in theory nothing should be presented except what the fictitious or historical personages experienced in that specific time frame.[20]

Characters are related only insofar as they live through the same block of time. They do not interact with each other, rather they all act simultaneously in separate (sometimes overlapping) spaces, and the narrative grows out of those actions. In its most extreme form, Solzhenitsyn's attempt to provide a feeling for the multiplicity of narratives that unfold simultaneously (the differentials of history) leads to a narrative almost entirely bereft of forward momentum. It takes 370 pages to narrate February 27, 1917, for example, and 270 for February 28.[21] In this regard *The Red Wheel* is the historical equivalent of James Joyce's *Ulysses*.[22] While Joyce needs 750 pages for an intensive observation of a few characters in a single city on a single day, Solzhenitsyn needs about as much space for an equally rigorous presentation of Russia on a few historically significant days.

This method has the effect of exploding our assumptions of how narratives should be constructed. In the vast majority of fiction and historiography, the central axis of narrative is along the causal chain. Action A leads to (causes) action B, which in turn leads to (causes) action C, and so on. The scheme can, of course, be far more complicated, as when the story is not told in chronological order (i.e., to use Formalist terminology, *sjuzhet* does not coincide with *fabula*), or when more than one cause is advanced for a single result. Nevertheless, there is one story (sometimes two, but rarely more) whose unfolding provides the interest of the book. Among other important things, this causal chain model implies as well that narratives will lead somewhere (to an ending of some kind if the text is fictional, or to some culminating point if it is historiographical). Despite various philosophical attacks on its validity, this basic narrative schema continues to hold sway in both fictional and historiographic writing. Even in the case of *War and Peace*, Tolstoy's attempts to provide irrelevant details can only be successful because there is some central story to which they are irrelevant. But in *The Red Wheel* there is no central narrative, and there is therefore no way to judge the relevance or irrelevance of any material, fictional or historical. The only overt organizing principle is chronology; if something happened in the month of the knot, then it is eligible to be included—from the most momentous occurrence to the most trivial detail.[23]

For readers expecting a "normal" novel, this method is maddening. We tend to assume that related events will be found in at least relative proximity and find it hard to deal with fifteen to twenty plot lines developing (if that is the word) simultaneously. Even more surprising is the lack of connection between Solzhenitsyn's various fictional and historical narratives. In a traditional novel we know that all the important characters will eventually begin to interact, even if they are kept segregated for hundreds of pages. This compositional principle is rarely tampered with, even in a modernist text like *Ulysses*. But in *The Red Wheel* the equivalents of Leopold Bloom and Stephen Dedalus never meet. We keep waiting for the plot twists that will bring the fictional stories together, tie up the narrative knots, but they never come.

The stories themselves are broken up in such a way that separate views of the same event can appear at some distance from each other. Thus, for example, chapter 131 of *April 1917* is narrated from the point of view of A. I. Guchkov, minister of war of the provisional government. Guchkov, his strength waning, has been asked to answer questions at the congress of deputies from the front. At first he refuses, but then, on April 29, he decides to speak before them, to tell the whole truth about the military situation, and to announce his resignation the next day. As always, the chapter is focused entirely on Guchkov's words and on the thoughts that race through his mind as he gives his speech. After it is over, Guchkov thinks to himself: "No, the speech just didn't go over. And I went in with such emotion. Oh, how difficult, how difficult it is for us to make contact with the masses. They remain—like a sphinx. And we are surrounded by them as by a horde of strangers from the steppe."[24]

No other perspective on Guchkov's speech is provided, however, until six chapters later, when we are given the internal monologue of the fictional Frol Gorovoi, dated April 30. "Yesterday Guchkov, the minister of war, showed up—straight from his bed, he said, but businesslike. Still, however, there's no strength in him, he's calling for victory, but he can't lead the army, no way."[25] Separating these two views of Guchkov's speech are five chapters: one from the point of view of Kerensky, thinking about his speech before the delegates; a second from the point of view of the fictional Sasha Lenartovich, describing the internal debates of the Bolsheviks; a third devoted to Nicholas II's perceptions of the evolving situation while under house arrest in Tsarskoe Selo; a fourth consisting of 22 quotations drawn from various newspapers concerning the situation at the front; and a fifth from the point of view of the fictional Colonel Vorotyntsev at the headquarters of the general staff in

Mogilev, including both thoughts about his rocky marriage and about the rumors of Guchkov's resignation.[26]

Even more maddening to readers expecting a "normal" narrative is that individual stories are never told completely. We begin to see some dramatic action developing in the life of an individual character, but then the focus switches to someone else, and we may or may not ever return to the individual with whom we began to empathize. Or, the month in question simply ends and the budding story ends with it, for it is not the story that interests Solzhenitsyn, but the interaction of the story with the specified time period. Each of the fictional stories exists in a constant "to be continued" state—"to be continued," that is, until the last knot ends with none of the stories resolved. Worse yet for the traditionalist is the note that accompanies the 150-page summary of what would have been the other sixteen knots. Here Solzhenitsyn says: "But I nevertheless decided to acquaint the reader with a summary of the main events which could not be passed over were one to write out the succeeding knots fully. . . . I leave stories with invented personages out of the summary."[27] So much for our expectations of fictional closure. The effect of all these experimental compositional devices is only heightened by the relentless psychological realism of each individual chapter; any chapter taken at random seems to come from a traditional novel, but taken together they add up to a highly unconventional text.

On the historical side of Solzhenitsyn's work, things are not much more traditional. Of course, Solzhenitsyn is well aware that readers know how it all turned out, at least in the main lines. Thus, he has no need to tell us that the Bolsheviks eventually came to power, that the tsar and his family were murdered, and so on. But even here, the exigencies of the chronological format make for an oddly shaped narrative. When *April 1917* ends, for example, a peasant congress is just getting under way. As readers we might want to know what it accomplished, how it related to the Soviets, the provisional government, and so forth. We learn none of this, in part because the end of the month does not coincide with the end of the conference, and in part because relations between different groups are not really of narrative interest here. The point is cotemporality—for Solzhenitsyn's text to work, we need to feel that we have a comprehensive view of everything that went on during the month, from what turned out to be utterly trivial to what turned out to be momentous. At the same time, as noted earlier, Solzhenitsyn generally avoids the use of foreshadowing in the later knots.[28] This heightens the effect of presentness, of experiencing an inherently open-ended situation, rather than being presented with the results of a finished story.

Naturally, such a project is inherently utopian. In order to reproduce a period fully we would need to live it again, and living it again, were this somehow possible, would mean losing the mediated Archimedean position from which we can view the variety of events happening simultaneously in different places. Still, Solzhenitsyn's is a bold attempt to create a new kind of historiographical position. The illusion created is that of the slice, the synchronic cross section of a society at a moment in time. For students of "Western" historiographical and fictional traditions, Solzhenitsyn's exclusively temporal concerns must seem innovative. For a Russian reader, however, an obvious model suggests itself: the Russian chronicles. As anyone who has read these works knows, their principle of organization is temporal. The relevant unit is the year, and in theory each entry is shaped not by the "logical" contours of a complete story, but rather by what seems to us an artificial chronological unit.[29] It would, of course, be a mistake to say that the chroniclers always cut off their stories at the temporal boundary only to take them up again later, but this is undoubtedly their basic principle of textual organization.

A typical entry from the early part of the chronicles reads: "In the year 913. Igor began to reign, succeeding Ol'ga. In these same times Konstantin, son of Leon, became emperor. And after Ol'ga's death the Derevliane seceded from Igor."[30] There is only a coincidental temporal relationship between the beginning of Igor's reign and that of Konstantin, although they appear side by side. And should we wish to get the whole story of Igor's life and reign, we would need to cobble together information from multiple entries, each of which is cluttered with (what seems to us) unnecessary or irrelevant material. At the beginning of the chronicle, some years are even left blank: "nothing" happened, so the date stands alone. Finally, the main narrative text of the chronicles is extremely heterogeneous. Treaties, wills, and other kinds of documents appear verbatim, and no distinction is made between what we might think of as historical and legendary (fictional) stories.

As I discussed in Chapter 2, Karamzin's great contribution to Russian historiography was, at least in his main text, to break with the chronicle form. He organized his narrative into logically coherent units (i.e., thematic ones) and he subjected the chronicles to critical scrutiny in an attempt to separate the historical from the fictional. What Solzhenitsyn has done, in effect, is to turn his back on the entire modern period of Russian historiography and fiction that grows out of Karamzin's work and to create in its stead a new Russian chronicle. In *The Red Wheel* we are confronted by a heterogeneous text organized, in principle, solely along the chronological axis. Indeed, in the final two knots, the chronological focus becomes so important that the date on which the narrated events are occurring appears at the bottom of every page.

Like the chroniclers, Solzhenitsyn skips certain time periods (he jumps from August 1914 to October 1916, and from then to March 1917), implying thereby that nothing significant happened in the omitted months. Also like the chroniclers, Solzhenitsyn is unable to hold to the chronological format exclusively, particularly in the first knot. There, in introducing his fictional characters and in setting the historical scene, he finds it necessary to provide longer or shorter flashbacks from the lives of his heroes. The most notorious of these are the biography of Stolypin, printed in 80-odd pages of small type, and the 100-odd-page monologue of Tsar Nicholas II in *August 1914*.[31]

Solzhenitsyn clearly recognizes that by including these background materials he is breaking his own compositional principles. We can see an admission of this, as well as a justification
for it, in the parenthetical phrase that precedes the biography of
Stolypin: "The author would not have permitted himself such a
flagrant break of the novelistic form had Russian history itself,
her whole memory, not been flagrantly broken up previously,
and her historians destroyed."[32] At the same time, if we keep
the chronicle in mind as a possible model, we recall that there
too, the period before the beginning of Russian history (that
is, from the creation of the world until the year A.D. 852) was
narrated independently of the chronological framework. Solzhenitsyn's flashbacks, the most egregious of which come in a
section entitled "From Previous Knots," can be seen, therefore,
as the functional equivalent of the "prehistoric" sections of the
chronicle.

By the later knots, however, flashbacks have mostly been
eliminated and the chronicle form is adhered to more strictly.[33]
There are also other indications of Solzhenitsyn's growing concern to eliminate extraneous elements in the later knots. We
have already spoken of the elimination of the absolute voice
and the Tolstoyan references. Even more important, however,
is the avoidance of a string of chapters devoted to the same
character. In *August 1914*, for example, Solzhenitsyn will follow a single character in three or four successive chapters. This
creates the illusion that he is writing a more or less standard,
if fragmented, novelistic narrative.[34] But by *April 1917* no two
successive chapters are devoted to the same individual. This
greatly increases the sense of fragmentariness and emphasizes
the strictly chronological principle governing the selection of
fictional and historical material. It functions to make the narrative more like that of a chronicle and less like that of a narrative
history or novel.

Finally, there is the question of didacticism. Although the
chronicle compiler rarely inserted his own voice into the text,
the chronicle was by no means a disinterested, objective narra-

tive. As one Soviet scholar put it: "The chronicle existed primarily not for posterity, but for contemporaries, and chronicle compilations were used in political struggles."[35] That is to say, the chronicles had political agendas (which could be expressed overtly or covertly) that directly affected their narrative. Furthermore, these narratives did not come into being as objects for aesthetic contemplation, but rather for fairly specific political purposes. In these respects, the chronicle differed sharply from works of literature and history produced in the modern era. By reinvoking the chronicle form, Solzhenitsyn, in my view, hopes also to escape demands for either aesthetically balanced fictional texts or objective histories.[36] His concerns are entirely different. He wants to show, as Michael Scammell presciently observed even before most of the *Red Wheel* cycle had appeared, that "pre-revolutionary Russia had had not just two choices—for the tsar or for revolution—but a third as well: to build something completely different. Behind this was the further, unspoken thought that if the choice had existed then, perhaps—in however attenuated a form—it still existed now."[37] This guess has certainly been borne out by Solzhenitsyn's programmatic essay of 1989, "How Can We Reconstruct Russia." Only by writing from the archaic position of the chronicler, only by rejecting the formal constraints and aesthetic expectations attached both to fiction and to history (while nevertheless retaining the Russian tradition of combining them), is Solzhenitsyn able to create an adequate narrative form to describe the roots of the Soviet Union and to provide his own explanation for the disease from which his people suffered for some 70 years and from whose consequences they continue to suffer.[38] With Solzhenitsyn, the Russian literary historiographical project has come full circle. If Karamzin and his successors tried to make a European country out of Russia, at least as far as historical narrative is concerned, Solzhenitsyn has tried equally hard to return her to her roots, to revive the principle of Russia's never-quite-forgotten indigenous historical genre.

❦

Chapter Ten

Conclusion

To this point, I have attempted to demonstrate the existence of a specifically Russian literary tradition of intergeneric dialogue on historical themes, one which has been productive of important works by major authors over practically the entire modern period of Russian culture. Although each author takes a particular approach to the tradition, the core concept— that historical truth can be expressed only through a multigeneric perspective on historical events—remains remarkably constant. Several questions remain to be asked. How and why did this particular literary tradition manage to begin and to sustain itself? Is the phenomenon of intergeneric dialogue discernible in other areas of Russian culture that are related tangentially, or even entirely unrelated, to discussions of history? And finally, what are the advantages and dangers inherent in a cultural/historical worldview that understands truth as a multigeneric construct? Obviously, in a relatively brief conclusion I can at best provide sketchy answers to the above, each of which could be the starting point for an independent investigation. They are, I think, questions worth raising nevertheless, if only in the hope that others may be induced to provide more satisfactory answers.

The Russian émigré economist Alexander Gershchenkron once proposed a theory to help explain why economic development, when initiated in underdeveloped countries, did not proceed in the same manner as it had in Britain, America, France, and so on. He notes that "industrialization processes, when launched at length in a backward country, showed considerable differences, as compared with more advanced countries, not only with regard to the speed of development (the rate of industrial growth) but also with regard to the productive and organizational structures of industry which emerged from these processes." [1] It is not just that these countries do not develop according to the same timetable as the model nations; even if they try to start down the same path, their economies end up looking different. Gershchenkron attributes these differences to the inevitable need to modify the introduced system in light of "indigenously determined elements." [2] Naturally, these indigenous elements will be specific to each country, thus ensuring that the process will never produce the same result twice.

Substituting words with the root *culture* for those with *industry* in Gershchenkron's hypothesis produces a formulation that could well shed light on the Russian situation. We might theorize that although the Russians tried to borrow European culture and in many ways succeeded in doing so, their attempts were also often fated to produce different "productive and organizational structures," both because European ideas sometimes conflicted sharply with indigenous elements and because wholesale borrowing produced a skewed time perspective in which everything absorbed at one time appeared contemporary, no matter what its date of composition. In Russia, for example, Homer, Dante, Shakespeare, and Rousseau were, for all intents and purposes, contemporaries, since their works all became available in the last quarter of the eighteenth century.

In the realm of what we would now call literature, this strangely telescoped perspective produced all kinds of unusual hybrids, but because the native Russian literary tradition lacked both drama and poetry (and the folk tradition exerted scant influence on high literature at the time), European models of varying traditions interacted only among themselves on Russian soil. In the area of historical writing, however, the situation was further complicated by the recognition in the eighteenth century of the importance of Russia's indigenous multigeneric chronicle tradition. Of course, other European countries had had chronicles of their own, but this form of history writing had ceased to be productive long before the eighteenth century. In Russia, that tradition had died out as well, but through the work of pioneering historians like Tatishchev, Müller, and Schlözer, the chronicles were rediscovered and made available to wider audiences. Thus, for Russian writers at the end of the eighteenth and beginning of the nineteenth century, this indigenous tradition was as much a part of contemporary culture as were histories like those of Hume, Voltaire, or Gibbon. It would, of course, be a bit simplistic to say that the Russian intergeneric tradition of history writing was the result of the simultaneous reception of the chronicles and Shakespeare (in the work of Catherine the Great) and of the chronicles and the European historians of the eighteenth century (in the work of Karamzin). Nevertheless, the close interaction of elements deriving from different centuries and different cultures must surely have played a major role in initiating this approach to writing history.

Once a multigeneric model had become available, however, the Russians were quick to see certain advantages in it. Building on the achievements of Catherine and Karamzin, Russian writers turned what might have remained a few isolated accidents into a powerful national tradition. For it turns out that in contrast to industrialization (the goals of which are fairly clear—modernization, the creation of a functioning industrialized economy, etc.), cultural development is not teleologically oriented.[3] Therefore, while economic backwardness causes problems that must be overcome if a modern industrial society is to be produced, the lags and strange blips produced by late literary development can be seen, in hindsight at least, as having been a positive feature. Thus we might want to say that the Russian "failure" to adopt the split between history and imaginative literature that gradually became canonized in western Europe in the first half of the nineteenth century was quite fortuitous insofar as it allowed for the appearance of a multigeneric tradition that would have been unthinkable in Europe.

Interestingly enough, national history was by no means the only subject Russian writers chose to deal with through a kind of intergeneric dialogue. That is, a belief that truth can only be discovered through a combination of multiple genres (fictional and nonfictional) seems to have been a general feature of Russian thought. The clearest analogous example to the tradition of intergeneric treatments of history is the Russian approach to childhood (auto)biography.[4] Childhood descriptions came remarkably late to Russian literature. Indeed, the first full-scale description of childhood experience in Russian culture is Tolstoy's *Childhood* (1852). True, there had been a handful of fictional works in which child characters appeared before the publication of Tolstoy's work, but for all intents and purposes childhood experience was not a literary fact in Russia before the 1850's.[5] Nor was childhood an autobiographical fact, at least as far as can be ascertained from published autobiographies. As opposed to the lavish amounts of space given over to descriptions of childhood experience in autobiographies from the latter half of the nineteenth century, autobiographies written before the 1850's rarely devote more than a couple of pages to the subject, and these are generally confined to setting out factual detail, rather than attempting to recall the child's own perspective.

When Tolstoy considered how best to represent childhood—that is, the personal past—he evidently perceived the problem as related to that of how to relate the nation's past. The genre he chose to present the first detailed description of childhood experience in Russia—I call it the pseudo-autobiography—has clear structural analogies to the techniques Russian writers had already developed for dealing with history (and which Tolstoy himself would later perfect in *War and Peace*). In the pseudo-autobiography, the author employs first-person narration as in a standard autobiography, but the narrator does not possess the author's name. Instead, he is a fictional character who tells the story of his life, a life that, within the Russian tradition, at least, has more than a little in common with the life of the actual author. The pseudo-autobiography allows in theory for a complex three-way interaction. The narration can issue from the point of view of the child, or from the point of view of the adult narrator, who can modify, embellish, or correct the child's "memories," or from the point of view of the implied author, who can lend his fictional characters as many or as few of his own memories as he chooses.[6] The problem of personal identity that is always present in any autobiography—that is, to what extent the adult writer is "the same person" as his or her childhood incarnation—is both complicated and simplified in the pseudo-autobiography. On the one hand, the ambiguous relation between author and narrator makes the problem of identity between author and child even more problematic. At the same time, the now-obvious fictionality of the child's perspective tends to make the question of identity seem less important.

From an author's point of view, the pseudo-autobiographical genre is ideal. By mimicking the form of the autobiography, the narrative accrues many of its advantages. In particular, it encourages readers to indulge the perhaps irrational but nevertheless common tendency to accept first-person narration as being truer than other kinds of narration, perhaps by evoking memories of what Philippe Lejeune has called the "autobiographical pact"—the basic claims to truth of autobiography. At the same time, the author is not limited by actual recollections, and is free to create a composite figure whose voice is not bound by the limits of memory. Because of the fictional nature of the narrative, the author need not worry that readers will question the accuracy of the child's perspective. We do not ask how the narrator could possibly remember details of his feelings, conversations, and observations at the age of two or three;

instead of truth we demand only plausibility. The basis for the analogy between pseudo-autobiography and intergeneric dialogue on historical subjects is now clear. In both cases authors choose to juxtapose the perspective of narration as if from the inside and in the unfolding specific present (the voice of the fictional historical narrator, or that of the child) to that of narration from hindsight and with full knowledge of the outcome of the historical processes or childhood experiences being described. In both cases the reader is encouraged to consider both an overtly fictional perspective and a nonfictional perspective on the same events. Neither perspective alone is adequate for a full portrayal of autobiographical or historical truth; instead, truth arises from the dialogic interaction of fictional and historical or fictional and autobiographical perspectives.

Of course, this Russian tendency to flout the expected distinction between fictional and nonfictional genres in histories of the personal and of the nation's past (while all the time exploiting readers' awareness of the theoretical incompatibility of these two perspectives) can be seen as part and parcel of an even more general Russian tradition, one that was most famously characterized by Tolstoy in his justification of the formal peculiarities of *War and Peace*: "The history of Russian literature from the time of Pushkin not only provides many examples of such deviations from European forms, but it provides not a single example to the contrary. From Gogol's *Dead Souls* to Dostoevsky's *House of the Dead*, in the modern period of Russian literature there is not a single work of artistic prose rising above the mediocre that wholly fits the form of a novel, a poem, or a story."[7]

It remains to ask what the advantages and disadvantages of the Russian multigeneric approach are. Most obviously, this tradition has allowed for some of the most powerful works in the Russian, and in some cases, the world literary tradition. However impatient we may sometimes be with "loose baggy monsters" of the type of *War and Peace* or *The Brothers Karamazov*, we must ultimately admit that a great part of their power resides precisely in their looseness and bagginess, in their multigeneric combination of fiction and nonfiction, history and prophecy. Much the same thing can be said of the other works that have been analyzed in this book, and the list could easily be longer. In this respect at least, the combination of European culture with Russian native traditions has unquestionably produced a unique cultural system, one that has returned with interest its debt to outside sources.

It is much more difficult to assess the dangers inherent in this cultural outlook. In part this is because such an assessment requires us to propose an organic linkage between literary traditions and more general cultural worldviews. But in Russia, where there have been repeated attempts to borrow models taken from literature for use in real life, the possibility that such linkages exist must be taken seriously.[8] Certainly, it seems clear that there is at least a potential danger in a cultural system that implicitly denies the possibility of discovering historical truth outside of the dialogic interaction of narratives. The Russian writers discussed in this book used intergeneric dialogue to write history because they believed, deep down, that it would allow them to get to the truth. The system worked only because of a belief that there was truth somewhere to be had. If this core belief is abandoned while the intergeneric approach is retained, however, history simply becomes a series of narratives, and their intergeneric combination provides nothing more than an opportunity for a cynical and manipulative game. In the particular case of the Russian approach to history, we may well want to ask whether the apparent belief of the Soviet state apparatus that history is merely a series of narratives to be manipulated endlessly was a logical outcome (not the only one, to be sure) of the Russian literary view of historical truth as inherently dialogic.

A dialogic approach to the truth is considered to be a good thing in most circles these days. But as Morson and Emerson point out in their study on Bakhtin, dialogue is not necessarily an unalloyed good: "The most vulnerable side of dialogue, Bakhtin may have sensed, is its benevolence. For even a cursory reading of Bakhtin reveals that the implied potential other in his dialogues lives on friendly boundaries and continuums."[9] When this is not the case, when the other merely uses the form of dialogue either as a mask for authoritarianism or for full-blown relativism, it is not clear how the dialogic approach can defend itself.[10] With the recent downfall of the Soviet system, we can only hope that the cynical attitude toward historical truth that was one of its hallmarks will disappear as well, and that the powerful Russian tradition of intergeneric dialogue on historical themes will once again become part of the general search for the truth.

Reference Matter

Notes

Chapter 1

1. Review of "Vtoroi tom 'Istorii Russkogo naroda' Polevogo," in Pushkin, *Polnoe sobranie*, vol. 11, p. 127.

2. Chaadaev, *Stat'i i pis'ma*, p. 475.

3. Chaadaev, *Philosophical Letters*, p. 166–67. Translation modified with reference to the original in Chaadaev, *Stat'i i pis'ma*, p. 150.

4. Chaadaev, *Philosophical Letters*, pp. 166–67 (modified).

5. Quoted in Morson, ed., *Literature and History*, p. 24.

6. Groys, pp. 48–49.

7. Starr.

8. "Utopicheskoe ponimanie istorii," *Diary of a Writer*, June 1876, in Dostoevsky, vol. 23, p. 47.

9. "Nechto o Peterburgskom Baden-Badenstve," *Diary of a Writer*, July–Aug. 1876, in Dostoevsky, vol. 23, p. 58.

10. Letter from Philotheus of Pskov to Tsar Vasily III, quoted in Billington, p. 58.

11. Gary Saul Morson, "Literary History and the Russian Experience," in Morson, ed., *Literature and History*, p. 15.

12. See Oksman; Petrunina, *Proza Pushkina*.

13. Morson provides a comprehensive discussion of readers' perplexity in the face of this aspect of *War and Peace* in *Hidden in Plain View*, pp. 40–72.

14. For a summary of various extant critical approaches to the *Diary of a Writer*, see Frank, "Approaches to the *Diary of a Writer*," in *Through the Russian Prism*, pp. 153–69.

15. For the evolution of the historical novel, see Lukács; Scham-schula. For that of Russian historiography, see Miliukov; Mazour.

16. Some of the potentials for intergeneric dialogue and, indeed, the term itself are discussed by Morson in *The Boundaries of Genre*. He suggests the possibility that entire traditions "may also be constituted by *inter*-generic dialogues with neighboring genres regarded as hostile to [their] core philosophical assumptions" (p. 79; see also pp. 81–84).

17. Morson and Emerson, *Mikhail Bakhtin*, p. 220.

18. Bakhtin, *Problemy poetiki*, pp. 60–62.

19. Morson and Emerson, *Mikhail Bakhtin*, p. 304.

20. Emerson, p. 8.

21. The obvious example in England was the treatment of the French Revolution and the Napoleonic era, which was dealt with in works of major authors such as Dickens, Thackeray, Hardy, and Meredith.

22. L. N. Tolstoy, from the notebooks for *War and Peace*, in Tolstoy, vol. 13, p. 53.

23. An interesting problem arises when translation must play a role. For the English-speaking reader, say, *The Captain's Daughter* is simply a historical novel, because *The History of Pugachev* is almost completely unknown. The one obscure translation of the latter is never included in English-language collections of Pushkin's prose. But for the reader with access to both texts, the potential for interplay and dialogue is obvious.

24. "O sluchaiakh i kharakterakh v Rossiiskoi istorii, kotorye mogut byt' predmetom khudozhestv," *Russkii vestnik* pt. VI, no. 20 (1802), p. 290. The article appeared under the initials O.O., a common pseudonym of Karamzin's. Actually, Karamzin was echoing thoughts that had been stated by Lomonosov as early as 1763 (see Lomonosov, vol. 9).

25. Dostoevsky, vol. 24, p. 312.

26. Henri-Irenée Marrou, *De la connaissance historique*, cited in Shils, pp. 60–61.

27. Gossman, pp. 230–31.

28. "Since the 1830's, the historical methods of textual criticism taught by Leopold von Ranke in his historical seminar at the University of Berlin and used by him in his own books had become so famous that they determined, in part, the international professionalization of the discipline of history." Hans Schleier, "Ranke in the Manuals

on Historical Methods of Droysen, Lorenz, and Bernheim," in Iggers and Powell, eds., p. 111.

29. "Michelet's approach to history was not and could not be that of the modern professional. . . . The historian was still, as Michelet's reading and formation indicate, a man of letters in the old eighteenth-century sense of the term." Gossman, p. 163.

30. Gossman, pp. 192–93. It will be noted that both of these possibilities for historical narration were exploited by historians, leaving writers of imaginative literature no room at all for serious historical narrative.

31. For the classic study of the importance and influence of the historical novel, see Lukács. For a specialized study on the historical novel in Russia, see Schamschula.

32. The exception that comes immediately to mind is Victor Hugo's truly anomalous *Les misérables* (1862). For a discussion of this great novel from the point of view of the Russian tradition of intergeneric dialogue, see Chapter 5.

33. There are, of course, exceptions. One is Iury Tynianov, who went from academic literary criticism and history to writing historical novels (see Chapter 8). Another is Natan Eidelman, who started as a historian but wrote much historical quasi fiction.

34. See Mazour's summary of nineteenth-century Russian historiography, pp. 195–97.

35. Shils, p. 58.

36. See Schama's "Afterword" (pp. 319–26) explaining and attempting to justify his postmodern historical/literary angst. For an effort to see this kind of work as belonging to a specific genre of postmodern writing, see Hutcheon.

Chapter 2

1. "Patriarshaia ili Nikonovskaia letopis'," p. 9.

2. The Nikonian Chronicle is one of the fullest but also one of the last and the most untrustworthy of the Russian chronicles. As early as the 1820's, scholars had begun to disbelieve the historical accuracy of any statements in the Nikonian Chronicle not corroborated in other sources. Of course, for our purposes here, it is a matter of indifference whether Vadim existed or not.

3. Kheraskov, p. 179.

4. Glinka, "Introduction," p. 6.

5. Mazour, p. 28. 6. See Mazour, pp. 30–32.

7. Tatishchev, vol. 2, p. 13. 8. Likhachev, p. 9.

9. For a summary of Catherine's career as a playwright, see Karlinsky, pp. 83–92.

10. Ekaterina II, *Sochineniia*, vol. 2, p. 499.

11. Ekaterina II, *Sochineniia*, vol. 8, introduction.

12. Ekaterina II, *Sochineniia*, quoted in vol. 11, p. xx.

13. Ekaterina II, *Sochineniia*, vol. 9, p. 236.

14. Mazour, p. 33. For a summary of the history of the conflict in Russian historiography over the Norman theory, see Pritsak, pp. 3–7.

15. Mazour, p. 34.

16. Ekaterina II, *Sochineniia*, vol. 11, pp. 509–10.

17. Actually, this publication was the first only for the Oleg play. The Riurik play had been published a few months earlier (in 1786) in a separate edition.

18. Ekaterina II, *Sochineniia*, vol. 2, pp. 255–56.

19. *Rossiiskii featr* 1787, vol. 14, p. 169.

20. The courageousness of this break with Russian theatrical tradition is, by the way, an important and thus far overlooked piece of evidence in favor of Catherine's authorship of these plays. Ever since Pypin published his eleven-volume edition of Catherine's work, some have claimed that Catherine could not have actually written the works attributed to her. It is true, of course, that her Russian was not native and that someone in her secretarial corps must have heavily edited the texts. Nevertheless, it seems extremely unlikely that the second-rate writers who worked for her would have been daring enough to make such a radical break with Russian theatrical conventions. It seems to me that only someone in a position as high as Catherine's could have afforded to ignore those conventions and produce an entirely new kind of play.

21. Ekaterina II, *Sochineniia. Proizvedeniia literaturnie*, p. 320.

22. Ekaterina II, *Sochineniia. Proizvedeniia literaturnie*, p. 317. The political message of Catherine's play was noted and discussed as early as 1899 (see Zamotin, p. 14).

23. See, for example, the excellent article by Morgan. See also Denoon and Kuper.

24. See Marker, pp. 128–31. 25. Karlinsky, p. 140.

26. Gukovsky, pp. 362–69. 27. Karlinsky, pp. 140–42.

28. See *Rossiiskii featr* 1790, vol. 32, pp. 187–298. Much the same can be said about Kniazhnin's adaptation of Pietro Metastasio's *La Clemenza di Tito*, which was commissioned by Catherine herself. For more on this subject, see Karlinsky, p. 136.

29. Dashkova, p. 176. In a different place, however, Dashkova says that she never had the play read, simply assuming it would be unremarkable. See the notes to Dashkova, p. 458.

30. Another hint that Catherine was jealous about her literary priority vis-à-vis the Vadim/Riurik theme comes from the publication history of a play by Plavil'shchikov. The piece was first performed in 1795 in Catherine's theater under the incomprehensible title of *Vseslav*. However, when it was published in 1811 it was called *Riurik the Great, Russian Prince Called in 862 by the Varangians, Ruled 17 Years and Died in 879. (Riurik Velikii Kniaz' Russkii, Novgorodtsami iz Variagorussov prizvan v 862 godu, kniazhil 17 let i skonchalsia v 879 godu).* This pompous title was followed by an ambiguous note from the editor: "This tragedy was performed in St. Petersburg by court actors under the title 'Vseslav'; today it is published under the original title" (Plavil'shchikov, vol. 2, introduction [unpaginated]). One can only speculate as to what induced Plavil'shchikov to change his play's title. It is not farfetched to imagine, however, that one of the reasons was a lack of desire to step on Catherine's authorial toes. The play itself is another tired reworking of the Riurik/Vadim conflict. Plavil'shchikov had taken the role of Vadim in the aborted 1790 production of Kniazhnin's *Vadim*, so he was well aware of the theme's various dramatic treatments. His is, in most respects, much closer to Catherine's vision than to Kniazhnin's.

31. Karamzin, *Istoriia*, vol. 1, "Introduction," p. ix.

32. For a detailed survey of the prose of this period, see Lotman, "Puti razvitiia."

33. That reader was Konstantin Batiushkov, who said that "Oskol'd" belonged to "the highest achievements of letters." "We are carried into the times of the deepest past," he said, and added that the characters "live and act before your eyes." Batiushkov, pp. 80–81.

34. Murav'ev, vol. 1, p. 230.

35. Karamzin, "Marfa-posadnitsa," pp. 65–66.

36. Karamzin, *Istoriia*, vol. 1, chap. 4, pp. 69–70. In fact, doubts about the truth of the Vadim story had been voiced by Karamzin even earlier. For example, in an 1802 article published pseudonymously,

he stated flatly, "Vadim the brave also belongs to the fables of our History." "O sluchaiakh i kharakterakh v Rossiiskoi Istorii, kotorye mogut byt' predmetom khudozhestv," *Russkii vestnik* pt. VI, no. 24 (1802), p. 295.

37. The same can be said about the Vadim of Pushkin's extant fragments.

38. Ryleev, p. 329.

39. Ryleev, p. 330.

40. Khomiakov's source here was almost certainly Zhukovsky's "Vadim" fragment.

41. Khomiakov, p. 475.

42. Khomiakov, p. 475.

Chapter 3

1. *Pis'ma russkogo puteshestvennika*, p. 252.

2. Pushkin, *Polnoe sobranie*, vol. 7, p. 44.

3. For a thorough summary of the reception of Karamzin's work, see Black, *Nicholas Karamzin*, chap. 5, pp. 129–55.

4. For a detailed discussion of the objections of the future Decembrists N. M. Murav'ev and M. F. Orlov, see Vatsuro. See also Egolin, ed., pp. 557–600.

5. Quoted in Emerson, p. 40.

6. See, for example, the ample testimonies from professional historians in Pokrovsky.

7. For a collection of quotes documenting the importance of Karamzin's *History* for the major pre-Revolutionary Russian writers, see S. O. Shmidt, "Istoriia gosudarstva Rossiiskogo v kul'ture dorevoliutsionnoi Rossii," in Karamzin, *Istoriia*, vol. 4, chap. 1, pp. 28–43.

8. Letter from Zhukovsky to Dmitriev of Feb. 18, 1816. In Zhukovsky, vol. 4, p. 568.

9. Karamzin, "Marfa-posadnitsa," p. 60. Further references to this tale will be made by page number in the main text.

10. Historical accuracy as such is not at a premium. The notes to any edition of "Martha the Posadnik" give an idea of the extent to which Karamzin rearranged historical facts.

11. In describing Scott's attitude toward the conflicts he presents in his historical novels, Lukács says: "Scott sees and portrays the com-

plex and intricate path which led to England's national greatness and to the formation of the national character. As a sober, conservative petty aristocrat he naturally affirms the result, and the necessity of this result is the ground on which he stands. But Scott's artistic world-view by no means stops here. Scott sees the endless field of ruin, wrecked existences, wrecked or wasted heroic, human endeavor, broken social formations, etc. which were the necessary preconditions of the end-result" (p. 54). If one were to substitute Karamzin and Russia in the appropriate places this quote could easily stand as a characterization of "Martha the Posadnik."

12. Karamzin, *Istoriia*, vol. 1, "Introduction," p. xi.

13. This article appeared under Karamzin's pseudonym O.O. in *Russkii vestnik* pt. VI, no. 24 (1802), p. 290.

14. Karamzin, *Istoriia*, vol. 4, chap. 9, p. 134.

15. Karamzin, *Istoriia*, vol. 6, chap. 1, pp. 18–19.

16. Karamzin, *Istoriia*, vol. 6, chap. 3, pp. 80–81.

17. Karamzin, *Istoriia*, vol. 6, chap. 3, p. 86.

18. Karamzin, *Istoriia*, vol. 6, chap. 3, p. 86.

19. In Pokrovsky, p. 109.

20. See Black, "The *Primečanija*," pp. 138–39, for a summary of the ways in which the footnotes contradict the main text. Black, however, merely notes the presence of contradictions without speculating about their raison d'être.

21. Emerson, p. 39.

22. Pushkin, *Polnoe sobranie*, vol. 7, p. 94.

23. *Istoriia*, vol. 1, "Introduction," p. xiii.

24. Karamzin, *Istoriia*, vol. 1, chap. 4, p. 67.

25. Karamzin, *Istoriia*, vol. 1, "Introduction," p. xiii.

26. Karamzin, *Istoriia*, vol. 1, "Introduction," p. xiii.

27. Lotman, "Puti razvitiia," pp. 42–43.

28. Karamzin, *Istoriia*, vol. 1, chap. 9, p. 139.

29. Karamzin, *Istoriia*, vol. 4, chap. 1, p. 11.

30. Walicki, *A History*, p. 97.

31. Karamzin, *Istoriia*, vol. 1, chap. 4, p. 69.

32. Karamzin, *Istoriia*, vol. 5, chap. 1, p. 70.

33. For complete definitions of these categories, see White, *Metahistory*, pp. 7–11.

34. Of course, this is not to say that Karamzin does nothing more

than this. There are naturally many side channels and derailments in the course of the history. I am referring here merely to the main thrust of the narrative.

35. Karamzin frequently refers to the enormity of his task in the course of the introduction, and hints at it in the main narrative as well.

36. For a fuller treatment of poetics versus prosaics, see Morson and Emerson, *Mikhail Bakhtin*, pp. 15–23.

37. White, for example, says, "Romance and Satire would appear to be *mutually exclusive* ways of emplotting the processes of reality" (*Metahistory*, p. 9). But White was dealing with material drawn from Western Europe, and as I pointed out in the Introduction, Russia is in many ways a different case entirely.

38. It is true that Catherine the Great had done something similar even earlier, but her literary prestige was probably not sufficient for her work to serve as a model, particularly considering its relatively low literary quality.

39. Unlike Karamzin, Pushkin never officially received the title of imperial historiographer. However, as L. B. Modzalevsky points out in his commentary to Pushkin's posthumously published materials on Peter the Great, when in 1831 Pushkin asked for and received permission to work in the archives relating to Peter, "the poet's contemporaries took this fact to mean that Pushkin had been appointed Peter's historian" (p. 509). Pushkin himself was clearly inclined to believe that his reappointment to the civil service was effected in order to allow him to carry out historiographical research. As he wrote to Pletnev, "The tsar has taken me on. Not to serve in a ministry or at court, or in the army—no, he has opened up the archives for me and he is paying me a salary to poke around there and do nothing." Quoted in Veresaev, *Pushkin*, p. 108.

Chapter 4

1. This comment about Pugachev by the archimandrite Platon Liubarsky is quoted, presumably ironically, by Pushkin as an epigraph in his *History of Pugachev*. *Polnoe sobranie*, vol. 9, pt. I, p. 4.

2. As Riasanovsky says of the Pugachev rebellion, this "great uprising followed the pattern of earlier lower-class insurrections, such as the ones led by Bolotnikov, Razin, and Bulavin, which strove to destroy the established order. . . . At its height the rebellion encom-

passed a huge territory in eastern European Russia, engulfing such important cities as Kazan and posing a threat to Moscow itself" (*A History*, p. 260). Pugachev was a Don Cossack who pretended to be Catherine's deposed and murdered husband, Tsar Peter III.

Initially, Pushkin wished his nonfictional work to appear under the title *The History of Pugachev*. Tsar Nicholas I found that title unacceptable, however, and demanded that it be changed to *The History of the Pugachev Uprising*.

3. According to Pushkin's father, even as a boy Alexander "understood that Nikolai Mikhailovich Karamzin was different from the others. One evening Nikolai Mikhailovich was visiting. He stayed for a long time, and the whole time Alexander sat across from him listening to his stories and not taking his eyes off him. [Alexander] was not yet six." Veresaev, *Pushkin*, p. 46.

4. "We are visited by the pupils of the Lycée: the poet Pushkin and Lomonosov. Their kind openheartedness amuses us." Karamzin to Prince P. A. Viazemsky, June 2, 1816. Quoted in Veresaev, *Pushkin*, p. 90.

5. Pushkin, *Polnoe sobranie*, vol. 17, p. 16. Further citations from the collected works of Pushkin in this chapter will be indicated in the text and the notes by volume and page number (and part number for vol. 9) of this edition.

6. In a letter to Viazemsky dated July 10, 1826, Pushkin wrote: "Your short letter grieved me for many reasons. In the first place, what do you mean by my epigrams against Karamzin? It's enough that there is one, which I wrote at a time when Karamzin had quit having anything to do with me, and thus deeply wounded my self-esteem" (Pushkin, *Letters*, p. 313).

7. Letter to Raevsky of Jan. or Jun. 30, 1829 (Pushkin, *Letters*, p. 365). For some hints of exactly how Pushkin used Karamzin's *History*, see Striedter, "Poetic Genre," and for a splendid study on the question, see Emerson.

8. In September 1836, Pushkin wrote a letter to P. A. Korsakov asking for help in getting *The Captain's Daughter* through the St. Petersburg censorship committee, of which Korsakov was a member; Pushkin wrote, "I take the liberty of sending you the first part of my novel for your judgment, and I ask you to preserve the secret of my name" (16, 162). A month later, having read and liked the manuscript, Korsakov replied: "Please inform [me] . . . can I tell the

censor that this manuscript (by an unknown author) was presented by you, since the ending gives you away . . . as the editor of this story" (in Pushkin, 16, 177). Despite the fact that Korsakov was correct, Pushkin insisted on remaining in the shadows. "I would ask you not to mention the real name of the author, and to say that you were presented the manuscript through P. A. Pletnev, who has already been told" (16, 178). It is hard to see why Pushkin would have gone to such lengths unless he were attempting to free his novel from the obligations imposed by the tsar's personal censorship.

9. For a detailed discussion of how Pushkin transformed some of his sources, see Komarovich.

10. Among other reasons, Polevoi had earned the enmity of Pushkin and his circle by publishing his *History of the Russian People*, a work that competed directly with that of their old idol Karamzin. Pushkin wrote two articles devoted to Polevoi's history, one in 1830 and the other in 1831. He never published the review of the second volume, which was less negative than that of the first. Neither, however, could be considered positive. For a summary of Pushkin's relations with Polevoi, see Chereisky, pp. 317–18.

11. One possible exception has been noted by Sam Driver: "It is in the footnotes where the full horror of the rising is indicated by Pushkin's careful inclusion of some twenty-five pages of a report listing the atrocities of Pugachev and his men" (p. 64). Even here, however, the contradiction is only implied. Pushkin does not deny Pugachev's cruelty in the main text; he simply does not focus on it.

12. It is worth noting that the editor's note at the end of *The Captain's Daughter* might well have been suggested by a note that Pushkin had in fact once received from the historical novelist Ivan Lazhechnikov. "Not long ago I discovered that you are writing the history of Pugachev. I have a manuscript that might be useful to you. I don't know whether you have a copy of it already, but in any case I'm sending it along to you" (published in Pushkin {15, 122}).

13. For more on Pushkin's techniques of frustrating the reader's expectations in *The Captain's Daughter*, see Debreczeny, pp. 261–67.

14. Petrunina makes this very clear in her exhaustive analysis of the compositional history of *The Captain's Daughter*. See Petrunina, *Proza Pushkina*, pp. 246–56.

15. Letter to Mordvinov of July 30, 1833. Cited in Pushkin, *Letters*, pp. 599–600. This letter does not, by the way, mark Pushkin's

first mention of a desire to write about Pugachev. According to the memoirs of Princess M. N. Volkonskaia, as early as 1826 Pushkin told her, "I want to write a work about Pugachev" (cited in Veresaev, *Pushkin*, pp. 339–40).

16. For an amusing account of this "fact-finding expedition" to the Orenburg region, see Dal', "Vospominaniia," pp. 222–26.

17. Letter of Dec. 6, 1833 (Pushkin, *Letters*, p. 621).

18. One should also not overlook the financial considerations that might have prompted Pushkin to undertake his *History*. Karamzin had been handsomely paid as official historiographer, and Pushkin, who was perennially short of cash, could expect that some kind of government subsidy would be forthcoming should his historical researches bear fruit. This was, in fact, the case. Pushkin eventually received 15,000 rubles from the imperial treasury for the *History*. Pushkin's effusive letter of thanks to the tsar (by way of the unavoidable Benkendorf) attests to the subsidy and Pushkin's gratitude (15, 108). The role of Nicholas I in the publication of *The History of Pugachev* is described at length in Petrunina, *Proza Pushkina*.

19. Recall Pushkin's letter to Raevsky, cited earlier in this chapter, in which he said that a knowledge of Karamzin was a sine qua non for appreciating his play. For an excellent treatment of the relationship between Pushkin's play and Karamzin's history, see Emerson, particularly chap. 3, pp. 88–137.

20. There were, of course, sketchy accounts available in memoirs of some of those who had put down the uprising, and there was a lively oral folk tradition concerning Pugachev. But before the appearance of Pushkin's history, nothing remotely like a full-scale narrative description of the revolt existed.

21. Even if the events had not been ordered forgotten, it is likely that they would not have been well known, for while Russian historians of the first decades were very assiduous in their researches into older periods of Russian history, they almost completely ignored the period from the reign of Peter the Great to their own day.

22. Petrunina, *Proza Pushkina*, pp. 256–57.

23. Annenkov, p. 361.

24. Further evidence that Pushkin believed intergeneric dialogue to be the appropriate method of dealing with historical material can be found in the comments reported by the writer and lexicographer V. I. Dal' concerning his (Pushkin's) work on Peter the Great: "Push-

kin then got fired up in the full sense of the word, and, touching on Peter the Great, he said that in addition to a history, he intended to create an artistic work to commemorate Peter." Veresaev, *Pushkin*, p. 175.

25. Quoted in Petrunina, *Proza Pushkina*, p. 264.

26. "When Pushkin returned to prose in the late 1820's, beginning with *The Moor of Peter the Great* (*Arap Petra Velikogo*), there was an atmosphere in Russian literature quite different from what induced Pushkin to choose drama as the mode for *Boris Godunov*. By the 1830's, the tendencies toward prose were pronounced rather than incipient . . . and fiction of the 1830's was primarily historical fiction." Sandler, p. 250.

27. In the introduction to his history, Polevoi characterized Karamzin's work as follows: "It is actually a history of kings and not of the kingdom or the people. Karamzin, who was led astray by a false understanding of the political system of the past, considered that the proof of his love for the fatherland was his desire to touch up, or retint, the truth, and he often sacrificed the truth and a critical approach to his material in favor of an elegant narrative." Polevoi, vol. 1, p. xxxvi.

28. As Pushkin himself put it in his 1830 article on Zagoskin's historical novel, *Iury Miloslavsky*, "In our time we mean by the word 'novel' a historical epoch developed in an invented narrative. Walter Scott has attracted a whole crowd of imitators" (11, 92). For a thorough discussion of Scott and the historical novel in Russia in this period, see Schamschula.

29. Masal'sky, pp. 4–5.

30. See, for example, Gasparov's "The Apocalyptic Theme," pp. 16–25. Gasparov analyzes Pushkin's comic use of the apocalyptic theme, as opposed to his more conventional treatment of it in *Poltava*. Pushkin was also not above treating the same material in different ways within the confines of a single work. For more on this subject, see Lotman, "K strukture."

A recent dissertation points out that in his 1830 lyric "The Hero" ("Geroi"), Pushkin presents the attitudes of the "poet" and the "historian" regarding the proper way to view history. The poem's refusal to endorse either position can be seen as one more indication of Pushkin's conviction of the need for both. See Evdokimova.

31. For specific examples of the double meaning of this verb in

nineteenth-century usage, see the entry under *perepisyvat* in Dal''s celebrated dictionary.

32. Striedter, "Poetic Genre," pp. 299.

33. The lack of such a unifying voice was what Pushkin criticized in Polevoi's history. See the review (never published in Pushkin's lifetime) of the second volume of *The History of the Russian People* (11, 125).

34. The *dumy* had initially been published individually in half a dozen periodicals between 1821 and 1823. Ryleev prepared the collection in 1824 and it appeared in 1825.

35. Ryleev, p. 105.

36. Interestingly enough, Ryleev began composing the *dumy* under the direct influence of Karamzin's *History*. In a letter to Faddei Bulgarin, written after reading the ninth volume of the *History*, Ryleev said, "So that's the Terrible! So that's Karamzin!—I don't know which is more amazing, the tyranny of our Ivan or the talent of our Tacitus." In that same letter he enclosed the first of the *dumy*, the one concerning Ivan's archenemy Kurbsky, with the comment: "Here is a little piece of mine—the fruit of my reading of the ninth volume" (quoted in Ryleev, p. 14).

37. That the prose biographies were not, for the most part, written by Ryleev himself, but by P. M. Stroev at Ryleev's request, does not change the dual generic character of the *dumy*.

38. For a classic discussion of the interpenetration of literary and life genres in the lives and works of the Decembrists, see Lotman, "Dekabrist."

39. Gogol also applied for the position of professor of history at Kiev University at about the same time.

40. See Veresaev, *Gogol*, pp. 151–76.

41. During this period, Gogol and Pushkin saw each other frequently, and Gogol was aware of Pushkin's historical work. "Pushkin has already almost completed *The History of Pugachev*. This will be a unique kind of work in our country. It's a real novel!" (from a letter to M. P. Pogodin, May 8, 1833, in Gogol, vol. 10, p. 269).

42. "O prepodavanii vseobshchei istorii," in Gogol, vol. 8, p. 25. This essay was originally published in 1834 under a slightly different title in the *Journal of the Ministry of Education*. It was reprinted in 1835 in *Arabesques*.

43. Gogol, vol. 8, p. 38. According to Susanne Fusso, Gogol's

entire *Arabesques* collection is organized around what I would call an intergeneric dialogue juxtaposing the general to the specific. "Throughout *Arabesques*, whether the subject is history, geography, or art, Gogol reiterates the need not only to apprehend multifarious, individual, partial detail, but to use one's intellectual powers and artistic sensibility to assemble seemingly fragmentary data of experience into a unified whole" (p. 113).

44. In general, the critical literature on Gogol tends not to take his historical research, teaching, and articles seriously. Nevertheless, a reading of Gogol's letters from the first half of the 1830's indicates that he himself took his historical work very seriously, perhaps even more seriously than his fiction writing. For example, he informed M. P. Pogodin on Jan. 11, 1834: "I am completely immersed in Ukrainian and in universal history; and both of them have begun to move forward. . . . It seems to me that I will do something unique with universal history. My Ukrainian history is extremely frenetic, but, of course, it could hardly be otherwise." For more on this subject, see the rest of Gogol's letters to Pogodin and those to M. A. Maksimovich in the years 1833–35.

45. For a good discussion of Gogol's use of historical sources and of the importance of the interrelationship of history and literature in his oeuvre, see Karpuk; see also Seifrid.

46. It is interesting in this regard that both Pushkin and Gogol treated material that had not been touched by Karamzin. In Pushkin's case the reasons were temporal—Karamzin's history ends with the "time of troubles"—while in Gogol's they were spatial—Ukraine (at least in the period Gogol was interested in) did not fall into Karamzin's geographical purview.

Chapter 5

1. From the notebooks for *War and Peace*, in Tolstoy, vol. 13, p. 53. Further references to the works of Tolstoy in this chapter will be by volume and page number of this edition.

2. Henry James, "Preface to *The Tragic Muse*," p. 84.

3. Tolstoy, "Neskol'ko slov po povodu knigi 'Voina i mir' " (16, 7).

4. *War and Peace* was not, however, Tolstoy's first flirtation with the desire to be a historian. For a detailed discussion of Tolstoy the historian in the period before *War and Peace*, see Zaidenshnur, pp. 7–11.

5. That what is narrated in the past tense can be perceived by readers as present-tense action has been recognized to be a characteristic feature of third-person narration since the appearance of Käte Hamburger's classic study, *The Logic of Literature*. She calls this tense of narration the "epic preterite," and says that when it is used in the novel "the preterite is no longer perceived as stating the past" (pp. 64–81).

6. This draft is quoted in Zaidenshnur, p. 37. Of course, later in the novel Tolstoy introduces Platon Karataev, but even his appearance is motivated by his effect on future Rostov in-law Pierre.

7. The first such usage of the narrative "we" comes in the book's first chapter, when Tolstoy describes the conversation of Prince Vasily: "He spoke that refined French in which our grandfathers not only conversed but thought" (9, 4). The use of the first-person plural possessive pronoun helps make it difficult to determine whether this passage is fictional or historical. See further discussion of this passage later this chapter.

8. See Morson, *Hidden in Plain View*, pp. 9–36.

9. Morson, *Hidden in Plain View*, p. 13.

10. Berlin discusses the differences between hedgehogs and foxes and Tolstoy's ambiguous position on this continuum in "The Hedgehog and the Fox." In Berlin, pp. 22–24.

11. Eikhenbaum, p. 195.

12. Zaidenshnur (pp. 347–49) discusses two major historical digressions that Tolstoy chose to cut from the first volumes.

13. Morson, in *Hidden in Plain View*, cites a number of reader reactions, the most succinct being the following: "Taken as a whole, this *1805* [Tolstoy's original title] offers something strange and undefined. Evidently the author himself does not know how to define his work; its title says simply *The Year 1805*, by Count Leo Tolstoy" (p. 39).

14. The English novelist Arnold Bennett stated the problem quite well: "The last part of the Epilogue is full of good ideas the johnny can't work out. And of course, in the phrase of the critics, would have been better left out. So it would; only Tolstoy couldn't leave it out. It was what he wrote the book for" (as quoted in Berlin, p. 27). My only caveat is to say that Tolstoy did not try to work out his ideas in the epilogue; rather, he uses the epilogue to point readers toward the solutions that are found on other textual levels.

15. As quoted in Morson, *Hidden in Plain View*, p. 44.

16. For a convincing analysis of specifically what annoyed Bakhtin about Tolstoy, see Caryl Emerson, "The Tolstoy Connection in Bakhtin," in Morson and Emerson, eds., *Rethinking Bakhtin*, pp. 149–70.

17. Wasiolek, p. 112.

18. "The Hedgehog and the Fox," in Berlin, p. 24.

19. Cited in Zaidenshnur, p. 348.

20. Of course, by virtue of their presence in what we ultimately recognize to be a multigeneric text, even the completely harmonic passages are in principle dialogized. Take, for example, such quintessentially fictional scenes as the hunt or the ball at Iogel's. Although they are presented entirely by the fictional narrator, the reader certainly knows that they could, say, also be described by the historical narrator. Tolstoy does not choose to employ the historical narrator for these scenes, but we realize that he could have.

21. The historical narrator can even be present in fictional sections like the beginning of the hunt (10, 244). This works only because the reader has already been sensitized to this kind of narration in the truly historical scenes.

22. Morson, *Hidden in Plain View*, p. 134.

23. See Lukács, p. 39, for an explanation of why this method of composition is so central for the classical historical novel.

24. *Les misérables*, p. 269. This denial, by the way, can be seen as Hugo's unspoken justification of his switch in this section to historical narration.

25. Of course, in the twentieth century, the overwhelming majority of historians have learned how to do without individuals as central heroes. But they still tend to focus their causal explanations around collective heroes—the working class, the developing economy, demographic change, etc.

Chapter 6

1. From the notebooks for *Diary of a Writer*, in Dostoevsky, vol. 24, p. 312. Further references to the works of Dostoevsky in this chapter will be by volume and page number (and part number for vol. 29) of this edition.

2. Mochulsky, pp. 557–62. See also Belknap, *The Genesis*, passim;

Morson, *Boundaries of Genre*, pp. 31–32; and the notes to Dostoevsky (15, 407).

3. Mochulsky, p. 557.

4. Mochulsky, pp. 557–62.

5. "Postydno li byt' idealistom," *Diary of a Writer*, July–Aug. 1876 (23, 67).

6. See, for example, Dostoevsky's letters to L. A. Ozhigina and to S. D. Ianovsky of December 17, 1877 (in Dostoevsky, 29, II, 177–80).

7. Morson, *Boundaries of Genre*, pp. 49–50.

8. The August 1880 issue is somewhat of an anomaly, for it is entirely devoted to Dostoevsky's famous "Pushkin speech" and to his response to criticism of the speech (Dostoevsky had given the speech in June 1880). Because of its occasional nature, and because Dostoevsky made no effort to prepare other issues for 1880, the August issue should probably not be considered an attempt to start the *Diary* anew. It is actually the January 1881 issue, which was prepared after all work on *The Brothers Karamazov* was finished, that marks the true resumption of the *Diary*.

9. See the notes to Dostoevsky (15, 411–47) for a detailed discussion of the history of the composition and publication of the novel. *The Brothers Karamazov* is the only novel-length fictional work Dostoevsky wrote after beginning the *Diary*. It is true that he published something called *Diary of a Writer* in the journal *Citizen* in 1873. Therefore, one could say that the novel *A Raw Youth* (*Podrostok*, 1875) was also embedded in the *Diary*. But as the editors of the most recent complete works of Dostoevsky point out, the earlier *Diary* differs substantially from the *Diary* as it was reconstituted in 1876 (22, 264–65). In particular, the earlier version lacks the apocalyptic/utopian historiography that characterizes the later one. Thus, while the dialogue between the earlier *Diary* and *A Raw Youth* might be worthwhile to study, it falls out of this investigation. It is also worth noting in this context that the initial seed for *Diary of a Writer* appears in Dostoevsky's 1872 novel *The Devils* (*Besy*). In part I, chapter 4, section 2 of that novel, Liza tells Shatov of her plan to publish a kind of almanac that would be a digest of the entire Russian periodical press: "And if one were to compile all these facts for a whole year into a single book, according to a definite plan and a definite idea, with

headings, indexes, and a division into months and days, then such a compilation could trace the character of Russian society for the whole year" (10, 103).

10. In *The Boundaries of Genre*, Morson has provided a cogent analysis of the dialogic relationship between the journalistic and the fictional sections of the *Diary*. I will not repeat that analysis here. All I would wish to add is a suspicion that one of the reasons Dostoevsky turned to the novelistic form in 1878 may have been a certain dissatisfaction with the size limitations imposed on his fiction by the *Diary* format. Although it is true that Dostoevsky was capable of writing effective short fiction, he was a writer who, for the most part, needed the space that only a novel (or at least a novella) could provide for his greatest fictional work. The authorial preface that Dostoevsky provides at the beginning of the November 1876 issue of the *Diary* (which contained only the story "The Meek One") hints at the constraints of the *Diary* format: "I ask the forgiveness of my readers for having this time given only a story instead of the *Diary* in its usual form. But I really was occupied with this story for the entire month. In any case, I beg the readers' indulgence" (24, 5).

11. Dostoevsky (29, II, 178–79).

12. In a letter to Maikov of Dec. 31, 1867, Dostoevsky said, "For a long time now a certain idea has been tormenting me, but I've been afraid to make a novel out of it, because the idea is too difficult and I'm not ready for it, although the idea is most tempting and I love it. This idea is to portray a wholly beautiful individual. There can be, in my opinion, nothing more difficult than this, especially in our age" (28, 240–41).

13. Mochulsky, p. 381.

14. Ekaterina II, *Sochineniia*, vol. 8, introduction (unpaginated).

15. Karamzin, *Istoriia*, vol. 1, "Introduction," p. ix.

16. Karamzin, *Istoriia*, vol. 1, "Dedication," p. vii.

17. Karamzin, *Istoriia*, vol. 1, "Introduction," p. ix.

18. Ryleev, p. 105.

19. Khomiakov, "Predislovie k Russkim pesniam," in vol. 3, p. 166.

20. For an excellent discussion of history and parody in *The History of the Village of Goriukhino*, see Kropf. For a different view of the role of *The History of the Village of Goriukhino* in Pushkin's work, see Bethea and Davydov.

21. At the very end of the "Notes," for example, Pushkin tells the tsar that it was really only the *dvorianstvo* (aristocracy) who supported the throne, a word to the wise that seems designed specifically to counter the aristocrat-bashing that had been going on in the popular press for years, and to strengthen the claim that the aristocracy, rather than the bureaucracy, was the pillar of the throne (Pushkin, *Polnoe sobranie*, vol. 9, pt. I, pp. 369–76).

22. See Eikhenbaum, p. 115.

23. Quoted in Eikhenbaum, p. 154.

24. "Nechto o Peterburgskom Baden-Badenstve," *Diary of a Writer*, July–Aug. 1876 (23, 58).

25. "Opiat' v poslednii raz 'proshchaniia,' " *Diary of a Writer*, Nov. 1877 (26, 87–88). The *Diary* was by no means the first manifestation of Dostoevsky's belief that he was capable of prophecy. For example, after hearing of a crime that matched in many respects the action of *Crime and Punishment*, Dostoevsky wrote to Maikov on Dec. 11, 1868, "I have completely different ideas about reality and realism than our realists and critics. My idealism is more real than theirs . . . their type of realism does not know how to explain even a small fraction of real actual events. But we by our idealism *have even prophesied facts. We have actually prophesied them*" (28, II, 329; emphasis mine).

26. Riasanovsky, *A History*, p. 125.

27. Chaadaev, *Philosophical Letters*, pp. 166–67.

28. Morson, "Dostoevsky's *Diary of a Writer*," p. 30.

29. Berlin, p. 120.

30. Gleason, p. 157.

31. Walicki, *A History*, p. 107.

32. Clearly, Danilevsky and Dostoevsky had direct precursors in some of the more intellectually astute followers of the doctrine of official nationalism, particularly Shevyrev and Pogodin. For these men, however, a militant brand of national chauvinism (furnished with a basically Slavophile-inspired ideal of Russia's past) was, first and foremost, the foundation for concrete Russian activity in the present. Although they certainly spoke about a glorious future for Russia, this future was conceived of within the framework of the existing European political and social order, rather than as the final, messianic stage of world history. For a detailed discussion of official nationality, see Riasanovsky, *Nicholas I*, pp. 73–183.

33. For a full discussion of Danilevsky's version of Pan-Slavic

historiography, see MacMaster, pp. 177–250. For Dostoevsky's differences with Danilevsky (Dostoevsky thought Danilevsky was not chauvinistic enough!), see, for example, Dostoevsky, "Tolki o mire. 'Konstantinopol' dolzhen byt' nash'—Vozmozhno li eto? Raznye mneniia," *Diary of a Writer*, Nov. 1877 (26, 85–86).

34. Morson, *Boundaries of Genre*, p. 33.

35. "Primiritel'naia mechta vne nauki," *Diary of a Writer*, Jan. 1877 (25, 17).

36. "Utopicheskoe ponimanie istorii," *Diary of a Writer*, June 1876 (23, 47). Interestingly, Dostoevsky's belief in Russia as the universal civilization led him to break with his Slavophile predecessors over Peter the Great. The Slavophiles were basically isolationists who believed that Peter had betrayed the nation's traditions. For the universalist Dostoevsky, however, Peter's actions were praiseworthy, for in breaking down Russia's parochial isolation Peter had forged a broad foundation on which the edifice of universal Russian civilization could rise.

37. "Dve polovinki," *Diary of a Writer*, Aug. 1880 (26, 167–68).

38. Dostoevsky, *The Devils* (10, 109–10).

39. "'Anna Karenina' kak fakt osobogo znacheniia," *Diary of a Writer*, July–Aug. 1877 (25, 199). The same thoughts, expressed even more fully, are central to the famous Pushkin speech that appeared in the August 1880 *Diary* (26, 136–49).

40. *Diary of a Writer*, July–Aug. 1877 (25, 202).

41. It is true, of course, that Myshkin enunciates messianic Slavophile views at various points in *The Idiot*. But Myshkin's very isolation from society (as well as society's inability to appreciate his views) shows that these are mere utopian dreams. The author himself, we suspect, does not believe that the actual historical moment is ripe, even if the ideas expressed are similar to those that appear in *The Brothers Karamazov*. It was only Dostoevsky's thorough analysis of European and Russian society in the wake of the "Eastern crisis" of 1877 that convinced him that the proper historical moment had indeed arrived.

42. Mochulsky, p. 615.

43. "Moi paradoks," *Diary of a Writer*, June 1876 (23, 40).

44. *The Brothers Karamazov*, pt. II, bk. 5, chap. 3 (14, 210).

45. *The Brothers Karamazov* (14, 6).

46. Not all interpreters take the narrator's claim about the expected production of a sequel as a statement of Dostoevsky's intent.

For a good summary of opinions on the subject, see Belknap, *Structure*, pp. 98–102.

47. "Prodolzhenie predydushchego," *Diary of a Writer*, Sept. 1876 (23, 130).

48. This is why Dostoevsky notes that the institution of elders is not a modern invention, as some have charged, but rather that "in Rus', the institution of elders has existed from the most ancient times" (14, 26).

49. See particularly the article entitled "Utopicheskoe ponimanie istorii," *Diary of a Writer*, June 1876 (23, 46–51).

50. *The Brothers Karamazov*, pt. IV, bk. 12, chap. 6 (15, 128).

51. Jackson, p. 343.

52. "Tri idei," *Diary of a Writer*, Jan. 1877 (25, 9).

Chapter 7

1. Quoted in Cooke, p. 158.

2. This quote is, of course, from the celebrated early-Futurist manifesto, "A Slap in the Public's Taste" ("Poshchechina obshchestvennomu vkusu"). In Markov, ed., *Manifesty*, p. 50.

3. Perloff, p. 22.

4. No authoritative history or analysis of Russian primitivism yet exists. The movement's basic parameters are drawn in Nilsson.

5. Markov, *Russian Futurism*, p. 35.

6. Of course, a break with the models of the nineteenth century in favor of those of the almost forgotten eighteenth century was by no means limited to writings concerning history in this period— one could point to similar tendencies at work in the odic poetry of Maiakovsky, or in the painting of Alexandre Benois, for example.

7. Khlebnikov, *Tvoreniia*, p. 37.

8. Baran, "The Problem of Composition," pp. 95–100.

9. The only important formal difference between Solov'ev's "Conversation" and Khlebnikov's "Dialogue" is that the former contains five differentiated voice positions, while the latter is limited to two. That Khlebnikov was aware of the Solov'ev connection (at least at a later date) and saw Solov'ev as a precursor can be seen in *Zangezi*: "What Kulikovo was for the Tatars/the horror of Mukden became for the Russians./Like a prophet in eyeglasses/at his writing desk, Vladimir Solovyov/foresaw it all" (Khlebnikov, *The King of Time*, p. 221).

10. Khlebnikov, *Tvoreniia*, p. 585.

11. Khlebnikov, *Tvoreniia*, p. 588.

12. Khlebnikov, *Tvoreniia*, p. 589. Khlebnikov was very proud of this prediction, both when he made it and later, and his fellow Futurists shared the enthusiasm. For more details on this subject, see Duganov, pp. 140–41.

13. "To the Artists of the World!" in Khlebnikov, *The King of Time*, p. 146.

14. It was this aspect of the Futurist program that inspired Viktor Shklovsky's essay "The Resurrection of the Word" ("Voskreshenie slova").

15. Khlebnikov, *The King of Time*, p. 147.

16. Baran, "Temporal Myths," p. 71.

17. In regard to virulent nationalism, Khlebnikov's views were consonant with those of the Russian avant-garde in general. As Boris Groys puts it: "Contrary to the widespread notion of its 'Westernism,' the Russian avant-garde was extremely nationalistic" (p. 80).

18. Baran details Khlebnikov's early Pan-Slavic tendencies in "Temporal Myths," pp. 70–72. In addition, Khlebnikov's virulent opposition to F. T. Marinetti's visit to Russia was unquestionably related to his nationalism. See Markov, *Russian Futurism*, pp. 150–52.

19. Khlebnikov first applied this phrase to himself in a letter to Kamensky (Khlebnikov, *Sobranie proizvedeniia*, vol. 5, p. 303).

20. Markov, *Russian Futurism*, p. 149.

21. In this area Khlebnikov's utopian project overlaps with that of the Russian composer and mystic Alexander Scriabin, who attempted to create an instrument to link musical sounds with appropriate colors. Khlebnikov was enamored of Scriabin. His views on the composer are presented in Grigor'ev, pp. 131–42, although synesthesia, which in my view is the most significant connection, is not mentioned.

22. Khlebnikov, *Tvoreniia*, p. 623.

23. Khlebnikov certainly knew *War and Peace*, as a casual reference to Natasha Rostova in his notebooks proves (*Sobranie sochinenii*, vol. 4, p. 332). In this context it is perhaps also worth noting that although the poet is not very given to using biblical quotations, in this same *Tables of Destiny* (*Doski sud'by*) he quotes the phrase "Mne otmshchenie i az vozdam" (*Sobranie sochinenii*, vol. 4, p. 475), which, while not particularly prominent in the Bible, was well known to Russian readers as the epigraph to *Anna Karenina*.

24. The question of the relationship between these quasi-scientific writings and Khlebnikov's more purely literary work has been a vexed one. Vladimir Markov encouraged readers to see them as essentially unrelated (Markov, *Russian Futurism*, pp. 25–26), but I must agree with Raymond Cooke, who says that "although it might be argued that Khlebnikov's mathematical analyses of history should be separated from his artistic work, one of the most important elements of Khlebnikov's writings is, on the contrary, the integration of scientific and poetic interests" (p. 151). To this I would add that obviously artistic works like *Zangezi* can in fact be understood only by appreciating their intergeneric dialogue with such quasi-artistic works as *The Tables of Destiny*.

25. In Khlebnikov, *The King of Time*, p. 183.

26. For other examples of the same concern, see the 1915 prose pieces "Ka" (Khlebnikov, *Tvoreniia*, p. 532), and "Bitvy 1915–17 gg." (Khlebnikov, *Sobranie sochinenii*, vol. 3, 422–27).

27. Khlebnikov, *Sobranie sochinenii*, vol. 3, p. 425.

28. "In 1789 there was a ferment in Paris: it grew and spread, and found expression in the movement of peoples from west to east. Several times that movement is made to the east, and comes into collision with a countermovement from the east westwards. In the year 1812 it reaches its furthest limit, Moscow, and then, with a remarkable symmetry, the countermovement follows from east to west; drawing with it, like the first movement, the peoples of central Europe. The countermovement reaches the starting point of the first movement—Paris—and subsides" (Tolstoy, vol. 12, p. 297).

29. Solov'ev, "Tri razgovora" in vol. 2, p. 692.

30. Solov'ev, vol. 2, p. 642.

31. Indeed, Solov'ev himself seems to have been ambivalent on the subject, for although he predicted great destruction and death in the wake of the invasion from the East, this invasion was nevertheless necessary for his millenarian scheme. This perhaps helps explain the ambiguous epigraph that Solov'ev chose from his own poetry for the "Short Tale about the Antichrist": "Панмонголизм! Хоть имя дико / Но мне ласкает слух оно, / Как бы предвестием великой / Судьбины божией полно" (Panmongolism! Though the word is wild/It caresses my ear,/'Tis filled, it seems, with augurs/Of a gigantic divine fate). *Izbrannye sochineniia*, vol. 2, p. 736.

32. Markov and Sparks, eds. and trans., pp. 46–47. Among

dozens of other choices, we might note the appearance of this theme in Andrei Belyi's *Petersburg* and in Alexander Blok's "The Scythians" ("Skify").

33. Khlebnikov, *Tvoreniia*, p. 647. The names Khlebnikov chooses to mention here are, of course, quite significant. The Chaadaev of the "First Philosophical Letter" is the very model of a Russian obsessed with history. Pushkin figures here both as a writer in this same tradition and as the model of a Russian writer, while Pafnuty L'vovich Chebyshev (1821–94) was a famous Russian mathematician whose work included books on probability theory and mathematical interpolation.

34. Khlebnikov, *Tvoreniia*, p. 650. The "law of 28 years" referred to here was one of Khlebnikov's preliminary mathematical/historical formulations. It postulated that 28 years (or multiples thereof) separated the births of analogous figures.

35. Khlebnikov, *Sobranie sochinenii*, vol. 3, p. 471.

36. For example, Douglas calls the work a "story of transcendent faith in the human spirit" (Khlebnikov, *The King of Time*, p. 190). Baran, on the other hand, sees it as a far more ambivalent statement ("Temporal Myths," pp. 78–79 and 84–85), while Cooke, perhaps wisely, refrains from any overarching interpretation.

37. Khlebnikov, *The King of Time*, p. 191. Unless otherwise noted, all further quotations from *Zangezi* in this chapter will be cited in the main text by page number of this edition.

38. I have not been able to identify "Unkulunkulu," and my guess that this god is supposed to be Finnic is based only on the sound of the name. In any case, the god is clearly neither Roman nor Russian.

39. For more on Khlebnikov's work habits, see Cooke, 166–68.

40. Khlebnikov, *Tvoreniia*, p. 479. The punning sentence makes more sense in Russian, because the word Рог (horn) is a homonym for Рок (fate).

41. For more on the possible connection of this section with mantras, see Baran, "Temporal Myths," pp. 83–84.

42. The Russian is in Khlebnikov, *Tvoreniia*, p. 486. English in Khlebnikov, *The King of Time*, p. 212.

43. Like the "Tables of Destiny" excerpt in plane four that does not correspond exactly to any part of that work, this section may simply be a reworked variant of "Night Search."

44. The lines on p. 217 of *The King of Time* echo p. 329 in *Tvoreniia*.

45. Khlebnikov, *Tvoreniia*, p. 698.
46. Douglas, in Khlebnikov, *The King of Time*, p. 190.
47. Khlebnikov, *The King of Time*, p. 235.
48. Khlebnikov, *Zangezi*, p. 35. The promise of a sequel appeared in the first edition of the Supersaga. Subsequent editions and the Schmidt translation omit it.
49. See Vroon's articles.
50. Kamensky, *Put' entuziasta*, pp. 492–93. The basic accuracy of Kamensky's memoir is confirmed by a letter he wrote when he sent his manuscript to the critic A. A. Izmailov in 1915: "I created with the uncontrolled whirlwind of my rebellious soul . . . and it even seems to me that my book—my blood, will without bounds, a gigantic book—is needed by all now." Quoted in Kamensky, *Stikhotvoreniia*, p. 24.
51. Kamensky, *Sten'ka Razin*, p. 6.
52. Kamensky, *Sten'ka Razin*, p. 14.
53. Markov, *Russian Futurism*, p. 327.
54. Vroon emphasizes Khlebnikov's identification with Razin in "Velimir Khlebnikov's 'Razin'."
55. Kamensky, *Stikhotvoreniia*, p. 151.
56. As Kamensky puts it in the 1928 *Stepan Razin*, "Stepan and Frol [his brother], shocked by the unexpected, unimagined catastrophe . . . hid immediately, mentally swearing not only to revenge their father, but to get even at the same time with all the princes, boyars, generals, and nobles of the Muscovite state who could stand neither the Cossacks nor the whole Russian people, who were enslaved by the yoke of serfdom" (*Stepan Razin. Privol'nyi roman*, p. 12).
57. Quoted in Cooke, p. 158.

Chapter 8

1. "Kak my pishem," in Kaverin, ed., *Iury Tynianov*, pp. 196–97.
2. Erlich, p. 140.
3. For more on the internal tensions that broke up the Formalist school, see Gudkov, pp. 102–6.
4. Tynianov also discusses this relationship in the 1930 article "How We Write" ("Kak my pishem"). See the text in Kaverin, ed., *Iury Tynianov*, pp. 193–201. A concern with the relationship between science and art was not unique to Tynianov among the Formalists. It also informs Shklovsky's *Zoo*, for example.
5. Tynianov, *Arkhaisty i novatory*, pp. 591–92.

6. Chukovsky, in Kaverin, ed., *Vospominaniia*, p. 141.

7. Chukovsky, in Kaverin, ed., *Vospominaniia*, p. 141.

8. Boris Gasparov, in Gasparov, Hughes, and Paperno, eds., *Cultural Mythologies*, p. 5.

9. Monika Frenkel Greenleaf, "Tynianov, Pushkin and the Fragment: Through the Lens of Montage," in Gasparov, Hughes, and Paperno, eds., *Cultural Mythologies*, pp. 282, 287.

10. Tynianov, *Sochineniia*, vol. 1, p. 226.

11. Tynianov was by no means the only Futurist who tended to see in the past parallels with the present. As Eikhenbaum said: "History in this sense is a particular method for studying the present with the help of the facts of the past" (quoted in Gudkov, p. 100). Note, however, that as opposed to Khlebnikov and Kamensky, neither Tynianov nor Eikhenbaum sees knowledge of the past as a means to predict the future.

12. In Erlich, p. 177.

13. Tynianov, "Literaturnyi fakt," in *Arkhaisty i novatory*, p. 10.

14. Tynianov, "Dostoevsky i Gogol," in *Arkhaisty i novatory*, p. 413.

15. Quoted in Striedter, *Literary Structure*, p. 64.

16. Tynianov, *Arkhaisty i novatory*, p. 562.

17. Tynianov mentions Spengler in his 1921 article "Zapiski o zapadnoi literature," calling him "the German Chaadaev" (Tynianov, *Poetika, istoriia literatury, kino*, p. 125). According to the notes to that volume, "the Russian journals of the beginning of the 1920's were filled with comments on *The Decline of the West*, and they followed closely the reaction of German philosophy to Spengler's book" (p. 443).

18. Shklovsky, it would seem, had a far more highly developed sense of the need for total rebellion against the authority figures of the previous generation than did Tynianov. In part, this may have been because Shklovsky resented Vengerov's assessment of him as unqualified. See Shklovsky, "Gorod nashei iunosti," in Kaverin, ed., *Vospominaniia*, pp. 8–12.

19. According to the notes in Tynianov, *Pushkin i ego sovremenniki*, the article was lost in a fire in Iaroslavl in 1918 (p. 408).

20. After initial bouts of skepticism, Vengerov evidently came to appreciate Tynianov's work for his seminar. It is not clear whether this was because Vengerov was a truly tolerant scholar or because, like the

generations of critics Tynianov described in "Dostoevsky and Gogol," he saw influence but suppressed or did not recognize struggle.

21. Tynianov coedited the first collected edition of Khlebnikov's works (his only such work on a twentieth-century poet), included an article on him in *Archaists and Innovators*, and praised him extravagantly in the article "Promezhutok" in the same collection.

22. Tynianov, "Promezhutok," in *Arkhaisty i novatory*, p. 541.

23. "Promezhutok," in *Arkhaisty i novatory*, p. 542.

24. The idea of "literature of fact" was fully elaborated in 1925 and 1927 in the journals *Lef* and *Novyi Lef*. "The highest form of literary activity in this paradoxical theory, and the most useful 'in the epoch of socialism,' was factual reporting: the writing of sketches, biographies, diaries, travel notes, and the like. The concern of the writer should be with *facts* rather than with his own invention or fantasy" (Brown, p. 37). Although Tynianov was not a central figure in these journals, he did contribute to them and was in close contact with many of the journals' principals.

25. See "Kiukhel'beker i Pushkin," in Tynianov, *Pushkin i ego sovremenniki*, p. 260 and p. 410n27, for details.

26. "Frantsuzskie otnosheniia Kiukhel'bekera," in Tynianov, *Pushkin i ego sovremenniki*, p. 324.

27. Tynianov, ed., *V. K. Kiukhel'beker*, vol. 1, p. xxvi.

28. There is no question but that all of Tynianov's longer fictional works suffer from his overly copious knowledge. The reader frequently feels that Tynianov is too busy trying to include every little detail he knows about the period and not interested enough in telling the story.

29. The fact that Kiukhel'beker was a real person and Pechorin a literary character is, of course, immaterial in the Russian cultural context, where literary characters were frequently considered far more real than real people.

30. Kaverin and Novikov, p. 250.

31. Groys, pp. 48–49.

Chapter 9

1. *Avgust chetyrnadtsatogo*, vol. 2, p. 169.

2. "Neskol'ko slov po povodu knigi 'Voina i Mir,'" in Tolstoy, vol. 16, p. 7.

3. *Avgust chetyrnadtsatogo*, vol. 2, p. 545.

4. See the introduction to the section entitled "Na obryve povestvovaniia" at the end of *Aprel' semnadtsatogo*, vol. 2.

5. Quoted in Scammell, p. 993.

6. As Solzhenitsyn says in *October 1916*, before beginning yet another historical digression set off graphically in small print: "There is quite a lot of this material, already grown cold and seemingly linked but feebly to the October 1916 promised in the title, and it will not be exhausting only to those readers in whom the tense 1890's of Russian history still live, and who are able *to derive lessons for today from it.*" *Oktiabr' shestnadtsatogo*, vol. 1, p. 76. Emphasis mine.

7. In the afterword to *August 1914*, Solzhenitsyn says: "The author's father was introduced under what is practically his real name, and his mother's family exactly" (p. 546). Even the method Solzhenitsyn used to disguise his father's name (turning Solzhenitsyn into Lazhenitsyn) is reminiscent of Tolstoy's (Volkonsky to Bolkonsky). Solzhenitsyn's mother's family, the Shcherbaks, appear in *The Red Wheel* under the name Tomchak.

8. *August chetyrnadtsatogo*, vol. 1, p. 403.

9. *Oktiabr' shestnadtsatogo*, vol. 1, p. 332. Emphasis mine. Solzhenitsyn's absolute voice does not always contradict Tolstoyan doctrine, however. Thus, also in *October 1916*, we get the very Tolstoyan-sounding "Who can now explain where it all started? Who started it? Whoever would slice the continuous flow of history at one cross section and say: Here! it all started from here!—that person will always be mistaken" (vol. 1, p. 74).

10. *August chetyrnadtsatogo*, vol. 2, p. 38.

11. *August chetyrnadtsatogo*, vol. 1, p. 383. Solzhenitsyn is polemicizing here with Tolstoy's comments in book 3, part I, chapter 1 of *War and Peace* (Tolstoy *Polnoe sobranie*, vol. 11, pp. 4–7).

12. Tolstoy, vol. 11, pp. 265–66.

13. *August chetyrnadtsatogo*, vol. 1, p. 11.

14. Sentences like "Isaaky loved his natal Sablia and their homestead ten kilometers from it; he loved farm work, and now during the school vacation he did not try to shirk mowing or threshing" (*August chetyrnadtsatogo*, vol. 1, pp. 12–13) make the presence of *style indirect libre* obvious.

15. *August chetyrnadtsatogo*, vol. 1, p. 87.

16. See the section entitled "Na obryve povestvovaniia" in *Aprel' semnadtsatogo*, vol. 2, p. 1.

17. *Aprel' semnadtsatogo*, vol. 1, p. 103.

18. *Aprel' semnadtsatogo*, vol. 1, p. 114.

19. Tolstoy, of course, sometimes did the same thing. See my discussion of narrative harmony and narrative dissonance in Chapter 5.

20. Here Solzhenitsyn's narrative is heir to Dostoevsky's *Diary of a Writer*, a work which, in the author's words, was to be "a diary in the literal meaning of the word, an account of the impressions that were experienced each month" (Dostoevsky, vol. 22, p. 136).

21. *Mart semnadtsatogo*, vol. 1, pp. 337–703, and vol. 2, pp. 1–270.

22. For a fuller discussion of *The Red Wheel* in the context of modernist literature, see Wachtel, "Continuity and Change."

23. Of course, Solzhenitsyn is not entirely faithful to this scheme. All of his long historical asides are an implicit admission that the mere presentation of a cross section of life is not sufficient. Nevertheless, he is clearly somewhat uncomfortable with these digressions, and they become rarer and rarer as the cycle continues. See later this chapter for an analysis of their function in the cycle.

24. *Aprel' semnadtsatogo*, vol. 2, p. 232.

25. *Aprel' semnadtsatogo*, vol. 2, p. 268.

26. This approach is quite common in *The Red Wheel*. Perhaps the most extreme version is the presentation of the wounding and death of Guchkov's assistant, Prince Dmitry Viazemsky, in *March 1917*. Viazemsky is wounded on the evening of Mar. 1. This incident is described in chapter 292 (vol. 2, p. 482). Viazemsky dies the next morning, but his death in the book comes in chapter 326 (vol. 2, p. 615). His funeral on the family estate Lotareva takes place on Apr. 24, 1917 in vol. 2 of *April 1917*, some 430 chapters or 2,075 pages later.

27. *Aprel' semnadtsatogo*, vol. 2, p. 1 of the section entitled "Na obryve povestvovaniia."

28. He does not avoid it completely, however, even in the final knot. For example, after presenting the speech of Vasily Shul'gin at the anniversary meeting celebrating the four dumas, Solzhenitsyn adds, in parentheses, "Sixty years later, when Shul'gin was already 95, I visited him in semi-exile in Vladimir—and he continually returned to that speech, asking where he could find it to reread it" (*Aprel' semnadtsatogo*, vol. 2, p. 146). For a similar moment, see vol. 2, p. 232. Still, such instances of foreshadowing are very few and far

between; there are perhaps two or three in the 1,100 pages of the last knot.

29. This is by no means to claim that other nations did not also have chronicles. In Russia, however, for a variety of reasons, the chronicles have remained part of the nation's cultural memory and are thus potentially available to modern writers. In addition to *The Red Wheel*, other works of modern Russian literature that depend on readers' knowledge of the chronicle form are Pushkin's unfinished *History of the Village of Goriukhino* and Mikhail Saltykov-Shchedrin's *History of One City* (*Istoriia odnogo goroda*).

30. "Povest' vremennykh let," p. 56.

31. In *October 1916* such flashbacks are rarer, although we still get a shortened biography of Guchkov, a history of the sources of the Kadet party, and a fairly long analysis of "Society, the Government, and the Tsar" that stretches back into 1914.

32. *Avgust chetyrnadtsatogo*, vol. 2, p. 169. We find a similar admission and an identical justification in the "Author's Note to the Second Knot": "The recent history of our country is so little known or so distortedly studied that for the good of my young countrymen I was forced in my second knot to exceed the quantity of historical material expected in a literary work" (*Oktiabr' shestnadtsatogo*, vol. 2, p. 587). See also a similar statement in *Oktiabr' shestnadtsatogo*, vol. 1, p. 76.

33. Even when flashbacks are included, they are significantly shorter and are generally presented as if they were ruminations in the mind of a character. See, for example, the flashback biography of Nakhamkis (Steklov) in *Mart semnadtsatogo*, vol. 4, pp. 150–55.

34. In this respect the first knot of *The Red Wheel* seems close to the project of Vasily Grossman in *Life and Fate* (*Zhizn' i sud'ba*). In the later knots, however, the similarity becomes far less marked.

35. Lur'e, p. 15.

36. The highly archaic language that Solzhenitsyn uses throughout *The Red Wheel* may also be seen as an attempt to escape the linguistic constraints of modern Russian, and thus as analogous to the structural archaisms I have concentrated on in my analysis.

37. Scammell, p. 793.

38. It is worth noting that Solzhenitsyn's chief rival for control of the hearts and minds of Russian émigré and Western readers, Andrei Sinyavsky, also had recourse to the Russian intergeneric tradition in his attempt to explain twentieth-century Russian history: thus, his

nonfictional *Soviet Civilization* (*Sovietskaia Tsivilzatsiia*) must be read in tandem with novels such as *The Trial Begins* (*Sud idet*) and *Goodnight* (*Spukoinoi nochi*).

Chapter 10

1. Gershchenkron, p. 7.
2. Gershchenkron, p. 26.
3. This is clearly the view of Gershchenkron. It is not difficult to imagine, however, another point of view from which the gaps and lags in industrialization are evaluated positively—as potentials for escaping certain pitfalls and evils of western economic development. I will refrain from a discussion of whether such a point of view makes sense in an economic context.
4. For an account of the Russian tradition of childhood descriptions, see Wachtel, *The Battle for Childhood*.
5. Karamzin's fragment "A Knight of Our Time" ("Rytsar' nashego vremeni," 1802), the first significant work of Russian fiction with a child protagonist, had no immediate influence. Ivan Goncharov's fragment "Oblomov's Dream ("Son Oblomova," 1848) is the only other important fictional description of a child in Russia to appear before Tolstoy's work.
6. This form was not unique to Russia, nor was it invented by Tolstoy. Claudio Guillen uses the term *pseudo-autobiography* to describe a feature of Spanish picaresque novels, although these works are not, in fact, autobiographical at all. In my sense of the term, an autobiographical component is necessary. Some European works that fit this definition include Benjamin Constant's *Adolphe* (1816) and Alfred de Musset's *La confession d'un enfant du siècle* (1836). Perhaps the most famous European example is Charles Dickens's *David Copperfield* (1849–50, translated into Russian in 1851), which undoubtedly influenced the young Tolstoy.
7. "Neskol'ko slov," in Tolstoy, vol. 16, p. 7.
8. For various examples of this tendency, see Lotman, "Dekabrist," or Paperno.
9. Morson and Emerson, *Mikhail Bakhtin*, pp. 469–70.
10. The problem is not, it should be noted, that dialogue is inherently relativistic; it is that the outward form of dialogue can easily be exploited for other purposes. See Morson and Emerson, *Mikhail Bakhtin*, pp. 233–34, for a discussion of Bakhtin's ideas on dialogue in relation to authoritarianism and relativism.

Works Cited

Annenkov, P. V. *Materialy dlia biografii A. S. Pushkina*. St. Petersburg, 1855.

Aries, Philippe. *Certitudes et incertitudes de l'histoire*. Paris, 1987.

Bakhtin, M. M. *The Dialogic Imagination*. Caryl Emerson and Michael Holquist, trans. Austin, Tex., 1981.

——— . *Problemy poetiki Dostoevskogo*. Moscow, 1979.

Baran, Henryk. "The Problem of Composition in Velimir Chlebnikov's Texts." *Russian Literature* 9 (1981): 87–106.

——— . "Temporal Myths in Xlebnikov: From 'Deti vydry' to 'Zangezi.'" In A. Kodjak, K. Pomorska, and S. Rudy, eds., *Myth in Literature*, pp. 63–88. Columbus, Ohio, 1983.

Batiushkov, K. N. *Izbrannaia proza*. Moscow, 1987.

Belinkov, A. *Iury Tynianov*. Moscow, 1960.

Belknap, Robert L. *The Genesis of "The Brothers Karamazov."* Evanston, Ill., 1990.

——— . *The Structure of "The Brothers Karamazov."* Evanston, Ill., 1989.

Berlin, Isaiah. *Russian Thinkers*. New York, 1978.

Bethea, David, and Sergei Davydov. "The [Hi]story of the Village Gorjuxino: In Praise of Pushkin's Folly." *Slavic and East European Journal* 28, no. 3 (Fall 1984): 291–309.

Billington, James. *The Icon and the Axe*. New York, 1970.

Black, J. L. *Nicholas Karamzin and Russian Society in the Nineteenth Century*. Toronto, 1975.

——— . "The *Primečanija*: Karamzin as a 'Scientific' Historian of

Russia." In J. L. Black, ed., *Essays on Karamzin*, pp. 127–47. The Hague, 1975.

Bloch, Marc. *The Historian's Craft.* Peter Putnam, trans. New York, 1953.

Braudy, Leo. *Narrative Form in History and Fiction.* Princeton, N.J., 1970.

Brown, Edward J. *Russian Literature Since the Revolution.* Cambridge, Mass., 1982.

Brun-Zejmis, Julia. "Messianic Consciousness as an Expression of National Inferiority: Chaadaev and Some Samizdat Writings of the 1970s." *Slavic Review* (Fall 1991): 646–58.

Chaadaev, P. Ia. *"Philosophical Letters" and "Apology of a Madman."* Mary-Barbara Zeldin, trans. Knoxville, Tenn., 1969.

———. *Stat'i i pis'ma.* Moscow, 1989.

Chereisky, L. A. *Pushkin i ego okruzhenie.* Leningrad, 1975.

Clive, John. *Not by Fact Alone.* New York, 1989.

Collingwood, R. G. *The Idea of History.* Oxford, 1946.

Cooke, Raymond. *Velimir Khlebnikov.* Cambridge, Eng., 1987.

Dal', V. I. *Tolkovyi slovar' zhivogo velikorusskogo iazyka.* 4 vols. Moscow, 1978.

———. "Vospominaniia o Pushkine." In V. E. Vatsuro, ed., *Pushkin v vospominaniiakh sovremennikov,* vol. 2, pp. 222–26. Moscow, 1974.

Dashkova, E. R. *Zapiski.* Moscow, 1987.

Debreczeny, Paul. *The Other Pushkin.* Stanford, Calif., 1983.

Denoon, Donald, and Adam Kuper. "Nationalist Historians in Search of a Nation: 'The New Historiography' in Dar es Salaam." *African Affairs* 69, no. 22 (Oct. 1970): 329–49.

Dostoevsky, F. M. *Polnoe sobranie sochinenii.* 30 vols. Leningrad, 1972–90.

Driver, Sam. *Pushkin, Literature and Social Ideas.* New York, 1989.

Duganov, R. V. "Poet, istoriia, priroda." *Voprosy literatury* 10 (1985): 130–62.

Egolin, A. M., ed. "Dekabristy—Kritiki 'Istoriia gosudarstva Rossiskogo' N. M. Karamzina." *Literaturnoe nasledstvo* (Moscow) 59, part I (1954): 557–600.

Eikhenbaum, Boris. *Tolstoy in the Sixties.* Duffield White, trans. Ann Arbor, Mich., 1982.

Ekaterina II, Imperatritsa. *Sochineniia.* A. N. Pypin, ed. 11 vols. St. Petersburg, 1902–6.

————. *Sochineniia. Proizvedeniia literaturnie.* St. Petersburg, 1893.

Emerson, Caryl. *Boris Godunov: Transpositions of a Russian Theme.* Bloomington, Ind., 1986.

Erlich, Victor. *Russian Formalism: History-Doctrine.* New Haven, Conn., 1955.

Evdokimova, Svetlana. "History and Myth in the Works of Alexander Pushkin." Ph.D. diss., Yale University, 1990.

Fanger, Donald. *Dostoevsky and Romantic Realism.* Cambridge, Mass., 1967.

Frank, Joseph. *Dostoevsky: The Seeds of Revolt, 1821–1849.* Princeton, N.J., 1976.

————. *Dostoevsky: The Stir of Liberation, 1860–1865.* Princeton, N.J., 1986.

————. *Dostoevsky: The Years of Ordeal, 1850–1859.* Princeton, N.J., 1983.

————. *Through the Russian Prism: Essays on Literature and Culture.* Princeton, N.J., 1990.

Friedman, Barton R. *English Writers on the French Revolution.* Princeton, N.J., 1988.

Fusso, Susanne. "The Landscape of *Arabesques.*" In Susanne Fusso and Priscilla Meyer, eds., *Essays on Gogol*, pp. 112–25. Evanston, Ill., 1992.

Gasparov, Boris. "The Apocalyptic Theme in Pushkin's 'Count Nulin.' " In *Text and Context: Essays to Honor Nils Ake Nilsson*, pp. 16–25. Stockholm, 1987.

Gasparov, Boris, Robert Hughes, and Irina Paperno, eds. *Cultural Mythologies of Russian Modernism: From the Golden Age to the Silver Age.* Berkeley, Calif., 1992.

Gearhart, Suzanne. *The Open Boundary of History and Fiction.* Princeton, N.J., 1984.

Gershchenkron, Alexander. *Economic Backwardness in Historical Perspective.* Cambridge, Mass., 1966.

Gibbon, Edward. *The Decline and Fall of the Roman Empire.* 3 vols. New York, 1946.

Gleason, Abbott. *European and Muscovite: Ivan Kireevsky and the Origins of Slavophilism.* Cambridge, Mass., 1972.

Glinka, S. *Mikhail, kniaz' Chernigovskii, tragediia v 5 deistviiakh.* Moscow, 1808.

Gogol, N. V. *Polnoe sobranie sochinenii.* 14 vols. Moscow, 1940–52.

Gossman, Lionel. *Between History and Literature*. Cambridge, Mass., 1990.

Grigor'ev, V. P. *Grammatika idiostilia: V. Khlebnikov*. Moscow, 1983.

Grossman, Vasily. *Zhizn' i sud'ba*. Moscow, 1988.

Groys, Boris. *The Total Art of Stalinism*. Charles Rougle, trans. Princeton, N. J., 1992.

Gudkov, L. D. "Poniatie i metafory istorii u Tynianova i Opoiazovtsev." In *Tynianovskii sbornik: Tret'ii Tynianovskie chteniia*, pp. 91–108. Riga, 1988.

Guillen, Claudio. *Literature as a System*. Princeton, N. J., 1971.

Gukovsky, G. A. *Russkaia literatura 18ogo veka*. Moscow, 1939.

Gumbrecht, Hans Ulrich. *Making Sense in Life and Literature*. Glen Burns, trans. Minneapolis, Minn., 1992.

Hamburger, Käte. *The Logic of Literature*. Marilynn J. Rose, trans. Bloomington, Ind., 1973.

Howe, Irving. "The Great War in Russian Memory." *The New York Times*, July 2, 1989, section 7, p. 17.

Hugo, Victor. *Les misérables*. Charles E. Wilbour, trans. New York, 1931.

Hutcheon, Linda. " 'The Pastime of Past Time': Fiction, History, Historiographic Metafiction." In Marjorie Perloff, ed., *Postmodern Genres*, pp. 54–74. Norman, Okla., 1988.

Iggers, Georg G., and James M. Powell, eds. *Leopold von Ranke and the Shaping of the Historical Discipline*. Syracuse, N.Y., 1990.

Jackson, Robert Louis. *The Art of Dostoevsky*. Princeton, N. J., 1981.

James, Henry. "Preface to *The Tragic Muse*." In *The Art of the Novel: Critical Prefaces by Henry James*. New York, 1934.

Kamensky, Vasily. *Put' entuziasta*. Moscow, 1931. Reprinted in *Vasily Kamensky: Iz literaturnogo naslediia*. Moscow, 1990.

——— . *Sten'ka Razin. Roman*. Moscow, 1916. Reprinted in *Vasily Kamensky: Iz literaturnogo naslediia*. Moscow, 1990.

——— . *Stepan Razin. Privol'nyi roman*. Moscow, 1928.

——— . *Stikhotvoreniia i poemy*. Moscow, 1966.

Karamzin, N. N. *Istoriia gosudarstva Rossiiskogo*. 5th edition. 4 vols. St. Petersburg, 1842–44. Reprint, Moscow, 1988–89.

——— . "Marfa-posadnitsa, ili pokorenie Novagoroda." In *Russkaia istoricheskaia povest'*, vol. 1, pp. 60–99. Moscow, 1988.

——— . *Neizdanye sochineniia i perepiska*. St. Petersburg, 1862.

——— . *Pis'ma russkogo puteshestvennika*. Leningrad, 1984.

Karlinsky, Simon. *Russian Drama from Its Beginnings to the Age of Pushkin*. Berkeley, Calif., 1985.

Karpuk, Paul. "Gogol's Unfinished Historical Novel, 'The Hetman'." Ph.D. diss., University of California, Berkeley, 1987.

Kaverin, V., ed. *Iury Tynianov. Pisatel' i uchenyi*. Moscow, 1966.

———, ed. *Vospominaniia o Iu. Tynianove*. Moscow, 1983.

Kaverin, V., and V. I. Novikov. *Novoe zrenie*. Moscow, 1988.

Kheraskov, M. M. *Izbrannye proizvedeniia*. Leningrad, 1961.

Khlebnikov, Velimir. *The King of Time*. Paul Schmidt, trans. Charlotte Douglas, ed. Cambridge, Mass., 1985.

———. *Sobranie proizvedeniia*. Iu. Tynianov and N. Stepanov, eds. 5 vols. Leningrad, 1928–33.

———. *Sobranie sochinenii*. V. Markov, ed. 4 vols. Munich, 1972.

———. *Tvoreniia*. Moscow, 1986.

———. *Zangezi*. Moscow, 1922. Reprint, Ann Arbor, Mich., 1978.

Khomiakov, A. S. *Polnoe sobranie sochinenii*. 8 vols. Moscow, 1885–1904.

Kinahan, Frank. "Douglas Hyde and the King of Chimps: Some Notes on the De-Anglicization of Ireland." In J. Edelstein, ed., *Imagining an Irish Past: The Celtic Revival, 1840–1940*, pp. 64–81. Chicago, 1992.

Kliuchevsky, V. O. *Kurs Russkoi istorii*. 5 vols. Moscow, 1904–21.

Kniazhnin, Ia. B. *Izbrannye proizvedeniia*. Leningrad, 1961.

Komarovich, V. L. "Zapisi ustnykh rasskazov o Pugachevshchine." In *Pushkin: Vremennik Pushkinskoi komissii*, vols. 4–5, pp. 18–24. Moscow, 1939.

Korpala-Kirszak, Ewa. *Sztuka pisarska Juriji Tynianowa*. Wroclaw, 1974.

Kropf, David. *Authorship and Literary Subversions in the Romantic Period: Pushkin, Scott, Hoffmann*. Stanford, Calif., 1994.

LaCapra, Dominick. *History and Criticism*. Ithaca, N.Y., 1985.

Langer, Gudrun. *Kunst—Wissenschaft—Utopie: Die " Überwindung der Kulturkrise" bei V. Ivanov, A. Blok, A. Belyj und V. Chlebnikov*. Frankfurt am Main, 1990.

Le Goff, Jacques. *History and Memory*. Steven Rendall and Elizabeth Claman, trans. New York, 1992.

Lejeune, Philippe. *Le pacte autobiographique*. Paris, 1975.

Likhachev, D. S. *Chelovek v literature drevnei Rusi*. In *Izbrannye raboty v trekh tomakh*, vol. 3, pp. 3–164. Leningrad, 1987.

Lindenberger, Herbert. *Historical Drama*. Chicago, 1975.

Lomonosov, M. V. *Polnoe sobranie sochinenii*. 10 vols. Moscow, 1950–59.

Lotman, Iu. M. "Dekabrist v povsednevnoi zhizni." In *V shkole poeticheskogo slova*, pp. 158–205. Moscow, 1988.

————. "K strukture dialogicheskogo teksta v poemakh Pushkina." *Uchenye zapiski LGPI* 434 (1970): 101–11.

————. "Puti razvitiia russkoi prozy 1800-x–1810-x gg." *Uchenye zapiski Tartuskogo universiteta* 104 (1961): 3–57.

————. *Sotvorenie Karamzina*. Moscow, 1987.

Lukács, Georg. *The Historical Novel*. Lincoln, Neb., 1983.

Lur'e, Ia. S. *Obshcherusskie letopisi XIV–XV vv*. Leningrad, 1976.

Macaulay, Thomas. *Selected Writings*. Chicago, 1972.

MacMaster, Robert E. *Danilevsky: A Russian Totalitarian Philosopher*. Cambridge, Mass., 1967.

Malia, Martin. *Alexander Herzen and the Birth of Russian Socialism*. New York, 1965.

Mandelshtam, Osip. "Petr Chaadaev." In *Sobranie sochinenii v trekh tomakh*, vol. 2, pp. 284–92. Washington, D.C., 1971.

Marker, Gary. *Publishing, Printing, and the Origins of Intellectual Life in Russia, 1700–1800*. Princeton, N.J., 1985.

Markov, Vladimir. *Russian Futurism: A History*. Berkeley, Calif., 1968.

————, ed. *Manifesty i programmy Russkikh Futuristov*. Munich, 1967.

Markov, Vladimir, and Merril Sparks, eds. and trans. *Modern Russian Poetry*. London, 1966.

Masal'sky, Konstantin. *Strel'tsy, Istoricheskii roman*. St. Petersburg, 1832.

Mazour, Anatole G. *Modern Russian Historiography*. Westport, Conn., 1975.

Merezhkovsky, D. S. *Polnoe sobranie sochinenii*. 12 vols. Moscow, 1914.

Michelet, Jules. *Oeuvres complètes*. 21 vols. Paris, 1971–82.

Miliukov, P. N. *Glavnye techeniia russkoi istoricheskoi mysli*. Moscow, 1898.

Mochulsky, Konstantin. *Dostoevsky: His Life and Work*. Michael A. Minihan, trans. Princeton, N.J., 1967.

Modzalevsky, L. B. *Komentarii k deviatomu tomu sochinenii Pushkina*. Moscow, 1949.

Morgan, Prys. "From Death to a View: The Hunt for the Welsh Past in the Romantic Period." In E. Hobsbawm and T. Ranger, eds., *The Invention of Tradition*, pp. 43–100. Cambridge, Eng., 1983.

Morson, Gary Saul. *The Boundaries of Genre*. Austin, Tex., 1981.

———. "Dostoevsky's *Diary of a Writer*: Threshold Art." Ph.D. diss., Yale University, 1974.

———. *Hidden in Plain View*. Stanford, Calif., 1987.

———, ed. *Literature and History: Theoretical Problems and Russian Case Studies*. Stanford, Calif., 1986.

Morson, Gary Saul, and Caryl Emerson. *Mikhail Bakhtin: Creation of a Prosaics*. Stanford, Calif., 1990.

———, eds. *Rethinking Bakhtin*. Evanston, Ill., 1989.

Mossman, Elliott. "Metaphors of History in *War and Peace* and *Doctor Zhivago*." In Morson, ed., *Literature and History*, pp. 247–62.

Murav'ev, M. N. *Sochineniia*. 2 vols. St. Petersburg, 1847.

Nilsson, Nils Ake. "Futurism, Primitivism, and the Russian Avant-Garde." *Russian Literature* 8-5 (1980): 469–81.

Oksman, Iu. G. "Pushkin v rabote nad romanom 'Kapitanskaia dochka.'" In *A. S. Pushkin: Kapitanskaia dochka*. Moscow, 1964.

Paperno, Irina. *Chernyshevsky and the Age of Realism*. Stanford, Calif., 1988.

"Patriarshaia ili Nikonovskaia letopis'." In *Polnoe sobranie russkikh letopisei*, vol. 9. St. Petersburg, 1862.

Perloff, Marjorie. *The Futurist Moment*. Chicago, 1986.

Petrovich, Michael Boro. *The Emergence of Russian Panslavism*. New York, 1956.

Petrunina, N. N. *Proza Pushkina*. Leningrad, 1987.

———. "Vokrug 'Istorii Pugachava.'" In *Pushkin: Issledovaniia i materialy*, vol. 6, pp. 229–51. Leningrad, 1969.

Pipes, Richard. *Russia Under the Old Regime*. New York, 1974.

Plavil'shchikov, P.A. *Sochineniia*. 4 vols. St. Petersburg, 1816.

Pokrovsky, V. I., ed. *Nikolai Mikhailovich Karamzin: Ego zhizn' i sochineniia*. 3d ed., 1912. Reprint, Oxford, 1981.

Polevoi, N. A. *Istoriia Russkogo naroda*. 6 vols. Moscow, 1830–33.

"Povest' vremennykh let." In D. S. Likhachev, ed., *Pamiatniki literatury drevnei Rusi (XI—nachalo XII veka)*, pp. 23–279. Moscow, 1978.

Pritsak, Omeljan. *The Origins of Rus'*. Cambridge, Mass., 1981.

Pushkin, A. S. *Letters*. Thomas Shaw, trans. Madison, Wis., 1967.

————. *Polnoe sobranie sochinenii.* 14 vols. Moscow, 1937–41.

Raeff, Marc. *The Origins of the Russian Intelligentsia.* New York, 1966.

Riasanovsky, Nicholas V. *A History of Russia.* 4th edition. Oxford, 1984.

————. *Nicholas I and Official Nationality in Russia, 1825–1855.* Berkeley, 1959.

Rogger, Hans. *National Consciousness in 18th Century Russia.* Cambridge, Mass., 1960.

Ryleev, K. F. *Polnoe sobranie stikhotvorenii.* Leningrad, 1971.

Sandler, Stephanie. "The Problem of History in Pushkin: Poet, Pretender, Tsar." Ph.D. diss., Yale University, 1981.

Scammell, Michael. *Solzhenitsyn.* New York, 1984.

Schama, Simon. *Dead Certainties.* New York, 1991.

Schamschula, Walter. *Der russische historische Roman von Klassizismus bis zur Romantik.* Meisenheim am Glan, 1961.

Seifrid, Thomas. "Suspicion Toward Narrative: The Nose and the Problem of Autonomy in Gogol's 'Nos.'" *The Russian Review* 52, no. 3 (1993): 382–96.

Serman, Ilya. "Russian National Consciousness in the 18th Century." In R. Bartlett and J. Hartley, eds., *Russia in the Age of the Enlightenment,* pp. 40–56. New York, 1990.

Shils, Edward. *Tradition.* Chicago, 1981.

Shmidt, S. O. "Istoriia gosudarstva Rossiiskogo v kul'ture dorevoliutsionnoi Rossii." In Karamzin, *Istoriia gosudarstva Rossiiskogo,* vol. 4, pp. 28–43.

Solov'ev, S. M. *Istoriia Rossii s drevneishikh vremen.* 15 vols. Moscow, 1959–66.

Solov'ev, V. S. *Izbrannye sochineniia.* 2 vols. Moscow, 1990.

Solzhenitsyn, A. I. *Krasnoe koleso. Uzel I, Avgust chetyrnadtsatogo.* 2 vols. Paris, 1983.

————. *Krasnoe koleso. Uzel II, Oktiabr' shestnadtsatogo.* 2 vols. Paris, 1984.

————. *Krasnoe koleso. Uzel III, Mart semnadtsatogo.* 4 vols. Paris, 1986–88.

————. *Krasnoe koleso. Uzel IV, Aprel' semnadtsatogo.* 2 vols. Paris, 1991.

Starr, S. Frederick. "You Can't Murder History." *New York Times Book Review,* July 19, 1992.

Stepanov, N. *Velimir Khlebnikov. Zhizn' i tvorchestvo.* Moscow, 1975.

Striedter, Jurij. *Literary Structure, Evolution, and Value: Russian Formalism and Czech Structuralism Reconsidered.* Cambridge, Mass., 1989.

———. "Poetic Genre and the Sense of History in Pushkin." *New Literary History* 8, no. 2 (Winter 1977): 295–309.

Tatishchev, V. I. *Istoriia rossiiskaia.* 7 vols. Moscow, 1962–68.

Terras, Victor. *A History of Russian Literature.* New Haven, Conn., 1991.

Theimer, Catharine S. "The Function of Time in *The First Circle.*" *Modern Fiction Studies* 23, no. 1 (1977): 63–72.

Tolstoy, L. N. *Polnoe sobranie sochinenii.* 90 vols. Moscow, 1928–53.

Tsyrlin, Iu. N. *Tynianov—Belletrist.* Leningrad, 1935.

Tynianov, Iu. N. *Arkhaisty i novatory.* Leningrad, 1929. Reprint, Ann Arbor, Mich., 1985.

———. *Poetika, istoriia literatury, kino.* Moscow, 1977.

———. *Pushkin.* Leningrad, 1974.

———. *Pushkin i ego sovremenniki.* Moscow, 1969.

———. *Sochineniia v dvukh tomakh.* 2 vols. Leningrad, 1985.

———, ed. *V. K. Kiukhel'beker, Lirika i poemy.* 2 vols. Leningrad, 1939.

Vatsuro, V. "Podvig chestnogo cheloveka." *Prometei* 5 (1968): 8–51.

Veresaev, V. *Gogol v zhizni.* Moscow, 1933. Reprint, Moscow, 1990.

———. *Pushkin v zhizni.* Moscow, 1936. Reprint, Chicago, 1970.

Vroon, Ronald. "'Sea Shore' ('Morskoi bereg') and the Razin Constellation." *Russian Literature Triquarterly* 12 (1975): 295–326.

———. "Velimir Khlebnikov's 'Razin: Two Trinities': A Reconstruction." *Slavic Review* 39, no. 1 (1980): 70–84.

Wachtel, Andrew. *The Battle for Childhood.* Stanford, Calif., 1990.

———. "Continuity and Change in the Russian Historical Epic: Tolstoy, Grossman, Solzhenitsyn." *Stanford Slavic Studies* 4, II (1992): 408–27.

Walicki, Andrzej. *A History of Russian Thought from the Enlightenment to Marxism.* Hilda Andrews-Rusiecka, trans. Stanford, Calif., 1979.

———. *The Slavophile Controversy.* Notre Dame, Ind., 1989.

Wasiolek, Edward. *Tolstoy's Major Fiction.* Chicago, 1978.

White, Hayden. *The Content of the Form.* Baltimore, Md., 1987.

———. "The Historical Text as Literary Artifact." In Robert H. Canary and Henry Kozicki, eds., *The Writing of History: Literary Form and Historical Understanding,* pp. 41–62. Madison, Wis., 1978.

————. *Metahistory*. Baltimore, Md., 1973.

Zaidenshnur, E. V. *"Voina i mir" L. N. Tolstogo*. Moscow, 1966.

Zamotin, I. I. "Predanie o Vadime Novgorodskom v russkoi literature." *Filologicheskie zapiski* (Voronezh) 39, no. 3–4 (1899).

Zhukovsky, V. A. *Polnoe sobranie sochinenii v dvenadtsati tomakh*. St. Petersburg, 1902.

Index

Library of Congress Cataloging-in-Publication Data

Wachtel, Andrew.
  An obsession with history : Russian writers confront
the past / Andrew Baruch Wachtel.
      p.   cm.
  Includes bibliographical references and index.
  ISBN 0-8047-2246-3 (cl.) : ISBN 0-8047-2594-2 (pbk.)
  1. Russian literature—History and criticism.
2. History in literature. 3. Russian in literature. I. Title.
PG2975.W33   1994
891.708´ 358—dc20   93-14174
                                                            CIP

∞ This book is printed on acid-free paper.